Ladies
of the
Leisure Class

Ladies of the Leisure Class

The Bourgeoises of Northern France in the Nineteenth Century

Bonnie G. Smith

Princeton University Press
Princeton, New Jersey

Copyright © 1981 by Princeton University Press
Published by Princeton University Press, Princeton, New Jersey
In the United Kingdom: Princeton University Press,
Guildford, Surrey

All Rights Reserved
Library of Congress Cataloging in Publication Data will be
found on the last printed page of this book

Publication of this book has been aided by a grant from the
Paul Mellon Fund of Princeton University Press

This book has been composed in Linotron Primer

Clothbound editions of Princeton University Press books
are printed on acid-free paper, and binding materials are
chosen for strength and durability

Printed in the United States of America by Princeton
University Press, Princeton, New Jersey

For
William Wallace Sullivan
and in memory of
Harriet Amanda Howard Sullivan

Contents

List of Illustrations

List
of Tables

I
The
Historical
Context

The Nord

Dunkerque

BELGIUM

Tourcoing
Armentières
Roubaix
Lille

Douai
Valenciennes

Cambrai
Avesnes

FRANCE

1
Introduction:
A World Apart

What is a bourgeois woman? The question first came to mind when I studied history with teachers who described the modern world in terms of class. They used the words "bourgeoisie" and "proletariat," in particular, to define relationships in the productive or market world. Here the question first arose: How was a wealthy woman properly called bourgeois when she spent most of her life at home without any direct connection with either the market or production? In terms of class analysis, what was her place? The problem deepened as I proceeded to look at "bourgeois" attitudes. Nineteenth-century men were nothing if not industrious, rational, and committed to accumulating capital. But I envisioned the bourgeois woman as someone who probably passed many idle hours, and who was more concerned with spending money than with accumulating it. And if she were rational, why the many depictions of the bourgeois woman as preoccupied with furniture and fashion? I could not jettison accumulated wisdom in a blind defense of her scientific mindset. Outside the classroom came other meanings of the word "bourgeois." There were the epithets: oppressors of the people, political swindlers, and the ubiquitous construction of the word bourgeois as synonymous with bad taste. But in no instance did any of these satisfy my craving for a picture of the bourgeois woman. Conventional definitions all applied to men of the bourgeoisie.

There is a way to connect the bourgeois woman with the marketplace world that shaped nineteenth-century history, and historians have made sympathetic efforts to locate her in that environment. They have seen her as the bearer of its children, the consoler of its hard-pressed businessmen, and occasionally as volunteer nurse binding up social wounds through charitable activities. In addition, the clothing with which she adorned herself and the decorative objects she strewed throughout her home contributed to the perpetuation of modern society by softening its increasingly stark contours. The bourgeois woman was also the leading consumer of industrial goods, and, increasingly guided by advertising, she developed a complementary relationship with her male counterpart. While the bourgeois man directed production, she was responsible for the purchase of commodities.

Such an analysis, for all its merit, does not exhaust the substance of bourgeois women's lives, however. It ignores their remoteness from production, and even their explicit dislike for industrial society and its attendant social change. Bourgeois women mistrusted market values and the world beyond the home. Instead of adopting an individualistic, rational, and democratic world view, they abhorred it. Instead of working to amass capital or to contribute to either the economic or political advance of industrial society, they devoted their lives to their families, and, as often, to the Church. Although physically part of an industrial society, bourgeois women neither experienced its way of life nor partook of its mentality. They inhabited and presided over a domestic world that had its own concerns.

To penetrate this world and its concerns I have chosen as a case study a group of women who lived in the French department of the Nord during the nineteenth century. As wives, sisters, daughters, and mothers of men engaged in the professions or in running businesses and heavy industry, these women constitute a sample of several thousand who could be investigated in terms more or less applicable to bourgeois women in most industrial societies.

To begin, I have looked at the simple, obvious characteristics of their lives. Specifically and primarily, the bourgeois woman of the nineteenth century engaged in reproduction, and her body experienced reproductive cycles more regularly and palpably than did the bodies of men. Menstruation, pregnancy, parturition, lactation, and menopause relentlessly ordered the configuration of female life. It does not require biological determinism to appreciate how deeply rooted in nature woman's activity is. Simone de Beauvoir treated this theme minutely in *The Second Sex*, and it would be foolhardy (especially in a study of French women) to disregard her insights. De Beauvoir's work begins with female biology and leads to an explanation of why men have viewed women as lacking humanity. Along the way she examines the various stages in women's lives as at least partially modulated by their physical fluctuations. It is interesting to connect de Beauvoir's thesis with another pioneering work, Alice Clark's *The Working Life of Women in the Seventeenth Century*. Clark argued that the home of that era was slowly losing many of its productive functions, and historians hastened to join her in calling the moderrn home "functionless." Others began to look at the psychological workings of the home or at its "spiritual" nature in an attempt to impute vigor to domestic life. Yet, Clark's depiction linked to de Beauvoir's theory suggests that the home constituted a reproductive arena, an area charged with the content of women's physical lives.

The biological charge to reproduce does not, however, preclude cultural activity. This is the conclusion of Sherry Ortner's article that seeks out and locates the cultural activities in the socialization of children.[1] Explicitly building on de Beauvoir's work, she argued that in this capacity women transmitted a civilized tradition, but that the private setting for this activity hid their contribution and perpetu-

5

ated the affinity of women and nature in men's eyes. Despite an admirable effort, Ortner failed to build on de Beauvoir's insight when she characterized women as merely trans-mitters of culture, as robots, one might say, in service to the exterior world of male values and standards. Indeed, one might expect a different turn from a feminist anthropologist, for the home remains unexamined, even in a tentative way, as a source of an indigenous and autonomous culture.

In fact, the culture of the home has been so obtrusive that it already has its name. During the nineteenth century the domestic world of reproductive women overflowed with artifacts and produced patterns of behavior, the sum of which has been labeled "domesticity." Domesticity flowered from this period until the present day. Bourgeois women, in particular, suddenly released from much of the productive activity that had accompanied their reproductive life, began to fashion a home life for themselves, their husbands, and their children. Initially the prerogative of the upper classes, domestic habits and thoughts became common to rich and working-class women alike, as fewer and fewer married women participated in the industrial work force on a sus-tained basis. As a result, by the twentieth century women found themselves almost exclusively concerned with inte-rior decorating, fashion, cuisine, etiquette, needlework, and child-rearing; and by extension, these occupations came to be considered intrinsic to the female personality, arranged and systematized as they were into a symbolic expression of women's biological mission and the reproductive course of their lives.

The presence of a domestic culture and the accessibility of domestic artifacts suggest, it seems to me, a more direct study of women than the approach taken by conventional economic or political history. Scholars have traditionally found that the biological functions of women have made a historical treatment of women's lives difficult. Because nei-ther discourse nor a record of intellectual, political, or eco-nomic achievement exists as evidence of their reproductive activities, scholars remove women from the historical stage and relegate their study to the natural sciences. In addition, the attachment of academics to rational (or even irrational) discourse as the only valid source of information has moved them to dismiss women's involvement with fashion and interior decorating as signs of mental inferiority and of the triviality of their minds. I share the concern for rational discourse to the point of attempting to put into words what women expressed through their system of domestic artifacts. The possibility that fashion and housekeeping habits have an expressive content demands that we consider them in order to increase our knowledge of the home as an internally coherent, symbolic form. Not only is it interesting to uncover different modes of speech, for instance; it is crucial if we remember what nineteenth-century men never failed to recognize: the culture of the home often stood in opposition to the imperative of industrial progress.

Recently, demographers in family reconstitution studies have attempted to recover the reproductive past, as well as the history of many inarticulate groups, through statistics. For all that this fruitful method has extended our knowledge, it does not fully illuminate the substance and meaning of the domestic universe. Aside from the incongruity involved in describing with numbers women who never thought in mathematical terms, statistics may mislead by assigning false significance to the sheer quantity and spacing of children of marriages. Although the bourgeois women we will meet in this study cared deeply about their children, reproduction and other bio-sexual determinants remained central to their lives whether they had one or ten children. Each expressed that centrality through a system of domestic symbols (a preverbal language, perhaps) that then reversed itself to form a set of rules and cultural standards binding all women. Although statistics are often helpful in charting behavior, insofar as they contain their own symbolic expression, they obstruct our view of this type of reversible cultural equation.

Along with reproduction and domestic life, women's religious practices provide another access to their culture. The bourgeois woman was nothing if not devoted to the Church. Like the fact of reproduction and domesticity, however, this circumstance has often failed to enlighten, and has even blocked investigation. Secularism, once blessed with a measure of humility, has tended to construe religious faith as the opiate of womanhood. Faith has earned more epithets than understanding; and thus, in contrast to the lucid rationalism attributed to modern men, women are called "fanatic," "superstitious," and "ignorant." Sometimes, as in Ann Douglas's work, *The Feminization of American Culture*, religion acquires a rational connotation when it is seen as an instrument of social power for the otherwise impotent woman.[2] But what is gained by this in terms of historical respectability for religion is lost for the anthropological investigation of the domestic mind. By modernizing religion and fashioning it to her own devices, Douglas misses its importance as a cosmological system, its decidedly antimodern thrust, and the congruence between domestic ritual and religious rites. Because women maintained a traditional and preindustrial way of life, and because religion had long offered an explanation of the universe based on preindustrial experience, we should expect, rather than distort or modernize, the coupling of domesticity and faith. Indeed, it might be necessary for us to face, as did Freud and many anthropologists, the persistent adherence of women to the Church with curiosity instead of with blatant or ill-disguised contempt.

Modern historians have fairly well established that the nineteenth-century bourgeois man not only tended toward freethinking but also supported republican and democratic government. From a narrowly construed class perspective, women should have moved in a similar political direction. Yet our still rudimentary knowledge of the nineteenth-century woman suggests quite the opposite. For example, most politicians, when confronted with the suffrage movement, opposed the vote for women out of fear that they would support the forces of reaction. This consideration particularly moved French republicans whose power depended on preventing the revitalization of monarchism—a cause widely supported by women. There is a contemporary, though perhaps trivial, indication of the dichotomous political tendencies separating the political views of men and women: while men read *Le Monde* and *Le Figaro*, women satisfy their monarchist instincts in the pages of *Jours de France*. Despite such evidence, both sexes have been placed under the bourgeois umbrella.

A similar lack of discrimination provokes charges that men and women of the bourgeoisie equally "oppressed the proletariat." Because women generally had little economic contact with the working class, the source of this oppression is found in their charitable activity, which allegedly blinded workers to the source of their misery. This interpretation confuses the possible effect of women's volunteer activities with the social vision prompting their efforts. Embedded in the word "charity" and in its practice was an interpretation of the social order as a static and hierarchical construct. Women sought to maintain these distinctions through charity, whereas men hoped by similar activities to achieve a certain measure of social homogenization, or at least to present it as a political goal. The intent of modern social welfare (beginning in the nineteenth century) to bring everyone to a minimum standard of living contrasts sharply with women's desire to perpetuate social hierarchy.

In theory, static hierarchy died at the hands of French revolutionary politicians. In its place they substituted a creed of liberty and equality. Bourgeois women, however, scorned both revolutionary doctrine and democratic institutions: " 'liberty,' we all know what that means," they warned.[3] They clung instead to rigid, even aristocratic notions of place and status, all the more surprisingly when many of their husbands had amassed their fortunes because of new mobility and opportunity. Their retrograde views were less manifestations of stubbornness than of the sustained connection between women and family. Family depended on fixed patterns of authority, and to women aristocratic government and hierarchic social order best reproduced their familial experience. Because this experience so molded their opinions, women saw the entire universe shaped in this hierarchical way through a chain of command that originated with God, passed through kings, and eventually reached to parents. Thus, when bourgeois women performed a charitable act, they envisioned it as an act in the spirit of hierarchy (*noblesse oblige*). Among their own kind etiquette performed a similar function of denoting place in this type of ordering by blood.

All these subjects receive full treatment in subsequent chapters, but I introduce them now in order to suggest a line of argument. The bourgeois woman lived in an atmosphere and acted according to precepts entirely at odds with the industrial, market, egalitarian, and democratic world— the world, that is, of her husband. In addition, she had little use for the primary article of faith of the nineteenth century: rationalism. The women we will meet believed that scientific knowledge was chimerical, especially when it challenged the proper ordering of things, including family, society, and political authority. For them science had a substantial value up to a point, but when it made little gods of men or when it placed the laws of nature above the will of God, then human society had gone astray. Most women in France, most bourgeois women, in this case, acquired their antiscientific values at the convent, that institution whose close parallel to domestic structures we shall attempt to uncover. However, their line of argument against science was not merely obstructionist, for it rested on an epistemological commitment to the inaccessability of certain mysteries—particularly those of birth and death, which remained hidden in the mind of the Creator. This will lead us to explain the intellectual darkness pervading a nineteenth-century woman's acquaintance with sexual matters, which sprang less from a male conspiracy of silence than from a theory of knowledge. Although their ignorance in this regard may have met with male approval, women championed their own innocence because of its positive connotations.

Women did more than merely champion innocence; they turned it into a cult. We have heard much recently about "the cult of true womanhood" built on a reverence for domesticity and the virtuous woman.[4] It is tempting to assign the origins of this cult to men who wanted their womenfolk home and sexually faithful to them. Although there is a male contribution to the insistence on chastity as a component of legitimate private property, such an interpretation does not explain the firm commitment of most middle-class women in most industrial countries to the cult of their own virtue.

Used loosely in descriptions of women's beliefs, the word cult has a precise philosophical and psychological purport. Freud, Cassirer, and several generations of anthropologists have contributed to the establishment of a connection between cult and mythical, prescientific attitudes toward man and nature. They see in particular the creation of or adherence to cults as indicating, in Freud's interpretation, a desire to merge the personality in a concept larger than the individual; or, in Cassirer's view, a lack of distinction between subjectivity and objectivity. Piaget also has isolated one stage of mental development in which the individual identifies with the whole of the universe and collapses its enormity into the self. Any of these interpretations allows for the growth of a religious attitude or for the adherence to a cult, for the individual comes to worship personal qualities that he or she projects on the whole of creation.[5]

In the past this particular state of mind has led to the generation of myth. The mythical mind anthropomorphizes nature by combining human qualities and events of nature in a mythical god or goddess. The person comes to worship these fictional creations and uses them to explain a myriad natural or human events. Entire categories of phenomena find their meaning in the activities of a larger-than-life being who, nonetheless, has human attributes.

I will suggest in the final chapter on the women of the Nord that the domestic novel plays a similar myth-making role in creating the cult of womanhood. Several hundred of the novels they wrote offer stories of larger-than-life heroines, and, it should be added, heroines whose story is duplicated so consistently in each novel that they come to form a single woman—an archetypal figure. I say this to differentiate between the mythical figures in the domestic novel and the human characterization offered in the great novels of the nineteenth century. The heroine's virtue confronts obstacles that test our credulity; her plight, unlike that of, say, Rastignac in *Père Goriot*, is to our eyes exaggerated to the point of being ridiculous. Yet the suffering heroine was a figure with whose image women could (and still do) identify, and in whose situation they somehow found themselves reflected. So, too, mythical heroes met dragons and demons, held the world, the skies, and the seas in their dominion, endured and triumphed. And in a prescientific age they exacted belief.

But how could modern women—how can they still—find the articulation of their world view in the plight of the virtuous heroine? The question leads us back to our starting point in the reproductive life of women. Freud, Cassirer, and Piaget have pointed to the genesis of religious belief in the mind still embedded in nature and in a subjectivity undifferentiated from the objective world, a failure to distinguish between itself and the universe. Our women of the Nord led lives embedded in reproductive functioning after the home ceased to be the place of production. No longer transforming nature, they emphasized their connection with it. While men abandoned their mythical or religious deities, women not only maintained their relationship with the Christian God, but invented a new cult of the virtuous heroine who ruled a domestically constructed universe.

In sum, my investigation of the bourgeois women of northern France will proceed as if they truly inhabited a world apart. This did not prevent the political and economic concerns of modern France from impinging on their lives. On the contrary, they and their husbands constantly found themselves in a difficult position in their relation to one another. On the one hand, French men did indeed find consolation in the home with its gentle evenings of song and poetry, and with its velvet cushions and delicacies. On the other hand, bourgeois women often menaced the uneasy equilibrium of a tension-ridden industrial order. As they championed reactionary causes—especially Church and king—and as they sometimes opposed rationalism and science—especially in the education of children—men saw in their partners a hostile and disruptive force. The conservative world view of the female half of the ruling class became increasingly worrisome to intellectuals and politicians who bore the burden of sustaining a market society. From their concern grew various efforts to reform women's education and to terminate the social influence women had gained through philanthropic activity.

With varying degrees of tenacity, and certainly with unequal weapons, the women of northern France fought these efforts to curb the influence of their world view and to change its character. The battle had interesting results. The attempt by men to alter the relationship between the market world and domestic life converted a few women to feminism as a means of emphasizing the importance of the female vision of society. Other women forged a tighter and more explicit alliance with reactionary institutions that could give force to their ideas, and a still greater number retreated from any activity in public life to unalloyed privacy in the home. But whatever their choice, the women of the Nord, in challenging the champions of modernization so directly, brought into stark relief the dichotomy that existed between men and women of the bourgeoisie, and testified to their own alienation from the modern world.

Such alienation had the important consequence of removing women from the historical stage. Their encapsulation in the home made them resistant to a mode of interpreting human experience that treats of public events and
thoughts in relationship to public time or chronology. Working-class women in the marketplace or feminists in the political arena more easily fill the requirements for historical
narrative. But an appreciation of women's lives demands
that we discuss a private world whose time was often more
natural and traditional than modern. Childbirth, periods of
illness, deaths, anniversaries, meals, and other household
occurrences formed a sequence of events significant to
women but inappropriate to a narrative shaped, say, by the
course of French political debate or by economic fluctuations. In fact, viewing home life exclusively through the
lens of public affairs or public time can only distort our
image.[6]

Throughout this book we shall be forced, then, to move
back and forth between two conceptions of time. When
discussing the household, the convent, or religious rituals,
the treatment of women will seem almost timeless, and
grounded in repetition or even biological rhythm. But simultaneously, as men, the market, or the political events
of France sought to or actually did influence the household,
we must be ready to switch, as the women of the Nord often
did, to sudden intrusions of public time. So too with space.
The household in a certain sense was removed from the
public forum, and was even immune to geographical differentiation. Homes in Dunkerque, Valenciennes, Lille, or
Roubaix had a similarity that contrasted sharply with the
differentiated loci of public events. So we must examine the
household in its own, often hermetic, terms, yet always
maintain a readiness to return to the public forum when
women enter it.

The problem of distinguishing, and yet showing the relationship between the domestic and public spheres occurs
repeatedly in the writing of social history. It becomes even

more intense when we introduce individual characters in a narrative. When I first studied a group of Northern women several years ago, I was intrigued by the details of their existence: the number of children they bore and how they raised them, the number of servants they employed and how they organized their households; their religious devotion and the expression of that devotion in social work and volunteer societies; school routines and the subjects they studied. My first effort in women's history consisted of relating these details for the bourgeoises of Lille and of noting the divergence between their lives and those of their husbands. But it soon struck me that the difference between the historical male and the historical female was more pronounced than I had realized. The mass of details themselves yielded no "great" individual women. Few consistently worked in public or shaped important events. Nor could the life of a single woman be charted in its entirety in any historically significant way. Instead the often gossipy details contained layers of a common experience. And this situation points to a perilous course to be followed between the extremes of meaningless antiquarianism (which tempts all social historians) and ahistorical stereotyping.

If it avoids these perils, social history extends the narrative of the past in a new direction. It humanizes that story in a way that economic, political, and intellectual history have often neglected. In the case of the women of the Nord we may not find any great individual consciously acting in the public arena, but we will gain a picture of an important social group whose private way of life proceeded outside previous standards of historical significance. The story of these women offers an example of the formation of a distinctive *mentalité* within a group having close ties to nature. Beyond this anthropological task lies the historical one: to show how the world view of women unfolded in a particular social context—namely, a scientific and industrial society with a democratic political configuration. That context had a significant effect on their lives. In the first place, a complex

15

division of labor relegated them to the exclusive task of breeding children, where once they had complemented their reproductive charge with domestic production. Second, it surrounded them with new ideas: democracy, individualism, natural rights, and the like. Domesticity can be seen as the result of new conditions of reproduction, just as feminism is currently being interpreted as a byproduct of political modernization: that is, of natural rights applied to women as well as to men.[7]

In any book about women, even one that deals with the household, the question of feminism lurks in the wings. Such books search for signs of suffering, bonding, and the seeds of rebellion in the household, and see domesticity as a construct that fosters an awareness of lost opportunity. This book, too, grows out of an interest in finding the connection between feminism and domesticity, the two striking phenomena of bourgeois women's lives in the nineteenth century. But it seeks an explanation of why feminism followed so closely on the heels of domesticity more satisfactory than *ad hoc propter hoc*. In many ways feminism reiterated not only modern political themes, but also those of the reproductive mentality of bourgeois women.

Part I sets the scene. The Nord was one of the most industrialized regions of France; the men of the bourgeoisie adhered to the general creed of capitalism, and their wives for a brief moment shared in the process of managing the family enterprise, a subject taken up in Chapter Two. The transition from mercantile to industrial manufacturing, however, terminated the relationship between home and business, and made for a separation of the sexes and a sharp definition of functions. In Part II our narrative concentrates on the life of women after their acceptance of an exclusively reproductive life without an explicitly public orientation. We examine, first, the activities of the household and try to explain their coherence as a cultural system. This private experience of women was knitted together in various ways. First, religion provided a cosmology and metaphysics for their mundane chores and satisfied their human craving for explanations of experience. Second, the tight fusion of domestic and religious values bred in Northern women a commitment to extend their scope beyond a single home into the households of the poor. They became vigorous ladies of charity. Home, cosmos, and society constituted a tripartite axis of the domestic vision.

In Part III we watch the propagation of domesticity. Instruction in the domestic, religious, and charitable way of life came most often from the educational system which, as the century progressed, centered on the convent. This one institution eclipsed all others by the end of the nineteenth century, and we can explain its triumph only in the context of the world created by women in the home and through the Church. Finally, the sum of women's experience found its voice in the sentimental novel, and the women of the Nord were no different from women in every industrial society in their use of this genre to give an ideological expression to domestic life in all its fullness.

The story that unfolds will not always be pleasant, and it may be tempting to explain away the reactionary, ignorant, militant, and even foolish activities of women by saying that they were the dupes of priests or oppressed by men or the victims of capitalism. Outside forces are not irrelevant, but too often they become the sole explanatory factor in women's lives. Because there is little evidence for a conspiracy theory of women's history, using this type of explanation amounts to a childlike wish to escape responsibility for one's own plight. More than sixty years ago Edith Wharton, herself a bourgeois woman, wondered "when our sex is coming out of the kindergarten."[8] We can start that process by analyzing domestic life as, in good measure, a female creation and as evidence of the continuing ingenuity of human agency.

2
The Nord and Its Men

Among tourists, the Nord has a reputation for dreariness and a dearth of good restaurants, but for historians willing to bear those misfortunes the region offers a colorful spectacle. A narrow strip of land bordering Belgium and stretching from Dunkerque to Cambrai, the Nord came to France in the seventeenth century as a prize of Louis XIV's wars against the House of Orange. It provided France with defensible northern boundaries, but two centuries later the importance of the Nord had grown beyond territorial considerations. Its fertile soil produced grain and sugar beets that supported livestocking, refineries, and brewing. Beneath that soil lay another source of wealth—minerals—whose discovery and exploitation alone could have made the Nord one of the most prosperous areas of Europe. Notwithstanding the importance of the mines (and its miners, who inspired Zola) and the food refineries, enormous though it was, the Nord possessed a distinctive legacy. Before it had revealed its special riches to France, it had been Flemish, and Flanders meant textiles.[1]

Northerners often considered themselves closer to Flanders and its traditions than to their French compatriots. Latecomers to the French nation, they especially contrasted their habits of hard work and thrift to those of the hyper-civilized Parisians. Even today some Northerners recount their history not in terms of manners, intellectual achievement, or cultural excellence, but as a steady commitment to commerce, and particularly to the Flemish heritage of commerce in textiles. Linen and wool had made them prosperous by the time they became French. It was on this foundation and with an ancestral sense of entrepreneurship that they moved into cotton, metallurgy, banking, coal, chemicals, and railroads.

Urban life, too, had flourished before the arrival of Louis XIV's armies. Dunkerque with its shipping wealth, Valenciennes with its renowned lace, and Lille with its accumulated commercial and manufacturing privileges each presented a graceful face to inhabitants and visitors alike. Flemish, not French, architecture first molded the lines of narrow brick buildings with their sculpted facades, and determined the outlines of heavily wrought city gates. To sustain and enhance their way of life, the more prosperous citizens endowed institutions not only for worship, but for charity: hospitals, retreats, and refectories for the indigent, aged, or wounded still stand amid the chambers of commerce or factories of the nineteenth century and the highrise apartments of the twentieth.

Yet despite, or perhaps because of, a highly commercial past, nineteenth-century "progress" would stun the Nord as it did almost no other region of France. Ripe for the introduction of modern industry, its urban institutions were ill-prepared for some of the consequences. The growth of textiles, the discovery of new coal seams, the appearance of sugar, chemical, and metallurgical factories brought an influx of population to the Nord unequaled in other parts of the country. Instead of the decline faced by many French cities, Lille experienced a trebling of her citizenry, while towns such as Roubaix and Tourcoing underwent a hothouse growth that converted them to miniature Manchesters.

Only Manchester provides an appropriate comparison for the transformation at work in the Nord during the nineteenth century. A replica of Manchester's prosperity and

Manchester's misery fell upon these cities in equal portion. The misery is well chronicled, for its sudden appearance summoned reporters and reformers—Villermé, Jules Simon, and Zola, to name only the most famous—to chart its depths and propose remedies. What they saw in Lille, Roubaix, or Marchiennes forms a familiar story: indigence throwing as much as one-third of the population onto relief during business depressions; a disease-ridden populace supporting and feeding its illness in dank cellars of seventeenth-century buildings and in cities whose outdated walls shut out fresh air and light; a permanent army of unemployed composed of the prematurely aged and those maimed by dangerous factory conditions; women who were hags at twenty-five; ill-fed and poorly cared-for children who, if they lived past two, had already achieved a miracle; and finally the prostitutes, juvenile delinquents, and criminals, whose numbers were supplemented later in the century by anarchists and even a few assassins of industrialists.[2]

If this grim story is familiar, so too is its other aspect: an undreamed-of prosperity, an increasingly sophisticated technology, and a new productive apparatus growing out of the combined effort of worker and industrialist. In this story it is the industrialist who commands attention. For him and for every commercially minded man of the Nord, the nineteenth century was a rich and creative time to be alive. During its early years, many *haut bourgeois* devoted themselves to the new opportunities in textiles. Some, like the Descamps, Barrois, or Crépy families of Lille expanded their families' operations of the eighteenth century by employing new workers whom they managed in cottage spinning and weaving and whose products they sold. Others— the new families Motte, Le Blan, Thiriez, Dufour, Faucheur, Scrive, and hundreds more—moved into the factory production of textiles. Before the end of the Second Empire (1870) they had secured the preeminence of the Nord and of their families in the industrial world.

There were other success stories besides the textile *pa-*

tronat: the sugar refiners like Béghin and Bernard; the great public-works entrepreneur Brame; the bankers Pajot, Scalbert, Joire, and Verley; the brewers, professional families, and great wholesalers. Fortunes were established—and, of course, fortunes were lost. But many of the successful then proceeded to new ventures during the Third Republic as they invested their capital in railroads, the newly discovered mines, and the proliferating metallurgical establishments. The textile magnate Alfred Motte-Grimonprez before his death in 1886 had joined ranks with the likes of the Serrets in the *hauts-fourneaux* or the Dujardins in turbine engines. So too the great printers of Lille, the Danels, invested heavily in the mines of the Nord and the Pas-de-Calais. Such were the ways of a dynamic and industrious bourgeoisie.[3]

Here we need to pause, as the men of the Nord occasionally did, to acknowledge the spectacular conquest of material life and to consider the bourgeois man. Few among them did not deliberately spend most of their lives acquiring capital. Most boasted that they were the hardest workers in their factories or other enterprises—the first to arrive in the morning, the last to leave at night. We have the testimony of Narcisse Faucheur-Deledicque, who recounts days that lasted until midnight as he took inventory of stock;[4] of Marie Feron-Vrau, who tells the same story of her parents;[5] of the industrialist Scrépel who arrived at the plant at 6:45 A.M. and left after sunset.[6] Their devotion to industrial time, in which each minute brought a new acquisition, was such that they often surrendered seasonal vacations for work, while their wives and children went to spas, seaside resorts, or country houses to escape the humidity of Northern summers.[7] They measured time, as the letters of Alfred Motte-Grimonprez tell us, sometimes in terms of family events, but more often in terms of business and the public world: the cycles of prosperity, the opening of a new plant, strikes, or the effect of political events on the market.[8] A single-minded commitment to wealth motivated most bourgeois men in the Nord and established the pattern of their lives.

This pursuit was filled with peril as well as opportunity. Every businessman competed with his neighbor, friend, or brother, and according to Jean Lambert's study of the textile industries, that competition resulted in a rate of business failure and bankruptcy of well over fifty percent in the nineteenth century. Because Northerners were slow to adopt the public corporate structure that would bring in outside capital in return for shares in the company, business failures were often catastrophes that permanently ruined families. By the twentieth century, when successive business slumps had done their work, some entrepreneurs in the Nord had been driven to mergers, to making heavy credit arrangements with banks, and even to transforming their firms into *sociétés anonymes*.

In the meantime, the reluctance of these entrepreneurs to resort to these modern measures has led historians to characterize Northern enterprise as family-oriented.[9] In particular, they cite the commitment to self-financing as evidence of a determination to exclude outsiders from influence or knowledge of family business. Often brothers (and even sisters) shared in the management of firms, and parents worked diligently to transmit to their offspring a healthy business or inheritance. In other cases—and here the Mottes of Roubaix provide a good example—parents helped their children start their own companies. Jean-Baptiste and Pauline Motte-Brédart's five offspring established separate enterprises and pursued them with varying degress of success—Alfred Motte-Grimonprez and Motte-Bossut outstripping Adèle Dazin-Motte, who herself did better than the less fortunate Etienne Motte-Desurmont or Pauline Delfosse-Motte.[10]

This example (there are hundreds like it) refines the notion of family enterprise. Like the Mottes, families in the Nord did not rise or fall together, but instead witnessed a constant occurrence of prosperity, mediocrity, or failure among its members. Each child, although financed to some extent by parental success, relied on his or her own entrepreneurial talent. Family members might loan each other capital or might (expecially in the case of women) have financial interests in siblings' firms because of inheritance. But in the long run Northern businessmen were highly individualistic and competitive.[11] Conservative business methods, especially the preference for self-financing, should not blind us to this fact. The bulk of their efforts served less the sentimental end of supporting flagging relatives than the personal one of amassing a fortune. The family served as a vehicle—the word needs to be stressed—for the conveyance of individual achievement in the form of property to the next generation. In viewing their families in this utilitarian way, the Northern businessman was similar to his counterparts in every capitalist country. More importantly for our study, this pragmatic sense of family contrasted with that more human and less economic definition that informed the world view of women of the Nord.

While working for their personal success, capitalists in the Nord demonstrated an intuitive awareness that their private aims called for efforts on the political front. Industry removed production from the household, socialized it, and thereby linked economics with public policy. Institutionalizing bourgeois gains in the French Revolution, the Napoleonic Code had created a legal system under which private property could flourish. But still, social and political questions demanded constant vigilance. Tariffs, for example, were uppermost in Northern businessmen's minds, and whenever free-trade policies threatened, their representatives, of a variety of political hues, formed a solid phalanx against competition from English technology.[12] So too local problems, especially the condition of the working class, were particularly crucial to prosperity. Both the material condition of workers and demands arising from those conditions led to a quest for public policy that would harmonize the imperatives of socialized production, private profit, and political order.

But although closely united in their commitment to capitalism, political and industrial leaders in the Nord often chose different routes to solve the social question. What plagued, inspired, and therefore divided them most were memories of the *ancien régime* and of an ongoing political debate. In short, like most Frenchmen they associated themselves with legitimist, Orleanist, Bonapartist, or republican traditions, and proceeded throughout the nineteenth century to fight political battles along lines that had been drawn during the Revolutionary and Napoleonic periods. As has been demonstrated in Sanford Elwitt's book on the Third Republic, the central and most persistent battle involved the creation of a political form in closest harmony with the economic system itself.[13] The question was ultimately resolved in the triumph of republicanism, with its mirror image of capitalist characteristics—opportunity, mobility, and individualism.

In the Nord a bitter struggle preceded this triumph, for there the forces of reaction were particularly well organized. The families Scrépel, Scalbert, Vrau and Feron-Vrau, Mabille and Thellier de Poncheville, and some of the Bernard families formed the leadership of the legitimist and Catholic wing of the bourgeoisie. While they were active (and well watched by the police) during the Second Empire, during the Third Republic their efforts reached a peak, until in Lille the bourgeois forces were so divided that socialists gained control of the mayor's office in the 1890s. This victory produced the expected reaction throughout the Nord. Everywhere the bourgeoisie came to understand the dangers of intraclass political struggles in the face of a socialist menace that threatened to destroy the most fundamental building block of the capitalist system—private property. By the early twentieth century they had put aside political squabbles, and ran successful and united bourgeois republican tickets headed by men such as Emile Delesalle of Lille and Eugène Motte of Roubaix.[14]

The difficulty in hammering out a political consensus has often obscured the achievement. Instead, the Northern *patronat* has acquired the reputation for political reaction and an attendant commitment to the most retrograde brand of Catholicism. It is not difficult to trace the origins of this opinion, for the small group of monarchist Catholics was extremely vigorous, especially through its newspapers, the *Dépêche, La Vraie France*, and, finally, *La Croix*. More than this, centrists made good use of the presence of these bourgeois reactionaries to gather support for their own politics. They pointed constantly to the dangers of a monarchist coup, rallied the working class around the threat of clericalism, and thus insured the stability of the republic by exaggerating the reputation of the right.

In addition, businessmen sometimes used Catholicism in an attempt to solve the social question. Publisher Edouard Lefort organized religious *patronages* for young working men, and he and Kolb-Bernard were instrumental in founding the Society of St. Vincent de Paul for Christianizing working-class families.[15] In the 1880s, alongside these two groups, grew the Association catholique des patrons du Nord, whose members instituted the *syndicat mixte* in their factories. A Catholic union of both workers and industrialists, the *syndicat mixte* tried to revive old-regime corporatism in which the social classes would merge through worship, cooperative programs such as wholesale buying of household commodities, and various types of instruction. Under such names as Notre Dame de l'usine or the Corporation St. Nicholas, the syndicate theoretically brought the classes together in harmony rather than conflict.[16]

Outside the formal structure of the syndicate, other Northern businessmen designed with extraordinary vigor a host of institutions to assist their workers. Their housing, savings plans, and factory schools have been used as evidence for the endurance of traditions of Catholic charity in

25

the Nord.[17] No interpretation could be more distorted. Organizations such as the Lefort *patronage* or the Society of St. Vincent de Paul had few supporters either among the industrial bourgeoisie or the working class. As Pierre Pierrard has demonstrated, both organizations declined after a few enthusiastic years, and even then the bulk of adherents came from small shopkeepers and their employees who saw the *patronage* as a way of social or economic advancement. Despite the grand publicity efforts of the Church, neither group came near its goal of Christianizing an industrial population.[18]

An even greater distortion occurs when the *syndicat mixte* is taken as indicative of a bourgeois commitment to the Catholic world view. Begun in the Third Republic under the leadership of Leon Harmel, the union never attracted a large following among the Northern bourgeoisie. Few of the major factory owners and businessmen adhered to the *syndicat*, although it gained support among the owners of small workshops. A greater number of prominent industrialists, even financial supporters of the Church such as Alfred Thiriez, opposed its methods of promoting interclass harmony.[19] Yet this one organization is frequently mentioned, following the lead of Catholic publicists, as evidence of bourgeois commitment to the Church.

In fact, the Association des patrons catholiques du Nord arose in the 1880s not because the bourgeoisie was committed to Catholicism, but for the opposite reason. Harmel's followers—the families Scrépel, Bayart, Vrau, and Feron-Vrau—started the organization out of fear for the future of a society led by so agnostic a bourgeoisie as existed in the Nord. The general indifference to religion on the part of most of their peers, they believed, set a bad example for the working class. As a corrective, the *syndicat mixte* would revivify the Catholic sense of order, and they set out unsuccessfully to persuade other industrialists of its virtues.[20] Finally, it should be added that the Catholic *patron* was not any less market-oriented than his less religious counterpart.

There was a certain convenience in using priests and nuns to bring discipline to industrial workers. Sometimes they served as personnel managers by screening potential employees, at other times they provided a structure to the factory environment that left industrialists free for other tasks. The *syndicat mixte* itself taught workers market skills such as the principles of wholesale buying, savings, and insurance. But most important of all, it solved an overriding need for labor discipline. As Louis Cordonnier reported amid the troubles of 1891, "those businessmen who look at us with an indifferent or mocking eye should take heed of the facts. . . . In my factory and in that of Monsieur Hendryckx, all employees have worked without making the slightest demands."[21] For Henri Bayart, another leader of Catholic businessmen, the *syndicat mixte* served a similar function: "it is a kind of insurance against socialism just as there is insurance against fire."[22]

Careful historians of northern France have long been aware of this Voltairian—that is, utilitarian—attitude toward religion. Jean Lambert and Jacques Toulemonde, two historians not only from the Nord but from families with close Catholic connections, have observed the nineteenth-century laxity of that region's bourgeoisie in matters of faith.[23] Their retrospective view finds confirmation in almost every contemporary commentary. Not only popular writers such as Pierre Legrand,[24] not only the high clergy such as Cardinal Régnier of Cambrai,[25] but the women of the bourgeoisie, whose own piety will attract us later, sounded the alarm on atheism. Hundreds of novels poured from their pens, and many of them traced the theme of male secularism. Writers—particularly Josephine de Gaulle, Mathilde Bourdon, and Julia Bécour—portrayed their male contemporaries in various states of religious decay. Other women formed prayer groups to ask for a special grace: that their husbands, sons, fathers, and fathers-in-law return to religion. In every case, these women made a point of contrasting the fallen state of men with the devotion of women to spirituality.

27

Facts bore out their concern. In the first half of the nineteenth century, not more than a handful of Northern bourgeois men joined the clergy. While a greater number later chose the religious life, there were still fewer than half as many monks and priests as women who went into convents.[26] Laymen, as the clergy in the Nord never tired of pointing out, usually took Communion only at Easter, if at all. Their wives sometimes experienced the sacrament weekly, and even daily. Men often ate meat on Friday, and sometimes deliberately broke religious prescriptions to demonstrate their freethinking.[27] The commitment to business rather than the quest for salvation determined the course of male life among the Northern bourgeoisie.

The businessman was less religious than rationalist, and never more rationalist than when confronted with the social question. The influx of Belgians, the working-class poverty, and urban decay each contributed its share to growing debilitation and militance among the working class. The threat to social order was patent, and so too was the insufficiency of old panaceas such as Catholic almsgiving or municipal institutions for charity dating from the *ancien régime*. Each constituted a piecemeal approach to an integral problem of the social order. So the industrialist turned his eyes to more coherent and comprehensive solutions: "we hope," wrote one industrialist, "that efforts of charity are practiced above all in the interest of the institutions of social economy and not in the interest of almsgiving; the latter rarely helps those who have need of it because they dare not take advantage of it; to elevate the individual by work, to combat alcoholism, to suppress pauperism and surround the worker with instructive works, this should be, according to us, the high calling of benefactors of humanity."[28]

Social economy: the words were on many bourgeois lips in the Nord as a remedy; and, strangely, this also has been seen as demonstrating a Catholic outlook toward social problems. Yet everywhere, as in the quotation above, social economy opposed the Catholic ideal of almsgiving, and instead proposed methods of teaching the working class to improve itself through enterprise. Like political economy, it postulated a society acting according to certain economic laws. But social economists proposed intervention to instruct the working class to see its own interest. Even Catholic laymen such as Eugène Mathon of Roubaix adopted, in tandem with their faith, this solution to social questions: "teaching the worker to manage his property, to balance a budget and administer it prepares him to understand better the play of economic forces."[29] It was in this spirit, and not in Catholic terms, that Northern businessmen established savings plans, cooperative buying, and retirement programs. The worker could learn to protect himself against indigence. Should catastrophe strike, he alone would bear responsibility for failing to act according to rational social and economic prescriptions.

In this way, bourgeois social programs not only purported to alleviate misery, they aimed at defusing working-class anger and violent outbursts. Instruction and critical thinking formed the backbone of the bourgeois creed. Northern industrialists foisted education on all members of society, certainly to meet technical exigencies, but also for civic ends. Opening the headquarters of Lille's Société industrielle in 1889, which took the lead in sponsoring educational programs for workers, Edouard Agache stated its positivistic attitude toward interclass tension: "Every thinking person today wonders anxiously as to what solution will put an end to the quarrel between capital and labor. If, as one might predict, we find no talisman that allows the instant transformation of social conditions, one can at least hope that the attentive study and knowledge of the laws of production and of those that regulate the division of profits will allow an amelioration in the present, and in the future will perhaps make for the progressive disappearance of the causes of this painful conflict."[30] In other words, understanding the laws of the market would lead to acceptance of depressions, lay-offs, speed-ups, and the omnipotence of capital. Workers, once instructed, could see that it was just as futile to rage at any of these phenomena as to rage at the weather. In initiating the host of programs that developed in the Nord, the businessman seemed to have donned a paternalistic garb in facing his workers, but he knew—and he wanted them to know—that their relationship was determined by laws of the market and not by those of the Christian family. In this sense he demanded that they operate in the same unsentimental and cutthroat world that shaped his own existence.

When businessmen in the Nord turned their eyes from the market, they did so to celebrate its achievements or promote its further advance. No spectacle matched, for example, the centennial of the Revolution of 1789, when republican municipal governments sponsored parades and dances, commemorative booklets and patriotic contests. In Lille, Emile Bigo-Danel organized this tribute to bourgeois secularism, while his wife remained one of the leading benefactresses of the Jesuits and vice-president of the maternal society that supported religious marriages.[31] The men also had their heroes, not just the revolutionaries of 1789 but more recent standard-bearers: Napoleon I, "father of industry,"[32] and Gambetta, champion of republicanism. But while a Northern deputy discussed the glories of Gambetta in the living room with his friend Clemenceau, his wife and her mother excused themselves to pray conspicuously for the poor deputy's eternal soul.[33] Men in the Nord wrote histories of the region, of its steady progress toward nineteenth-century prosperity and enlightenment. They publicized their family triumphs and local heroes in genealogies, while their women wrote spiritual diaries, pious works, instructive manuals, and, in their novels, lamentations of the religious apostasy of men. Both sexes engaged in the promulgation of ideology: that of women, as we shall see, served the cause of family and Church; that of men, the marketplace and its attendant politics.

Even male social institutions made their contribution to

facets of industrial life. Every Northern city saw the birth of some organization for the advancement of arts and science, in which members read papers on topography, disease, technology, and the history of industry. As France embarked on her imperial mission, geographic societies became the rage among the bourgeoisie. By no means an indulgence in whimsy, these societies aimed "to make [their members] love geography for itself, but also for the services it renders."[34] Men in the Nord followed vicariously and hailed the progress of Brazza as a daring explorer who would open new markets and sources of raw materials. Aside from these societies and the more official organizations such as the chambers of commerce, the purely social clubs were perhaps the most utilitarian of all. Card playing at the Salon des négociants, regular concerts at the Cercle du Nord, evenings at the theater, and Sunday rides with the hunt club—each removed businessmen from the warlike atmosphere of all against all and gave them the solidarity that was so elusive in the economic world itself.[35] The sum of social and professional organizations brought them together on a class (not familial) basis, and thus promoted the unity necessary to meet a parallel solidarity developing among workers.

There was hardly an area of society or urban life not touched by the concern for market utility. Even the physical configuration of cities changed to accommodate the needs of industry, which seemed to demand an end to the old intermingling of homes, businesses, and public buildings. Factories, as they expanded in size, moved to suburbs where they were surrounded by working-class housing. The progress of the Scrive enterprise provides a good example of this transformation: by 1840 two Scrive brothers had built a huge factory in Marquette, a suburb of Lille. The older factory that it replaced, which had been built by the textile pioneer, Antoine Scrive-Labbe, was converted from a building that had accommodated both workers and businessmen and their families to a residence for three Scrive offspring

31

and their children. Others of the Scrives moved to the new residential areas of the city developed on its western fringes by the creation of several wide boulevards and parks.[36] The inner cities of the Nord thus lost their homogeneous qualities, and became administrative centers for both public affairs and the commercial activities of industrialists. The transformation amounted to a public imitation of industrial space functionally ordered according to an increasingly developed division of labor. Production, exchange, administration, and reproduction each had its allotted area, as the process of industrialization created a differentiated urban order.

In undertaking this transformation, bourgeois men demonstrated an intuitive understanding of the most fundamental social divisions, and more important for our purposes, an awareness of the incompatability of home and marketplace. The removal of the home from its proximity to business was more than a matter of disliking soot, smoke, and uncouth workers. It acknowledged that the home was outside the economic (and therefore political and public) arena, once industry had socialized its productive tasks. Instead, home meant reproduction—a matter we will examine in greater detail—and, for men, relaxation. Like the hunt, theater, or musical life of cities, businessmen treated the respite afforded by the home with utilitarian respect. A kind of antimarket atmosphere filled with velvet cushions, useless objects, and piano-playing revitalized weary capitalists. And these same capitalists occasionally expressed the exact amount of sustenance they received:

> Lorsque tu viens rêveuse et pensive, t'asseoir
> Au piano parmi la paix grave du soir,
> Et que sur le clavier d'ivoire, ta main souple
> Court en faisant vibrer les notes qu'elle accouple,
> Assis derrière toi, dans l'ombre, les veux clos,
> J'aime, dans cette paix favorable au repos,
> Songer en écoutant la mélodie ailée

Qui pleure doucement; la lumière voilée
Par ta tête, projette autour de tes cheveux
Un cercle auréolé, nimbe mysterieux
Qui t'enveloppe entière, et le calme mystique
Se dégage de l'ombre où vibre la musique.
J'écoute, recueilli sous le charme sacré.[37]

Industrious, rational, secular, and committed to the acquisition of wealth, the businessman found release when nurtured in a very different domestic environment.

We are speaking here of a type of home that developed only after the factory became the primary focus of production. Before this transition in the first half of the nineteenth century, the household combined both productive and reproductive tasks. Because manufacturing and exchange occurred within its confines, the home constituted an economic arena. Therefore, when we first meet the subjects of our story—the bourgeois women—they are deeply engaged in the historical task of forging the industrial capacity of northern France and in the private one of reproduction. We find them working where we least expect them—at their husbands' sides. They appear not only driven by an equivalent desire for material conquest, but occupied in the direction of family business. This type of partnership, however, amounted to a false springtime that would not survive the triumph of industry.

3
The Productive Life of Women

Northerners are properly proud of their past. Few regions of the world can produce a claim to rival the stunning achievements of the men of the Nord. But Northerners never forgot the contributions of their women, whose story is still alive in the Nord today. Family chroniclers acknowledge that their personal fortunes are due to the combined efforts of their male and female forebears.[1] Far from lamenting women's efforts in industry as unfeminine, Northerners have consistently sung their praises. Listen to the words of Alfred Motte-Grimonprez, an outstanding Roubaisian industrialist, as he eulogized his mother more than one hundred years ago: "My mother was an extraordinary woman in the sense that, married to the most gentle man in the world and above all one completely hostile to industry, she was led by circumstances to direct *la fabrication* and the cotton mill herself. At the same time, she occupied herself with the education of her children and one could say that she inspired in all of us the love of science and the taste for hard work."[2] Pauline Motte-Brédart (1795-1871) was indeed extraordinary in having a husband so little interested in making money. She was less so in being both a female manager of business and interested in money herself. Right in her own family, her mother, mother-in-law, sister-in-law, daughter, and granddaughter occupied themselves with building fortunes. Everywhere in the Nord, noted Etienne Jouy in 1809, "one generally sees women directing businesses and exercising great authority in the *ménage*."[3] This was the legion of northern French businesswomen who probably inspired Michelet to comment that "in Flanders a woman is worth a man, and then some."

These women do not qualify as entrepreneurs merely by having money. They differ significantly from the female owners of Anzin stock or from someone like the legendary Henriette de Clercq of d'Oignies, whose property fortuitously perched atop rich coal seams discovered in the 1840s.[4] They differ, too, from wealthy widows and from women who became silent partners in joint-stock ventures. The businesswomen of the Nord so set themselves apart by their vigorous pursuit of wealth, rather than their enjoyment of it, that they acquired a collective reputation for shrewd business sense, industriousness, and even cunning. They shared these traits with other entrepreneurial women such as *modistes* or greengrocers, but again with a difference. The businesswomen of the Nord engaged in production, not merely in trade, and they amassed capital to invest and reinvest in the industrial capacity of France. In this sense they were capitalists of the first order.

In the late eighteenth and early nineteenth centuries, women's participation in business was common, and blended well with the structure of many enterprises. The Nord was no exception to the classic pattern of early production having close connections with mercantile activity. Well into the nineteenth century and long after the factory system had invaded the area, businessmen of almost any sort called themselves by the generic term, *négociant*, which now has the exclusive meaning of wholesaler. Such a term applied because in the putting-out system, that penultimate stage before the transition to the factory, the capitalist in textiles, for example, devoted most of his efforts to buying raw materials and selling finished goods, without exercising direct supervision of his workers.[5]

Such capitalists usually operated from the home and, indeed, for most enterprises no clear physical boundary existed between home and workplace. One illustration of this continuity is the complex of buildings owned by the *négociant* Delerue-Florin, 54 rue du Bois, in Roubaix. It consisted of a main building that had on the ground floor a salon, dining room, office, and workshop; on the first floor, three bedrooms, a small office, and workshop; on the second floor, a large workshop. Around the courtyard Delerue had buildings for carding, drying, and dyeing, a building with equipment to power machines, and a small shed for preparing cotton.[6] The Roubaix Mottes grouped their buildings in a similar manner, except that at the end of their garden was a cotton mill. In Lille two factory-homes—that of the Vrau family on the rue Pont-neuf and that of the Scrives on the rue Lombard—still stand, among others, as witness to this functional symbiosis.

Businessmen received help in their ventures from all members of the family because the occupation of *négociant* involved a multitude of tasks. In the case of weaving, the wholesaling house might purchase thread, oversee its preparation into warp and woof, its distribution to countryside workers, the receipt of and payment for woven fabric, and its further preparation in bleaching or dyeing. The *négociant* had only finished the job when, with his collection of samples, he had procured sales, expedited his product, and secured payment. An additional complication appeared early in the nineteenth century when many businessmen added to putting-out activities the management of small factories that they built in their courtyards or adjacent to their homes.[7]

Early industries, such as textiles, demanded smaller amounts of capital than did later enterprises such as metallurgy. They called, however, for enormous expenditures of energy by the patronal family—husband, wife, and even adolescent children. Many duties fell to the women; in the Nord, for example, they controlled all accounts and did all bookkeeping for the firm. Madame Motte-Brédart in the

1840s not only kept her own books but drew up the first balance sheet for one of her son's enterprises.[8] Alexandre Decrême, whose innovations in the manufacture of nankeen brought him many medals at industrial expositions and one of the largest fortunes in Roubaix, depended heavily on his wife's management of their financial affairs, for, as one historian noted, "she could count better than her husband."[9] In tandem with accounting, women such as Madame Toulemonde-Destombe distributed raw materials to workers, and received and inspected the finished product.[10]

Despite some division of labor within the entrepreneurial family, most often a complete partnership existed. Narcisse Faucheur-Deledicque, whose children and grandchildren would be very prominent in the Lille financial world, described this joint effort in his memoirs. In the 1830s and 1840s, he and his wife would work long hours, often until midnight, in their lace and linen thread business. Her perfect knowledge of the mill enabled him to leave on sales trips with confidence that production would continue smoothly.[11] Through many difficult years, a similar partnership built the fortune of the Vrau-Aubineaus, whose son would be a leader in establishing the Catholic university of Lille, and whose grandson would publish *La Croix*.[12]

Only sales remained in any sense the prerogative of men among Northern families. In Roubaix, Monsieur Motte-Brédart met customers at the stagecoach terminal while his wife ran their cotton mill. A generation later, his son-in-law, Dazin-Motte, entertained clients at a café while his wife tended their wholesaling operations.[13] Yet a few women did travel extensively seeking sales. Late in the *ancien régime*, Scholastique Duquennoy began traveling beyond the Escaut and Meuse with her father on his business trips. She arranged his credit with Tourcoing bankers, exchanged demand notes, and herself signed all their financial papers. Her marriage to Louis Lorthois in wool failed to divert her from her own business interests.[14] Madame Hollande-Dubois of Valenciennes provides an interesting example not only of a saleswoman but of one groomed for the job. From the age of sixteen she accompanied her father to Paris in the pursuit of customers for their batistes and lawns. The patriarch Dubois did not lack male offspring for this task; indeed, he had fathered twenty-one children. But his daughter proved adept, and by the 1820s she and her oldest brother had replaced their father in traveling throughout France for the Maison Dubois.[15]

Businesswomen had daily contact with their workers. Strict taskmasters, like their husbands, they inspected the quality of work with a careful eye, and rejected imperfections. Neither gentle nor sentimental, they would change dyers, for example, without hesitation when orders failed to be delivered on time. Records of the Conseil des Prud'hommes in Roubaix also show that women became involved in imbroglios with workers. Mme D. had a petition against her for confiscating the tools of a spinner who was allegedly behind in his work. A futile gesture perhaps, and one that brought the woman before magistrates. Others cribbed on wages for piecework if (said the defense) it failed to meet standards.[16] Even as late as the early twentieth century, the few remaining women in business, such as Mme Mahieu-Ferry in Armentières, took strong stands against unions and harassed workers.[17] Such behavior needs to be weighed against the argument that women's work in early production was completely analogous to the management of a household. Their activities carried women into a quite undomestic world of lawcourts and marketplace, and demonstrated a cost-accounting mentality that later women, devoted to jewelry and large dinner parties with musicians, cooks, and truffles, lacked. Women were dealing in business affairs that were more than housewifery writ large, and more than dollhouse-sized enterprises. Although the factories or mercantile firms they directed had not reached the proportions of contemporary conglomerates, Mme Lefebvre-Ducatteau of Roubaix employed 175 weavers, half of them dispersed, and dealt in millions of francs.[18]

At that same time in the 1840s, the Scrives, whose women were active in their various enterprises, engaged in transactions worth three and one-half million francs annually.[19] Size, however, does not tell all. It is more important to note that, in contrast to families in artisanal production or small trade, our subjects had entered the lists of those accumulating and reinvesting capital on a large scale in the service of industrial development.

This experience shaped the habits and mentality of the Northern bourgeoise. She lived in a world of price fluctuations, business cycles, labor problems, quality control, and bookkeeping, and her knowledge of economic exigencies had to be complete for the business to prosper. One such woman was Alexandrine Barrois-Virnot (or Virnot-Barrois, as she identified herself). Partner with her husband François in a large textile enterprise, she completely took over their business in 1790 when he left on a sales trip to recoup losses caused by the Revolution. Mme Barrois kept him informed not only of their own business position; during his absence she searched out new opportunities to make money.[20] Because Barrois was in daily contact with clients throughout southern France and northern Italy, she suggested that they branch out into oils and starches. In her letters she says that the price on starches varies every day between 25 and 26 livres, and that she has offered their services as wholesalers to Northern manufacturers for a commission of two percent. Couldn't Barrois, she asks, find some customers for her commodities?

During this trip, Mme Barrois ran into a series of problems, extraordinary problems arising from government policies and the normal problems of doing business. She has to replace workers at a higher salary, but she absorbs the deficit by dismissing someone who is underproducing. She bargains with clients to deal in assignats. It is not to our advantage, she informs her husband, to deal in anything else, gold being something to avoid in days of fluctuating paper money. Finally, Mme Barrois feels the weight of governmental instability during those days, and suggests moving part of their affairs to England where they will be more certain of the calm necessary for continued business success.

Mme Barrois shared the shrewdness and initiative of her contemporaries, both male and female. She also loved hard work. "I'm never so happy as when I have my hands full of work," she writes her husband. "Sometimes it happens that I'm a little tired at night: but I've noticed that then I sleep better and feel so much better the next day. . . . I have the spirit; I have the taste for work."[21] When her father visits, they talk about business. When she sees her neighbor, Mme Delemar, it is to compare black dyes and to request henceforth only the Geneva black for their cloth. She invites her cousin Julie to come, so that she herself will have more time for her work. This is the kind of woman Alfred Motte-Grimonprez had in mind when he spoke of his mother's inspiring "a taste for hard work." These women did it not by cajoling—although that device was also used—but by example. Imbued with this spirit, they refused leisure when it was offered them. Mme Hollande-Dubois, whose father had bred her for business leadership, declined to retire after her advantageous marriage.[22] And sometimes, as we have seen in the Motte-Brédart couple, women's zeal surpassed that of their husbands. Jean-Baptiste Motte-Brédart, devoted to gardening and charity work, constantly urged his wife to live on their capital. He considered their fortune sufficiently large to allow them a peaceful life of ease, but her commitment to activity and wealth precluded such a choice.[23] Even changes in management techniques, which finally drove women from active participation, failed to break the habits of a generation of women trained to work. Pauline Motte-Brédart's spinster granddaughter, Louise Dazin, maintained the tradition of paying her brothers' workers long after accountants had usurped her other duties in the business.[24]

Something about the early nineteenth-century businesswoman sets her apart from the modern career woman. Whereas the latter often operates in two worlds—the marketplace and the home—the former enjoyed a greater degree of unity in her life. The faithful correspondant, Alexandrine gave a description of her day:

> At the moment, dear friend, I wake up at seven o'clock in the morning, I breakfast, often while nursing one of the children and amusing the two others. I go next to my office to go over my books, to note the transactions in the journal, etc. After that I receive the No. 2s (the camlets); I number what there is or I send them to be dyed; I mark them, and finally do whatever work is at hand. When I have more time, like today, I spend a bit of my morning writing to you. At twelve-thirty I have dinner, and after that I pay all the workmen for the camlets from whom I purchased in the morning. Then I visit the dyeworks or mark the striped callemandes. Sometimes I go to the agent; when the weather is good and I have time I go see your mother and Mme Butard in Esquermes; or I stop at Papa's. Most often I remain here at night with Aunt Julie and my three children.[25]

Mme Barrois certainly had an order to her day, but also an easy passage from family to business. Visiting her father was not only familial; it often brought a financial proposition. So, too, she often combined social visits with inspecting the dyes of her suppliers, obtaining prices, or checking the credit of potential customers.

This pattern reappears in stories of other Northern businesswomen. Sophie Vrau-Aubineau only had to cross the courtyard, avoiding the pools of water from the *filterie*, to pass from home to factory.[26] Pauline Motte-Brédart's factory was newly constructed in the 1820s behind other workshops at the rear of her home. When her son, Motte-Bossut, built his "monster factory" in the 1840s, she only had to cut through the hedge to assist him with the books and other details of management.[27] The same type of arrangement

41

permitted the Toulemondes to take turns watching the warping mill during meals.[28] And it allowed women to open factory gates and admit workers at six in the morning. This symbiosis of home and factory facilitated the business-woman's task, but it had additional consequences for the direction of family life.

In contrast to the later nineteenth-century home, de-nuded of its productive aura, earlier in the century business standards infiltrated domestic life. The women of the Nord demonstrated a cost-accounting and utilitarian mentality in running their households. Witness, for example, Mme Motte-Brédart, who limited the amount of wine consumed at any meal: one bottle of fine wine for eight people, one bottle of ordinary wine for four. She harangued—the word is not too strong—her children about their expenses, made them record every expenditure, and then tallied their ac-counts for them. To the young Alfred away at school, she wrote a letter not only scolding his extravagance, but cor-recting his account sheet. "There in reality is what you have cost us."[29]

How strange to run across women who constantly re-minded children of how expensive they were. They seem even stranger in contrast to later generations of women, who only reminded children of how dear they were. Strange, too, a woman like Alexandrine Barrois, who thought of cloth-ing in terms of utility. After an arduous voyage of hundreds of miles and several months away from home, François Barrois wanted to return with gifts for everyone, especially with a silk dress from Paris for his wife. She refused with the discouraging response, "what would I do with it?"[30] Barrois' sentimental generosity ran up against his wife's business mentality, which developed from those hours keeping books, checking in workers, and inspecting bolts of fabric. This attitude would die with the last generation of women to have a connection with production.

It can be argued that sheer necessity demanded such thrifty, even mean, habits. Before the days of limited liability, separate accounts for business and home, and general fin de siècle prosperity for the great Northern families, the spectre of bankruptcy haunted all members of the bourgeoisie. Business failure meant not just the seizure of company assets, but those of the family as well. A few pennies saved on meals could easily be used to bolster a lagging enterprise, and who was in better position to control both business and domestic accounts than the bourgeois woman? She listed expenditures for raw materials in the same column as the butcher's bill, and tried to save on one as she saved on the other.[31] Marie Feron-Vrau illustrated this general situation with stories of her childhood. In the 1840s, the Vrau family firm was in precarious straits.[32] Accordingly, meals were frugal and luxury unknown. Industrial economy influenced the domestic economy, and vice versa.

Yet in the case of the Barroises and Motte-Brédarts, no such necessity shaped the frugality of their women. Both families had large fortunes, and in the case of Alfred Motte-Grimonprez, he wondered after his mother's death about her constant lessons in money, her harping on business conditions. He had thought the family poor to the point of destitution, so harsh were the restrictions she placed on such extravagances as taking riding lessons—she refused them as wasteful. He and all his siblings were astounded at their parents' death to find out that in fact their legacy was close to a million francs.[33] Being his mother's son, Motte-Grimonprez should not have been surprised. Her habits, like those of her contemporaries, derived not just from fear, but from a shared business attitude toward all aspects of life. This attitude also would be absent in the next, nonproductive generation of women.

In the early part of the nineteenth century, the busy bourgeoise of the Nord often put her infants out to nurse, although we have seen Mme Barrois caring for hers at home. Sunday was the day when parents, occupied during the week, made their visits to children in the countryside or those off at boarding school.[34] Women contrived in those

43

days to rid themselves of child-care responsibilities. For the infant, it meant a wet nurse; youngsters were entrusted to servants; and adolescent children went away to school, and sometimes stayed there for a year or more without returning home. This system allowed the businesswoman of the Nord time for her other pursuits, and she guarded that time jealously, almost to a point that modern observers would call parental neglect. Mme Motte-Brédart's youngsters all went to boarding school and complained about their exile, in their case to no avail. After eighteen months without seeing her home, Adèle Motte (later the prosperous businesswoman Adèle Dazin-Motte) threatened that she would die without a trip home. Her mother, hard-pressed in her work, offered the cold consolation that if the Lord were ready to take Adèle to His side, she could best prepare herself for heaven by staying with the good sisters of St. Bernard.[35] Other children—among them Adèle's own daughter—have left stories of roaming the streets of Northern cities while their mothers worked, of making the most of their excursions with servants, and of playing in workshops and factories without supervision. Occasionally the consequences were unfortunate; a Toulemonde child was killed in its parents' machinery.[36] But Northern businesswomen, unlike their sentimental descendants, did not see themselves as their children's "guardian angels."

Instead of being cute, small children were nuisances. When a child bordered on maturity, however, it captured its mother's attention. Then, businesswomen began the task of instructing their offspring in the ways of the market. Several generations of Motte women shaped the next generation's business mentality. In the case of Mme Motte-Brédart, she continued this tutelage into their adult years: Motte-Bossut's first balance sheet is drawn up in her hand. But other families shared the tradition; such training made Rosalie Parent a valuable asset to her husband, Henri Cuvelier. Married in 1847, she had learned the cloth business from her parents, and from that experience she proceeded to organize the bookkeeping system and serve as office manager for Cuvelier's extensive wine trade based in Haubourdin.[37] Women integrated their sense of parenthood with the general business orientation of their lives. Utility was as much a watchword in their attitude toward children as it was in selecting clothing, planning meals, or making household expenditures. For at least as long as they remained in business, the women of the Nord tried to hand their stern traditions on to their children.

These women led full lives, and ones that seemed to preclude heavy commitments to either Church or charity. This is not to say that they were irreligious and uncharitable, but evidence does not appear, as it does with their descendants, to suggest that the businesswoman spent much time beyond the market world. A few times in the course of her letters Mme Barrois mentions that she has gone to mass,[38] and Mme Motte-Brédart writes "God be praised" at the end of her oldest son's first balance sheet.[39] Aside from such indications, there is little evidence of their concern for religion. The first maternal society began in Lille in 1817; the first *crèche* was formed in Douai in the 1840s; the *salle d'asile* made tentative beginnings in the mid 1830s in Dunkerque and Lille. But none of these organizations, eventually supported by the volunteer efforts of women, flourished until after mid-century, when they spread throughout the Nord and gained the adherence of hundreds of now thoroughly domestic women. Then, also, the number of masses increased, and religious sodalities, prayer groups, and even religiously oriented political activities of women formed out of what seems to have been a new religious commitment. Before that time, the businesswomen of the Nord were occupied, as were their husbands, with making money while taking care of their families.

What terminated this business activity? Pierre Legrand of Lille noted in 1853 that the *bourgeoise* of yesteryear who had tended the books had suddenly metamorphosed into the lady clad in silks and absorbed in social and religious

45

life.[40] Motte-Bossut had trouble with his daughter-in-law's inability to stay within a budget, and he compared her spendthrift habits with the frugality of the previous generation. Aside from women in small commerce, by the late nineteenth century only one group, the widows, maintained the prerogatives of their mothers and grandmothers. Mme Bernard of Santes, widowed at the age of twenty-eight, continued the family sugar-beet operation as she raised her eight children.[41] In Lille, Mme Dujardin-Phalempin won the medal of the Legion of Honor for her contributions to industry through outstanding management of a heavy machine plant.[42] For more than three decades, Mme Alfred Reboux edited the family's *Journal de Roubaix*,[43] while in Armentières the widow Mahieu-Ferry continued to run "with a firm hand" the weaving enterprise started by her husband's mother and father.[44] Something had happened in the Northern business world (and perhaps in most industrial societies) to cause such a marked transformation in habits and mental attitudes.

The cause of this transformation and its timing are difficult to chart, but even while women were managing businesses, harbingers of a future division of labor were in the air. A certain discomfort with the presence of women in business made itself felt, sometimes in barely perceptible ways. For all that Mme Colle had won a medal in the Napoleonic era for her techniques in sugar production, for all that Mme Lefebvre-Ducatteau gathered medals year after year for her textiles, no evidence exists that women of the Nord ever sat on those departmental juries or national commissions that awarded them distinctions for their industrial achievements. Neither did they participate in the chambers of commerce, nor arbitrate labor disputes. Indeed, some women felt the presence of both legal and other prejudice against their activities. In an exasperated letter to her husband, Mme Barrois complained that one of their customers would only settle a small account with Barrois himself.[45] Married women never held business licenses in their own name, and even widows resorted to male representatives for public transactions—Mme Hufty's son, for example, petitioned for her mining concession around Fourmies.[46] Although these customs left women free to run their enterprises without interruption, the spirit of the Napoleonic Code, which placed considerable restriction on a woman's independence and on her ownership of property, suggested the turn that industrial management would take.

Not that the law determined industrial reality. Instead, the course of industrial development seems in retrospect to have dictated the retirement of bourgeois women to the home. A prejudice against women acting in the marketplace appeared in the Napoleonic Code. That, coupled with the tendency of industrialism toward a complete division of labor, pointed women toward an exclusively reproductive life. Here was a ready alternative for women when production lost its labor-intensive quality—or at least when the need for capital equaled that for a contribution on the part of all members of the family. Capital, human labor treated as a commodity, specialization of function to the detriment of a wide range of human skills—each new aspect of industrial life made its contribution. In the end it amounted to a world of production increasingly dehumanized, and the confinement of sympathetic concerns to the home.

The division between public and private—and these well-worn terms are still pertinent—has been explored. In the Nord it meant the separation of residential and industrial areas, the productive from the reproductive, the human from the mechanical. But the change had specific ideological configurations, as well. Local leaders, such as Alexandre Faidherbe of Roubaix, spoke against "the scandalous interventions of women in public and private business."[47] Josephine de Gaulle and Mathilde Bourdon, to name just two Northern writers, began charting the beauties of unrelieved motherhood in their works.[48] Instead of praising the accomplishments of businesswomen, they celebrated the religious and charitable duties of the housewife.

47

These changes in the structure of industry and the ideological climate soon affected the lives of bourgeois women throughout the Nord. In 1861, Mme Vrau-Aubineau retired after thirty-four years in the linen business, but her departure appeared to be forced. She suffered from migraine headaches for the rest of her life, and was cared for by her daughter, Marie Feron-Vrau, who took no part in managing the factory.[49] In Roubaix, the daughters, daughters-in-law, and granddaughters of Pauline Motte-Brédart slowly moved to complete domesticity. Pauline Delfosse-Motte (1825-1903) was excluded from business by her husband Aimé, who thought women had no place outside the home. Adèle Motte-Bossut (1819-1892) had "delicate health complicated by extreme nervousness" and so remained away from her husband's factory. The wife of Alfred Motte-Grimonprez, Léonie, (1833-1899) was "good, sweet and an excellent wife," but no businesswoman like her mother-in-law. Only Adèle Dazin-Motte (1819-1893) continued in her mother's footsteps. Her daughters and daughters-in-law, however, are praised almost exclusively for "practicing domestic virtues to perfection," for being "of a total femininity," or for being "born to be *mère de famille*."[50] Some women on retiring turned their managerial skills toward philanthropy: Mme Briansiaux-Bigo became president of the kindergarten society in Lille and supervised the care of thousands of working-class youngsters; Mme Descat of Roubaix lent her energies to founding day-care centers.[51] Others chose a completely domestic life. Where once women of the Nord had lived in modest quarters, produced a modest number of children, and filled their days with thoughts of business opportunities, after the mid-nineteenth century they inhabited enormous homes, resembling a cross between castle and bank, gave birth to ever larger numbers of children, and devoted their energies to domesticity.

If we seriously consider this shift in the tenor of life, we cannot fail to recognize the extent of its import for women. For the first time in history, the productive aspect of their lives virtually disappeared, with the result of making their existence focus on the task of breeding. Instead of minimizing sex roles, which one author has hailed as the benefit of industrialization, the development of industry accentuated the division of the world by gender.[52] This reorientation meant that the activities of one segment of the population emphasized the exclusive use of the biological as opposed to the intellectual faculties. Rather than marching in tune to the progress of civilization, rather than absorbing ideas of liberalism, individualism, and rationality that accompanied that march, women retreated to the world of nature and biology.

Something was certainly lost in the transformation, specifically the business mentality with its standards of rationality, "the love for hard work and science." But with the newly exclusive reproductive charge came a new world view and new habits. We have labeled them "domesticity." How reproduction and domesticity were inextricably connected is the story of the next chapter.

II
The
Domestic
System

4
Domesticity: The Rhetoric of Reproduction

The domestic woman, especially the woman of wealth, is a more familiar figure than her business-oriented ancestor. By 1870 her portrait is finished, revealing a carefully corseted lady in a plaid taffeta dress, slightly gathered across the stomach, full in back, her lacy shawl arranged to display a white collar attached with a cameo; a small veiled hat on her head, a plush purse dangling from her gloved hands.[1] She is about to make her afternoon visit—in fact, several of them. The children have been dispatched, some to school, some to the care of servants; she has drawn up an *ordre du jour* for the household staff, attended mass, written letters and entries in her diary, presided over the noon meal. In the evening she will sit with her family listening to one of the children read from the Comtesse de Ségur's *Evangile d'une grand'mère*;[2] while listening she will embroider a cushion and eventually summon the servants for evening prayers. This daily ritual is punctuated by visits from the seamstress, knitting for the poor, mending, making lists of repairs, purchases, and projects, and preparing an occasional lavish entertainment at which she and others of her female guests will play the piano and sing.

From the nineteenth century on, people have looked at this portrait and read from it the meaning of the home and the role of woman. The soft folds, delicate lace, plush cushions, and caressing voices contributed to the vision of the home as haven; men returning from work and children from school passed from the outside world with its demands and pressures to the refuge of the home; while one world ruthlessly suppressed personal and psychological needs, the other encouraged and even fulfilled them, providing sustenance and refreshment for industrial society's managers and young trainees. Yet such a picture, taken as it is from a male perspective, does not depict what the home meant to the woman who never left its confines.

Alternatively, the home has been read not as the opposite of the market world but as its complement; one, the world of consumption, the other of production. The tafetta dress, the cameo, the china and silver, even the Comtesse de Ségur's little book had all sprung from the machine. In this view, the home is seen as a repository for industrial goods, and the taffeta-clad lady becomes the parasitic consumer who fortifies the market economy with her spendthrift habits.[3] Thus, the home and, indeed, the domestic system as a whole, had an economic function of increasing the profits of capitalists everywhere. Within the domestic system, however, deployment of cushions, pianos, china, and books in a room have no economic significance, nor does the arrangement of a cameo on a dress have any connection with the market. While purchase or exchange may be an economic act, consumption is not. The artifacts of the home were not equivalent with the artifacts of the market for the woman who manipulated the cushions and cameos; they were not the same to her as balance sheets, gross national product statistics, or any other mathematical calculation; and no market indicator will ever recapitulate the lush but systematic interior of the household.

This view of the home, in which the signs of domesticity are equated with industrial order, has been buttressed by Thorstein Veblen, whose interpretation has come to dominate explanations of the lavish home and its equally lavish woman.[4] In his view, the attractive bourgeoise and her attractive children and home, like trophies of war, indicate male social position and acquired power. The excess of goods, domestic personnel, and the like not only satisfied the normal human craving for security and comfort, but were used by upper-class men much as the barbarian used his trophies to distinguish himself from others. Only the barbarian's use of physical force separated him from the modern male of the leisure class. In all other ways, and especially in the use of goods and women as symbols, modern man perpetuated primitive traits: domesticity—conspicuous consumption—was above all else a sign of family wealth.

Veblen's interpretation is intriguing, not so much for the scorn with which he treats men's psychological cravings as for his suggestion that artifacts in the home may convey meaning. He has not misread a plush reality from the plush surfaces of the home; he understands that the surface is not reality itself, but symbolic of reality. However, for Veblen, that reality is a male one. The artifacts of the home reveal the attitudes of the bourgeois man. But the taffeta-clad lady eludes him, as she eludes Veblen's epigones, who can only depict her as a puppet of her husband's needs for signs of power.

One may extend Veblen's thesis of the symbolic content of domestic artifacts by realizing that they were themselves a female creation, expressive of female realities. It was the bourgeois woman who bought the velvet cushion and embroidered it, who decided on the lacy black shawl, who played the piano at evening social gatherings for which she had supervised the meal planning, table decoration, and seating arrangements. What message did women convey in their choice and use of symbolic devices? Were they testimonials to some power women had acquired either politically or in the market?

If we are not to make the same mistake as Veblen and others, that of falling into a false or incomplete explanation

born of our own preconceptions, we must regard the artifacts of the home as modern anthropologists have for several
generations regarded tribal artifacts and rituals. The use of
beads, feathers, animal fur, strips of leather, indicates organized symbolic systems; in these systems expressions of
hunting, agricultural, kinship, and religious organization
are observed. In other words, artifacts express meaning, but
a meaning that resides in social organization and patterns
of activity. So, too, we must examine the "inner physiology"[5]
of the home, for only by understanding the underlying
mechanisms of domestic life can we unravel that tangle of
lace, drapery, lavish entertainment, household staff, and
needlework to arrive at the truth of what the home meant
to the woman who created and organized it.

Beneath the artifacts of women lay the reality not of economic activity but of reproduction, and concern for perpet-
uating the family. In the nineteenth century, the home became the exclusive focus for the legitimate procreation of
the human race. Within its confines men and women engaged in sexual intercourse; women gave birth to children
at home and nurtured them there in the hope that they
would survive the perilous course of childhood; they nursed
the sick and closed the eyes of the dead. Because women
preserved the ties of blood within an encapsulated space,
they tended to see the home as a microcosm, a holistic
universe to which the industrial world was a subordinate
support system. As industry extracted more and more of the
productive functions of the home, the latter's reproductive
essence stood only more purified and enhanced. We must
look, therefore, at the reproductive experience of women for
explanations of domesticity, just as we might look at farm
life for insight into peasant rituals and modes of expression.

Considering reproduction involves recognizing that it is
a natural act, and that a person who acts on nature, who
produces or has control of natural forces, may think differently from one who is nature's victim. Whether one manip-
ulates a tool or is manipulated by the weather, floods, or

blight shapes a state of mind. In this respect, the bourgeoise who devoted her life exclusively to reproduction, who was, so to speak, at nature's call, will have a different outlook from her ancestors who had some ability to act upon the world in their business life.

Yet to understand the bourgeoise, the social context in which she reproduced is important. Just as the worker produces in a social relationship with the industrialist, the bourgeoise procreated within a matrix of institutions, with the advice, consent, and cooperation of different people. In approaching this woman, the tendency has been to see her unsympathetically and even ahistorically as a culpable reproducer of babies to insure the transmission of private wealth. This interpretation locates her within a social milieu, but it ignores the effect that this context for reproduction had on her own mentality. The demands of society, its institutions, even the bourgeois woman's relatives, all helped create the taffeta-clad lady of the Nord, and they influenced the way she in turn constructed and interpreted the domestic world.

Reproduction

When the young women of the Nord married, they did so without illusions of love and romance. They acted within a framework of concern for the reproduction of bloodlines according to financial, professional, and sometimes political interests. Instead of leaving themselves victims of the personal whims of the young, the bourgeoisie of the Nord arranged marriages out of their need to conserve wealth within the region, in order to finance the expansion of industry, and to forge social solidarity. That system operated successfully, for example, in generations of the Scrive family. Antoine Scrive-Labbe, the daring innovator in textiles, contracted alliances for his children among his business associates in textiles. As the family's interests expanded into other financial endeavors, so marriage partners came from more diversified fields (see Table 1). Regionalism, for the most part, remained the norm.[6]

Children reaching an eligible age expected their parents, often in concert with other relatives, to undertake the search for marriage partners. Usually the bridegroom's family initiated the discussion, and within each cluster of families one member often served as broker for all related children. In the family R., for example, an uncle in the clergy arranged marriages for his brother, for his nieces and nephews, and finally for his grandnieces and grandnephews.[7] Custom dictated an initial meeting between these representatives, followed by a dinner or other social engagement between the families and the two children. The subject of marriage never arose at such an event. If the two families remained interested, they then pursued detailed inquiries into the religion, morality, and health of even distant generations. The presence of madness or congenital disease might disrupt a proposed alliance. Or, if the young man were known for profligacy of any sort, again a rupture might ensue. Any of these considerations paled, however, in the light of overwhelming financial assets or social position. The parents of Louise R., for example, although they thought her too young to marry at the age of eighteen, agreed to a proposal of marriage into a highly successful sugar-refining family because of its many advantages, and the marriage took place within a few months.[8]

Given this economic rationale, people throughout the Nord ridiculed, in fact inveighed against, marriages occasioned by love. Fortunes remained too tenuous, bankruptcies occurred too often for the *coup de foudre*, the lightning bolt of love at first sight, to be seen as anything other than one more gratuitous—and avoidable—disturbance.[9] The northern novelist, Mathilde Bourdon, devoted several of her works to the disasters ensuing from such a lack of common sense and family feeling. Girls must look only to the guidance of their parents, she thought, and divert their eyes from members of the opposite sex.[10]

58

Her warning derived from concrete instances of well-known disruptions of the social order resulting from the fact of falling in love. In the first place, initial meetings of families did not always work smoothly; thus the girl who engaged her heart to a young man before parental approval was certain risked a cruel deception that might spoil her for another venture. Then again, children who thought for themselves might produce a family scandal of enormous proportions. In the middle of the century, for example, two cousins, grandchildren of the wealthiest man in Lille, fell in love during their summers together on their grandfather's estate. Their request to be married, although approved by their respective parents, brought opposition from uncles and aunts who refused their consent for financial reasons. This seemingly innocent request ultimately tore the family apart to such an extent that the police were summoned to keep the children from seeing one another. Quickly the errant daughter was married to a wealthy invalid and subsequently became a nun, while the young man, later a highly successful national politician, never married. Such was the strength of money, such the power of family considerations in the matter of marriages.[11]

Few ever protested this system; instead, most people cited its advantages. What could better assure a successful union, they maintained, than the careful selection of partners by parents who shared financial, political, and social connections? Marriage bound a community in important ways that the romantic young might neglect to consider. Stunning examples of the success of this system reverberate throughout the history of northern France. The Barrois-Virnot union in the late eighteenth century produced through the united efforts of husband and wife an enormous family fortune and a series of most affectionate letters written while the husband went off on sales trips.[12] In the late nineteenth century, the careful marriage of Germaine Bernard to Paul Feron-Vrau, which combined the religious and political predilections of the two families, resulted in a common leadership in Christian factory management, Catholic politics, and urban religious fervor.[13]

This practical rationale for marriage seemed to gain almost complete assent from Northern children. Throughout the century, fewer than three percent of Northern women married out of birth order—an indication of parental control of marriages. Consistently they married by 21, again an indication that parents conceived of and enforced an appropriate age for such a union. Only the generation that came of age during World War I married significantly later (see Table 2). Little room existed, however, for much personal choice on the part of women even had they desired it. Convent-educated and closely chaperoned, they had little contact or experience with men. Such ignorance encouraged submission to parental domination. Although the young women had the final say in such matters, although they received an evening to consider the marriage proposal, such an evening usually passed in prayer and resulted in assent.

Young women prayed on the occasion of marriage proposals because they viewed marriage as a solemn duty rather than a joyful stage of life. Few young people in the Nord married for any reason other than that their parents wished it and had deemed it time for such an event. For men, organizing a household meant an end to the liberty of bachelorhood. For young women, it marked a separation from the warm atmosphere of their parents' home and the beginning of responsibility. Like Marie D., they soberly, if briefly, examined the suitor with whom they would spend their lives: "after exchanging a certain number of words, the mother went to find her son who impressed me as being young, even though he is almost twenty-eight years old. I would have preferred someone much older than I and he gave the effect of being younger, or was that just an idea. . . . I ascertained however that he spoke easily and intelligently and with the greatest simplicity." That same afternoon the young Monsieur D. proposed, and, encouraged by the company of aunts and cousins present at the meeting, Marie D. accepted the proposal the next day. "I believe I have found," she wrote to another relative, "gathered together all the conditions for a completely intimate happiness, placed, in addition, under the most Christian auspices so that there can be no better guarantee."[14]

Only a short betrothal period separated proposal from marriage. During that time a couple might exchange visits to begin an aquaintance, for like Marie D. and her fiancé, or like Jules Toulemonde and Adèle Dazin of Roubaix, often they had never met before. Sometimes, if separated, they wrote letters: "It's you and only you who always appears before my eyes. Ah, if I could hope that your thoughts wander in the same way, with or without permission, I wouldn't ask for more."[15] This kind of intimacy was probably rare and reserved for letters; in public the couple addressed each other as Monsieur and Mademoiselle until their wedding. And, in any case, the betrothal served less to produce intimacy than to prepare a household. A fiancée passed the time busily readying her trousseau, labeling dozens of linens with intertwined initials, assembling a year's wardrobe, and gathering other necessities to last decades of married life. Although young women also made and received courtesy calls connected with their approaching change of status, these only supplemented the more essential task of furnishing a home. For the household had to stand ready from the outset for the important role of receiving children who were expected to arrive as quickly as possible.

The Catholic Church's doctrine on reproduction as the primary purpose of marriage could not have accorded better with the needs of the Northern bourgeoisie. Children guaranteed that the family enterprise, including all its financial and production secrets, would remain free from outside influence and scrutiny. Until the late nineteenth century, when managers played a greater role, family firms demanded a minimum number of children to handle different aspects of the trade. Parents, then, soon after marriage, began questioning newlyweds about the imminence of a new heir. Any delay in pregnancy brought handwringing, plaintive letters to relatives, and disguised speculation about possible sterility.[16]

Such speculations often started after four or five months of marriage, for throughout the century the typical bourgeoise delivered her first child within eleven months (see Table 3). Moreover, Northern women seemed to take to heart the commitment to produce offspring: right through the first decades of the twentieth century they gave birth to large numbers of children. In the 1840s, when women were still active in the family business, the average number of children born into each family was five, but by the end of the century women bore an average of seven children (see Table 4). Yet, curiously, as women produced more and more children, the business necessity decreased: mergers had occurred and new business techniques had been adopted to release the *patronat* from the pressing need for numerous heirs. In fact, the increasing number of offspring at this time engendered a scramble for positions and the entry of many sons of the bourgeoisie into allied fields such as law, medicine, and notarial practice.[17] The dowering of large numbers of daughters also taxed family resources.

How, then, to explain the attachment of a utilitarian-minded bourgeoisie to such an impractical phenomenon, especially when the option existed of limiting their families? The Nord was notorious for its large clans of dozens of children. Was it a kind of luxury the wealthy allowed themselves—these tribes, like the Bernards, which in the twentieth century held reunions for hundreds, even thousands, of members who were no more distant than second cousins?[18] Was the Nord scrupulously following the dictates of the Church on matters of reproduction and sexuality? Or did the transition to an exclusively domestic life shorn of productive function play its role as well? For the women of the Nord had borne fewer children, and cared for smaller families, during the days when they worked alongside their husbands in business. This control of births appeared in families managing both secure and unstable enterprises. Those women who began their reproductive lives after 1870, who never entered the factory or kept business accounts, had begun reproducing with a vengeance, one would almost say. By that time the development of Northern industry had brought an amount of wealth and comfort that converted their function to an exclusively sexual and reproductive one. It should not be surprising, then, that within this framework of both necessity and possibility they made the most of their reproductive charge independently of the changes that had occurred outside their domestic domain. The social order now allotted them this exclusive role, the Church encouraged it, their bodies permitted it, and domestic symbolism enhanced the bearing of children within a system of female rites and rituals that constituted a language of reproduction.

Women of the bourgeoisie gained a certain kind of power from the reproductive act. The social order, though it might command them to reproduce, was by that command placed at their mercy. For economic and psychological reasons, if for nothing else, the cult of the heir glorified the woman who reproduced the father's image, the receptacle for his capital, his eternal life in a mortal world. From the moment of betrothal, attention focused on the woman, her trousseau, her wedding attire, and her radiant smile. Thereafter the mother in the Nord held center stage in the family. It was to her house that grown children flocked unfailingly on Sundays—a practice that continued long after a father's death. "At home my son obeys me," claimed one woman of her illustrious son,[19] while another man complained that Northern society reeked of matriarchy in which women decided all questions of marriage and vocation, parental largesse, and parental love.[20]

Because of this psychological, social, and physical dependence, what could have been more natural than the accretion of power to the woman, reproducing a bourgeoisie that could not escape her force? She was entrusted with its life in the most literal sense, and she carried out that charge in a multitude of ways. One example is Madame B., who, while delegating many households tasks to servants, maintained close track of her eight children. She kept a notebook on the strengths and weaknesses of each, wrung from them their most intimate thoughts, heard their lessons, rewarded and punished their actions. In all genuine modesty, Mme B. viewed herself as a guardian angel charged with surrounding her children with her presence so she might protect and mold them through her example as a Catholic woman. To "purge them of all evil thoughts and actions," she rewarded the obedient at the end of each week and punished the disobedient by withholding her love in the form of a goodnight kiss. Mme B.'s power over her children, then, consisted both of this knowledge of their most intimate thoughts and of the ability to reward and punish. It did not derive from teaching them the love of science and hard work.[21]

In addition to weaving this psychological net, Mme B., like all women of the Nord, held the cord of life, or at least she stood as its most visible representative. Not the man who ran the factory and produced the income, but the woman with domestic knowledge seemed to spell the difference between life and death. For their families women provided the connection with food, clothing, and shelter as well as the human components of love and socialization. Each child knew that his mother, in that age of frequent illness and precarious mortality, would spend long hours at a sickbed, and that she shared information on cures and remedies with her friends and relatives. She would know about Bordeaux wine, veal stock, or pomades for their maladies, and would be skilled in the use of leeches or cupping glasses.[22] Even when carrying a mending bag or correcting a servant, women of the Nord symbolized victory in the struggle for human survival. When combined with their nurturing skills, even peripheral signs invested them with vital power.

These marital, reproductive, and household patterns offer certain insights into the position of women in industrial society. In the first place, their position lacked autonomy. They neither made decisions about their marriages nor could they, because of their exclusively reproductive role, claim an economic position of their own. Although the dowries of Northern women usually were part of a *communauté des biens*, husbands administered family funds. Thus, in a market world, and from a psychological point of view, they were dependent. Reproductively, however, they had enormous power and a central role when it came to the perpetuation of life. They increased that power by producing larger families, but also by multiplying their attentions to human problems as they knitted their children's socks, cared for them in illness, and provisioned the household with all the necessities of life with a domestic vigor unknown to the preceding generations of business-oriented women.

This same ambiguous position informs the world of domestic artifacts; power and fragility both are expressed in fashion, interior decoration, and cooking, as is the centrality of reproduction itself. Women lived with pregnancies either imminent or actual, and as well with the attendant cycles of reproductivity: menstruation, lactation, menopause. Reproduction and sexuality were the source of their power, and also the font of their weakness, for childbirth killed many bourgeoises and reduced the vigor of countless others. The women of the Nord had cause to express a convoluted attitude toward reproduction and toward nature, attitudes that also dominate the arrangement of symbols in the domestic interior.

The daily activities of the Northern bourgeoise brought her close to nature. Her days were spent involved in the physical problems of her family—nourishment, illness, shelter, life, and death. In addition, women felt their companionship with the natural world through reproduction. While the market society moved toward mastering nature and producing "man-made" goods, its women remained caught in nature's cycles, concerned with the ravages it could work on them and their families. Nature could be their enemy; it could also serve as the source of female glory. In any case, it was central. Thus, we find the recapitulation of nature and of natural themes in domestic life, a concomittant stress on mastering a natural foe, while at the same time articulating, and even enhancing, its dominance as the focal point of the home.

As we enter the Northern bourgeois home and observe its daily life, we can regard its operations as part of a symbolic system. Each activity had its functional aspect, but as the thrust of human, as opposed to animal, activity tends toward cultural creativity, so we find webs of meaning, networks of communication, and expressions of human concern overlying many domestic undertakings. This gave household procedures a multiple significance of which women were often acutely aware.

Language

Bourgeois women recognized the descriptive importance of their demeanor, dress, and domestic interiors. "The furnishing of a room," wrote Julia Bécour in one of her novels about bourgeois life in Lille, "describes a person."[23] But not just any person or member of the family. Rather, it was the bourgeois woman herself, the *maîtresse de maison*, who acquired a reputation or definition from her household. Clever, neat, seductive, matronly, or even egotistical—any of these qualities and more were read from the arrangement or selection of domestic artifacts.

Increasingly throughout the century, the necessities consumed in the household acquired a thick layer of symbolism. At the beginning of the century bourgeois women working in business with their husbands preferred simple food—in fact, thought of it in utilitarian terms, if they thought of it at all. After their installation in the home, however, they

took new interest in *cuisine soignée*. Not that women in the
Nord did more cooking; indeed, except for making a cake
for a special occasion, most of them did none at all. They
purchased many of their desserts for parties at Meerts in
Lille, for example, or hired extra cooks for large social
events.[24] New wealth, of course, paid for the hands that
fashioned roses from truffles or leaves from angelica. But
while truffles, lobster, vol-au-vents created by other hands
garnished their dinner tables, the praise accrued to the reputation not of the cook, the pastry chef, or the *charcutier*,
but to that of the mistress of the house. That elegant cuisine
eventually permeated all layers of domestic society attests
to its ultimate importance as a symbol of domesticity. Cooking was a transformation of the natural into a sign of life-
giving capacity, and some women chose it as such. Since
it was a sign, little did it matter whether they had performed
the transformation directly. A clever enhancement and
repression of nature, an enhancement and repression in a
very physical state, formed part of their reflection. Society
saw them and they saw themselves in the glazed salmon
and in the carefully chosen strawberries that graced the
table.

So, too, with the gleaming furniture, polished silver, thick
carpets, or brocaded drapes. Once coated with wax for protection, lustrous furniture carried an important message
about a *maîtresse de maison*. In her youth, a Northern
woman learned the formulas for household maintenance—
three solutions for removing candlewax from linen table-
clothes, or the use of angelica to sweeten a chamberpot—
that were then performed under her supervision and to her
credit. The shining interior of a home mirrored the character
of its woman. As the nineteenth century progressed, the
necessity grew for constant redecoration and rejuvenation
of the home. Mme S. renewed her interior with carpeting,
drapes, objets d'art, dessert forks, fancy needlework displays, portraits, paper flowers, and liqueur glasses, among
other things. In Douai Mme Demont greeted summer by

draping the foyer in green wool and pompoms to simulate moss and flowers. Other women ushered in seasons with new chair coverings, draperies, and furniture rearrangement. Basic items of furniture, purchased at marriage, were expected to last a lifetime, but they were revitalized with a constant replacement of linens and dresser scarves to disguise their declining years, and perhaps, to add to the image of freshness, youth, and fertility of the housewife.[25]

No woman in the Nord ever went without her needlework. While Mme Demont and her mother sat by the window and watched passersby, the former worked at needlepoint coverings for the chairs; the latter knit her son's and grandson's socks, all in grey yarn, which supposedly wore better. Most women, with the help of a seamstress, made all their daughters' clothing. Others carried a bag of knitting or mending over their arm, and when the morning rounds were over or when a spare moment arose, took it out to work on. Mme R., daughter of a wealthy textile manufacturer and wife of a prosperous lawyer, was one of these women devoted to mending on all occasions.[26] Her attentions certainly served a utilitarian purpose, but why did she do a task that any one of her ten servants might have done? In one way she made a small saving of some symbolic importance, but in another sense she spoke through mending of her attachment to being female. By the end of the nineteenth century domestic symbolism was the only imperative underlying these activities: factories and workshops produced clothing that the Northern bourgeoise could easily afford, and most households contained small armies of servants.

When visitors joined the family circle, or when women were themselves guests, sewing continued, but in the form of fancywork. They made especially delicate household linens, embroidered small flowers on silk to line baskets sold at the charity bazaar, worked beads onto small purses for a friend. Here domestic symbolism was compounded, for not only did the appearance of busy hands speak about a woman's daintiness and generosity, but each work itself might contain a message. Anemones represented innocence and candor; a red geranium, melancholy; a white lily, innocence; a lily of the valley, the return of happiness. The combination of white and green meant proven virtue, while pink stood for tenderness and brown for humility.[27] Speaking a symbolic language of their sex, women of the Nord conveyed to their audience its oblique message through their activities.

It was fashion, however, that served as the most insistent and increasingly popular way of drawing attention to a woman's presence and of speaking about that presence. Novelists in the Nord used clothing as a convention for swiftly delineating their characters' personalities and stamping them as good or evil, and women themselves captured eyes not only with clever tricks of lace and ribbon, but with the sheer mass of hoops, crinolines, and bustles. Fashion formed a communication system among women, and even among men and women, a system that became the quintessential expression because it surrounded the female form itself. As fashion seduced women by its potency, observers noted the displacement of fancy needlework in the Nord by the whirring sounds of the sewing machine.[28]

The trend was new. In 1790 Mme Barrois-Virnot, co-manager of the family wholesaling fortune, had replied to her husband's suggestion of a new dress from Paris that she had no need for anything so elaborate. A century later such simplicity of taste and utilitarian considerations had succumbed to a fondness for a series of ornate garments. Although the bourgeois woman might limit herself to five or six dresses, those five or six were sometimes refurbished daily to fit the latest style or a sudden whim. With the help of the nefarious machine, women and their seamstresses turned skirts, added flounces or lace, recut bodices, or redesigned sleeves. Although not in the habit of buying all their clothes in Paris, they might treat themselves to one extraordinary frock from the capital. Because they lived in the provinces, the bourgeoises of the Nord received patterns from the *Journal des Modes* to follow the latest styles.[29] Provincial life did not stop them from spending enormous sums on jewelry, hats, lace, and sumptuous fabrics.

Some women in the Nord rejected the proliferation of garments and the emphasis on fashion. Always a good indicator of the feelings of the most conservative women, Mathilde Bourdon often spent a few lines in her books cautioning readers on the perils of fashion, and turned an entire work into a diatribe against the sewing machine. It was not, however, that Bourdon discarded clothing as a symbolic system, but rather that she recognized its importance. "You can tell at a glance," she wrote, "a woman's character by her clothing."[30] Thus, Bourdon inveighed against the statements that excessively dressed women made about themselves.

In harmony with Bourdon, an alumnae group of the Sacré-Coeur boarding school asked its members to avoid the whirl of fashion: "Don't follow *la mode* servilely." They demanded of each member of the Children of Mary a commitment to "simple elegance" in dress. Indeed, their photographs display an adherence to this principle: dark silk garments, hair pulled back neatly.[31] Yet even then, among women noted for their austerity, appear false curls on some, and tiny, almost invisible tucks and lace insets, rippled sleeves, and ribboned caps. Each asserted herself with clothing, however disguised. Dark silks, hair sleeked back, a certain kind of jewelry meant "simple elegance." Other women, posing corseted and decolletée, intricately coifed, used the same language to offer a different message.[32] Following *la mode* displayed a knowledge of female language, showed an obedience to the female code, and demonstrated an ability to speak by its rules; but it may be noted that resistance to a particular vogue implied the same acknowledgment of its symbolic potency as did acceptance.

The suspicion with which the alumnae of Sacré-Coeur regarded fashion had another significance, for these women recognized therein a challenge to the integrity of female symbolism. Increasingly *la mode* had fallen under the domination of industry and industrial values, and those alumnae protested the rhythm of ceaseless change demanded by capitalist control of fashion. Refrain from rushing to Paris, they urged; find a nearby dressmaker who knows you and your character.[33] An interloper from the world of money and men had placed its foot on the threshold of the home, and this interloper seemed to be drawing many women away from the fullness of their domestic responsibility. Yet other women, seduced by the new offerings of industry—hundreds of yards of lace or hats laden with cherries, feathers, ribbons, lace, and a veil—rushed toward the connection with a world that offered all the tools for their sexual embellishment. How could one resist the rich profusion of raw materials of domestic symbolism that opened the possibility for great female artistry, that provided the opportunity to garnish their bodies with all the signs of reproductivity? By the end of the nineteenth century, women of the Nord were thus of two minds about fashion. Denouncing its inroads, one group continued to use the metaphor of clothing to make statements about their "simple elegance." Another faction followed its dictates scrupulously and reveled in the abundance of possibilities for making statements. The latter group found its reward in local social columns. Mme Salembier's costume of black silk incrusted with black lace on white taffeta and a black straw hat garnished with white lilacs received detailed treatment in the account of her daughter's wedding.[34] A single image was multiplied as others copied it.

Being *à la mode*, however, entailed enormous expense, and seemed to stand in sharp opposition to the bourgeois sense of thrift and utility. At base it conflicted with the interests of self-financing for industry, of legacies for heirs, and of domestic economy. Mme S. spent many times her food budget on hats and dresses, while Mme T.'s new brooch cost more than her husband's wardrobe for three years.[35] Simultaneously, the women of the Nord professed a commitment to thrifty household practices. They made savings by mending and remending stockings and linens, limiting the amounts of food or wine consumed at their tables, and drilling into their children economical habits. Moreover, they gave the impression of venerating their account books more, even, than their children. "Dear friends," Marie Tou-lemonde wrote to her sisters in the convent, "Mother doesn't have time to write to you, but she loves you all the same and charges me to give you a big hug. Unfortunately for you, Saturday is the day for accounts . . . and this afternoon we will be driven from our rooms for the usual cleaning."[36] The account-book ritual followed a set order: a notation of every household expenditure went into a particular enve-lope according to the nature of the expense—food, house-hold, personal expenses of each family member, small treats and pleasures, charity, and the like. On a fixed day each week the *maîtresse de maison* recorded these expenditures in appropriate columns in her account book, and at the end of each month she totaled them and compared the sums with her cash balance. "My mother did this religiously," recalled one elderly Roubaisienne, "and she became panic-stricken if the figures failed to tally. Although she claimed that my father would be furious, he hardly ever looked at the book and then only perfunctorily."[37] This obsessive at-titude toward an account book on the part of the wife of one of the wealthiest men in the Nord, owner of a newspaper, chairman of the board of directors of mines and of banks, paralleled the view of most Northern women, who were determined to leave a patrimony as large as they had re-ceived.

Although one can not fault their sincerity in this profes-sion, in fact the account book had almost no impact on inheritance, nor were Northern women utilitarian in their expenditures. At the beginning of the century, when do-mestic and business funds were joined, when the wife had charge of accounts, and when household savings affected the amount of capital available for entrepreneurial development, domestic economy played a significant role. Savings from self-imposed restrictions on luxury of any sort—wine, food, clothing, vacations—were devoted to amassing capital, and at that early point women were as active as their husbands in imposing such austerity. In a sense, the privations fit a functional way of life that ignored the kinds of symbols later surrounding domesticity: fashion, *cuisine soignée*, piano lessons, and painting on leather meant nothing to a Mme Barrois, Mme Motte-Brédart or Mme Vrau-Aubineau. The balance sheet and its sums of gold signaled success to them, and told of that success to their peers.

For the late nineteenth-century women, however, domestic austerity played almost solely a symbolic role in lives rich in symbolic content. It inflicted small sacrifices that would produce compensating luxuries. It allowed for fashion, new carpeting, more silver—all the symbolic refurbishing of the female space. But financial exigencies, budgetary restrictions, and concern for where each penny went had little real influence on expenditures. When Mme S. ran short of money, she simply added more to her account. When the totals failed to tally, she entered the shortage (and often it was considerable) as "missing." Women did gain credit, however, if they showed particular skill, and an ability to combine "thrift with charm" spoke about them in much the way that fashion or needlework did.[38] By this time the notion of domestic economy was a sham, relating to nothing substantial in actual economic practice. All garnish, all symbol, the well-kept account book stood for the presence of a woman concerned with her family and her domestic charge. In the anachronistic perpetuation of this relic of women's economic power, the emptiness of real economic content only served to highlight a woman's reproductivity. When husbands checked their wives' balance sheets, they smiled, not at their economic earnestness, for their wives spent fortunes. Men smiled at the femininity of women with so little economic sense. Remembering his mother in this way, Fernand Motte wrote, "my mother, still astonishingly

73

young and beautiful, had very refined tastes; she loved clothes, beautiful furniture, and lavish dishes. Especially she knew nothing about the value of money, and in minutes she could organize, like a maestro, the waltz of our money."[39] In the case of many such women the account book and all its contradictions rivaled the use of a bow, a jewel, a modulated voice as a female sign.

Even—perhaps especially—the servant system, which seemed to mushroom in the nineteenth century, acquired an evocative capacity in contrast to the utilitarian concerns that had earlier determined the use of help in bourgeois households. For example, Mme S. provides an example of a woman in the 1840s who employed servants according to her need. With one child she relied on one live-in domestic, and supplemented her services with dayworkers such as a seamstress, a laundress, cooks, and serving maids when the necessity arose.[40] By the end of the nineteenth century, however, several servants became the norm as dayworkers were incorporated into the home, and as their number came to include not only the usual cook and housemaid, but in addition live-in gardeners, ladies' maids, valets, and chauffeurs.[41] Although some might propose that this specialization of labor in the household duplicated that in industrial society, another factor was at work. Numerous servants provided an enlarged image of their mistress. She was all places at once, caring for family matters.

A faithful servant acted as a maternal surrogate in many situations: walking the children to school, dressing, bathing, feeding, and sick-nursing them. Because this proximity influenced the next generation of the family, it was important to find domestics of high moral character. They performed the household functions of cooking, cleaning, sewing, laundering, and ironing, which motivated the search for servants who also had a certain dexterity, cleverness, and skill. But each of these qualities was doubly imperative, because the correct performance of tasks (or the incorrect performance) reflected the image of the housewife, and served to determine her reputation. Even in those areas that suggest the necessary and substantial—in cooking, sewing, or cleaning—servants expressed the symbolism of the household. Each task in the home carried a double import by serving simultaneously functional and metaphorical purposes. Cooking, sewing, and cleaning fed, clothed, and sanitized family members, but they also created domestic symbols: shining furniture, glazed salmon, bows, flounces, and pleats. With the help of servants a bourgeois woman could arrange, polish, and adorn her home and herself; each adornment expressed and heightened the female presence. Thus, servants helped focus attention on the central female figure in the domestic world.

This reciprocity, this partnership between servant and mistress, perpetuated a traditional "moral economy" within the household, quite distinct from the cash tie binding employer and employee in the labor contract. Centuries of custom lay behind domestic work-life. The tie between housewife and servant rested on notions of duty (*devoir*), obligation, and correct behavior, and to that extent resembled old-régime corporatism. The relationship was not a contract between equals but a partnership of unequals, not a temporary arrangement for individual self-interest but a mutual dependency aimed at the good of the whole. Like the head and the hand working together to benefit an individual, the servant and mistress cooperated for the good of the family of which each was a member. The bargain between them was not exhausted by a certain number of hours' work and a salary, but only by the achievement of the general welfare, a goal that made the relationship almost unlimited. The personal nature of the bonds sometimes alleviated the worst features of this authoritarian structure. Yet when confronted by the attractions of contractual labor, this type of familial relationship became "the servant problem."

This telescoping of the servant into her mistress, intensifying as it did their reciprocal relationship, was typical of other hierarchic patterns of social organization. Children

75

were included in their parents, reflected them, and, it was hoped, glorified them, just as inhabitants of a kingdom served the purposes of their superiors and eventually those of the king. In Christian doctrine, human beings had received a graded allotment of talents to be used to glorify the Father at the pinnacle of the hierarchic chain. In this sense each individual was affiliated with a higher being, but could not equal his superior. The servant affected the magnificence of the bourgeois woman, but could never rival her mistress because of the qualitative differentiation that determined the organization of family members.

Because the relationship was close both in ideal and in practice, choosing their servants preoccupied Northern women. Although the "servant problem" did not arise until the twentieth century, a suitable servant was sufficiently rare to provoke an endless quest. Convinced of the debilitation of the urban population, families in the Nord sent frantic letters to relatives in the countryside asking for healthy, robust, moral, and tractable domestics. Or they would trade servants, especially wet nurses, who were always difficult to find. One woman wrote to her mother in the country: "Maria wants absolutely to have a nurse from the Aveyron; I proposed finding a woman near Bergues, Blanche spoke to her about the wife of Péronne; she won't listen to any of this and has charged me to beg you to find one; for my part I would be very grateful. The age of the milk doesn't concern Maria; . . . but if you can't find anyone better she will take the nurse of little Henry despite the portrait Blanche has drawn of her character." In the case of nurses, women relaxed their standard of morality to the end of obtaining an unmarried rural mother, a first offender, whose milk would be good.[42] When the services of the *fille mère* had been secured, however, her morality, like that of all servants, became the charge of the bourgeois woman.

The charge to scrutinize household help closely and carefully appeared in both domestic manuals and novels. Nov elists, particularly, emphasized this urgency with stories of disaster falling on young wives remiss in their duties toward servants: a child's mortal illness, a household thrown topsy-turvy, a young housemaid turning to crime could all result from a lack of supervision.[43] All evidence indicates that Northern women performed this task scrupulously. They organized, as in the city of Lille, prayer groups for the female domestic help,[44] but to even greater efficacy, they bound their servants to the family by providing the servants' children with education, by furnishing clothing, and by nursing and burying faithful domestics.[45] In return, servants performed an endless round of tasks and were expected to behave according to a rigid code of behavior.

Dire warnings on servants' conduct were given for reasons other than actual threats to the smooth functioning of the home. The message conveyed by servants about their mistress had an important content, and so care must be taken in their selection. Above all else, servants perpetuated the reproductive motif of domesticity through demonstrations of "morality," that is, through their sexual restraint. They constituted a ubiquitous definition of the reproductive woman in the sense that a negative defines a positive. While a servant could replace her mistress in most areas, there was one task exclusively in the domain of the lady of the house. She alone could reproduce legitimate heirs. The picture of the idle upper-class woman coddled by toiling domestics thus signified and fortified her reproductive splendor. She existed only to reproduce, while her opposite—the nonreproductive and productive—self existed in others. The household staff projected her presence in all their activities, including their incapacity in the sexual and reproductive sphere.[46] The servant, in the long run, was not just functional; she served as the negative metaphor for reproduction.

Fashion, too, presented the dominant message. Especially the shape of the dress echoed female fertility. Empire styles had often been sexually revealing in disposing of petticoats

77

and conforming to the lines of women's bodies, as did the tight hose of men. As ideas of equality for women were firmly disposed of, as industrialization worked its division of labor, male clothing became asexual and utilitarian, while the shape of female clothing changed dramatically. Reproductive contours appeared in the form of ever-widening skirts. Only in pregnancy, when breasts and abdomen swell to reach spherical proportions is the female figure uniformly round. This roundness was duplicated in the skirts of the 1840s, 1850s, and 1860s. Following that, the spherical shape receded to the back of the skirt. With that change around 1870, an opposition of pregnant contours appeared in the higher waistline, which metaphorically accommodated the elongated and impregnated uterus and in the dramatic roundness in the bustle. By the end of the century, symbolic fullness shifted to the upper half of female garments. A new kind of corset continued to emphasize the rounded derriere, while flattening the stomach, but it also created the illusion of breasts swollen with milk. Yards of fabric suddenly appeared on sleeves, which were spherical over the upper arm. The women of the Nord followed these changing styles while their husbands remained wedded to bourgeois garb: utilitarian, spare, stripped of the sexual emphasis in previous male clothing, and virtually unchanging for almost two centuries.[47]

The women of the Nord thus accentuated their reproductive function in two ways. They indulged in large-scale, even conspicuous procreation; and they highlighted reproduction by giving it a central place in domestic symbolism. The relentless translation of reproduction into a domestic language system had the effect of removing the activities of women from natural history and making them clearly cultural. By speaking through the accoutrements of her environment, a woman could be reproductive and sexual in a symbolic way long after she had ceased to reproduce life; or she could opt never to engage in reproduction except through domestic symbolism. In many industrial countries domesticity flowered simultaneously with the limitation of childbirth, and perhaps even as a function of birth control. But in the Nord the vigorous bourgeoises worked through both explicit reproduction and metaphor.

The quality of the reproductive experience was described metaphorically by these women. For one thing, it gave them power, and domestic symbolism highlighted the power of women. Full skirts, bodices, huge sleeves gave substance to female claims to importance by increasing their physical size to at least double that of men. Women wearing hoop skirts, crinolines, bustles, or trains filled the social space and made people aware of their presence. Women were so powerful that sometimes doorways could not let them pass; they overflowed the small chairs, cushions, and footstools of mid-century. As skirts became less voluminous, women's furniture became more massive. At the *fin de siècle*, women of the Nord began filling their homes with huge buffets, cupboards, armoires, and larger sofas and chairs. Because women saw themselves reflected in objects, they multiplied those objects as testimony to force: magazines, plants, little comforts became popular ways of presenting a forceful image through sheer increase in number.

Yet objects so thoroughly reflected women that they had to tell of weakness as well as strength. Pictures of the Northern bourgeoise show her dressed in voluminous clothing, but her dress at mid-century has embroidery and tiny tucks in the bodice that give a delicate air to the bulk. She has an abundance of miniscule false curls escaping from her bonnet. In 1870 her semibustled overskirt is ringed with small bows; the sleeves of her dress are tightly fitted to make the arms slim, and they end in a row of intricate pleats at the wrist. She wears, too, a small half-hat with a wisp of veil, a tiny feather, a narrow ribbing. At the end of the century her massive upper torso is weakened with shirred fabric, her skirt banded with slender ribbon, and the imposing hat undermined by fluttering ostrich feathers, a cluster of grapes, more veil and ribbon, and a final fragile encasement in the sheerest of tulle. This emphasis on fragility terminated in the hobble skirt, but throughout the century layers of clothing reduced the importance of the body itself while simultaneously creating mass. The corset also made a woman tiny and insignificant. And the sum of all garments testified to female imprisonment, to an unliberated ego, and was voluntarily worn by all women to testify to this aspect of their lives.

Women repeated the motif of weakness in meals, interior decorating, and needlework. They worked small, pretty objects such as purses, slippers, handkerchiefs, baskets, and linens for themselves, their relatives, friends, or fiancés. Such intricacies, so the story went, could only come from the gentle hands of woman, and they contributed to her mystique. Observers also noted the tendency toward delicacy in cuisine. The truffle or the rough angelica stalk assumed innumerable fragile forms in bourgeois kitchens. Mme S. always chose the airy, light vol-au-vent and purchased tiny, though luxurious, pastries for her dinner parties. Nothing remained bulky or unrefined by female hands; instead, the number of courses in meals increased to demonstrate substance, while each course exposed a feminine daintiness. This transformation was accompanied by a more complex table setting and adornment. Tables were laden with a greater number of tiny utensils: individual but small table lamps, salt cellars, bone dishes, finger bowls. The hostess directed the ensemble with minute, barely perceptible gestures: she inclined her head, rang a small silver bell, touched a utensil, or placed her forefinger to her lips to give commands.[48] Each sign perpetuated the juxtaposition of power and fragility.

Every large piece of furniture had its delicate counterpart. Bureaus, tables, buffets, and mantles carried their array of small objects, ranging from clocks and candlesticks to Sèvres china statuary and extraneous pieces of silver. Between them lay delicate doilies, embroidered scarves, or some other piece of fragile fabric. Chairs and sofas had their coverings in florals, stripes, and brocade (which though strong had a delicate relief), and their fringes, flounces, and trims duplicated the rhythms of female dress. They might have, like all household linens, an extra layer of dainty embroidery. When more massive furniture appeared, the women of the Nord increased the tiny objects—especially plants, books, and vases of flowers—to maintain the balance of oppositions. The entire treasure of delicacies might not appear simultaneously. Some, like those of Mme Demont of Douai, were carefully stored in tissue and boxes to emphasize that they were too inordinately fragile to tolerate customary display.[49]

Servants also contributed to the convoluted feminine metaphor. Like the aristocrat's retainers, they expanded a woman's presence. In their obedience to her orders and even whims they provided a demonstration of her power. Conversely, however, servants gave repeated testimony to female fragility. They performed the mean tasks of life, and thus expresed her delicacy. Too refined to touch a soiled child, she could kiss it goodnight.[50] Others kept her gardens in order, so that she could pick the flowers—or *faute de mieux*, she made artificial ones.[51] In the Nord the bourgeois woman abstained from handling fowls, roasts, and vegetables for meals. She did, however, supervise the delicate tasks of making fruit preserves or liquors, and her only culinary forte—if indeed she had one—was fashioning an intricate, dainty dessert.[52]

Because weakness and power grew from the reproductive charge, and because that charge itself grew from their biology, women also expressed their closeness to the natural world in domestic symbolism. They decorated their homes in floral motifs and repeated it in their clothing. Anniversaries, weddings, birthdays as indicative of natural cycles were occasions—from the female perspective—for floral symbols of nature.[53] They chose flowers for embroidery or as a pattern to decorate cakes or refashion food. Sometimes small fruit—especially grapes and cherries—substituted for flowers on hats, dresses, linens, or needlework. A women's group in the Nord selected the daisy as its emblem.[54] At these happy signs of plant life, however, they stopped. For although nature surrounded them, it did so in a threatening way by regulating and even endangering their lives.

The women of the Nord endured natural regulation, bodily changes, and perils in complete ignorance. Sent off to boarding school as preadolescents, or to visit a relative when childbirth approached, teen-aged girls often thought the babies were purchased, found, or mysteriously delivered. The fears, mystery, and even secrecy surrounding sexual and physical life led by all women in the nineteenth century can never be overemphasized. Northern bourgeois women went to the marriage bed ignorant of the sexual act. If she was bold, a mother might prepare her daughter for the event in the following manner: tonight your husband is going to do something to you. He has the right. If it becomes too terrible, pray to Jesus Christ. Many women were uninstructed in the results of sexual intercourse, or they made no connection between that and pregnancy. When pregnancy did occur, women generally faced the prospect of childbirth in secret terror. Again a mother might give her daughter a generalized or vague description of what would happen, or the doctor offered as instruction the command to make a fist, to scream as loud as possible, and to push. Besides that slim knowledge, women knew that others had died in childbirth: Mme B. on the birth of her tenth child; Mme O. at twenty-two in the delivery of her first; Mme R. seven days after the birth of her third daughter. Stories of suffering and pitiful agonies passed down through families in whispers. No one thought of revealing miscarriages, and pregnancies went hidden from public view as women remained at home at least from their sixth month.[55] Women tried, in short, to tame the natural by hiding it.

For every expression of the reproductive and natural there was an attempt to disguise its potency in the shrouds of metaphor. The corsets, bustles, and petticoats produced accentuated hips. They also masked them in an envelope of fabric and converted the reproductive woman into a composite of lace, silk, feathers, and jewels. Through the use of artificial materials and a set of rules, in this case the rules of fashion, nature (woman) became convention. Doilies and dresser scarves also spoke and hid, while the rules of etiquette regulated and stylized, and thus transformed the sexual encounters of men and women on social occasions. The sexual symbolism of the home is perhaps most famously illustrated by the Victorian ladies who recognized the sexual potency of table legs and covered them from sight. Thus, while desiring to speak of reproductivity and of nature, women tried also to make it invisible. Despite its reproductive centrality, the bed lay down hallways, under canopies and drapes, and behind closed doors. Women sought to erase that centrality of the natural by placing water closets severely out of view, or by insisting that their children shower in their clothes so that sensuality would never escape.[56]

Concealment was not their only weapon. When the women of the Nord took a truffle and disfigured it, when they had a fowl dismembered and covered with sauce, they had worked a transformation on nature. By transforming it into a human sign, they thereby conquered their enemy. The same process occurred when they deformed their own bodies with corsets, covered them with layers—and imprisoning layers at that—of fabric, lace, jewels, feathers, and false fruit. The natural body emerged as a tamed artifact. Women created elaborate chignons. They rearranged the wood, cloth, and glassware in their homes as a sign that they, not nature, were in control. In this way domesticity became the cultural expression of women, for like most people they attempted to modify the natural situation in which they found themselves. From this attempt developed a system of signs—preverbal signs—articulating their concerns and expressing the scheme of their lives: reproduction, family, power, weakness, and weddedness to nature.

Adding a bustle to a dress converted the natural into the conventional, and human conventions have formed the network of communication among people from the most primitive to the most sophisticated. But the first layer of meaning in such symbolic systems has usually commenced with the struggle to differentiate between the human and the natural world.

When nature seemed to have its way, however, they nursed their sick families, made broth and poultices, and even applied leeches themselves. But wherever possible they sought to prevent invasions of nature that could bring chaos and worse. The women of the Nord were renowned for the cleanliness of their households despite the soot and smoke from factories. Servants scrubbed, polished, and waxed every surface inside the house, doused sidewalks with water, and swept doorsteps.[57] In addition, the bourgeoise knew a hundred formulas for avoiding cockroaches, mice, and other small animals. Precautionary also was the advice of Mathilde Bourdon, counselor of Northern women: "Make sure," she warned women who spent hundreds on baubles and lace, "that nothing is wasted . . . that nothing spoils . . . that nothing deteriorates." Beware, she said, of nature.[58]

Natural chaos could appear in other ways. Mme L. believed that if she removed the ordering support of her corset, her flesh would dissipate, spread, and dissolve.[59] Natural functions had to be ordered to master them. Sexual life was confined to the central bed, in a specified room. So too the water closet had its own fixed location. Other techniques, like an inflexible etiquette and the recurring, single placement of utensils regulated eating and the social intercourse of human beings. Bourdon summed it all up: the home was not a place for laissez-faire, but for order.[60] Only that prevented the disasters which, as women knew, nature in all its many guises could bring.

In this way domesticity transcended functionalism and

moved into ritual. Saturdays in the Nord were for house-cleaning, whether necessary or not; another day was for laundry, for mending, for visiting. A late nineteenth-century Mme Motte religiously kept her account book, though her son said that she had absolutely no sense of money. When the fashion column announced that English embroidery on garments had been dethroned,[61] women followed its advice and ritualistically gave such dresses to the cook. Schedules, fashion, corsets, etiquette, polishing acquired a life of their own and shaped a woman's life. They formed the sum of domesticity, but domesticity itself became a magical rite serving to master nature. Once it was installed as an efficacious system, one could not accept the bustle and then dispense with proper table arrangement, *haute cuisine*, and waxed furniture. All parts of the ritual had to be included if it was to work its magical triumph over nature. Leave one part out, the magic was broken. Here the high priestesses moved in—the Catharine Beechers, Mathilde Bourdons, or Lady Campbells—both to reiterate the formulas and to make their warnings. Bourdon especially liked to juxtapose examples of the success that followed the proper adherence to ritual and the disaster awaiting women who threw aside their schedules, who ignored servant morality, or who broke the rules of etiquette.

After these wanderings through the domestic world, let us bring the components together to see how they functioned as a type, however primitive, of linguistic system.[62] Language begins by drawing attention to the speaker. A yell, a discourse, even a few words said in a modulated voice say "I exist." Certainly the women of the Nord performed this first charge of language well as they filled domestic space with signs of their existence. Truffles, draperies, cleanliness, polish, and lace meant that a woman ruled the household. Observers gave her due praise for being a woman, so feminine, and so committed to duty.

In recognizing the hand of woman in the house, such observers also were witnesses that domesticity met the second requirement of language: it conveyed meaning. Domesticity expressed the feminine, and we have seen precisely what the feminine experience consisted of. It meant reproduction and concern for the family. Reproductive contours distributed themselves throughout the household; so did those of the family. The latter was the focal point of all interior order. In the decoration of a home the dining room contained a buffet along the walls with the table and chairs at the center, around which the family would congregate. In the *salon*, commodes, clocks, and small tables appeared on the periphery, and the chairs and small sofas for the family were grouped around a central point. A bed occupied the focus of a bedroom, with dressers and armoires along the walls. Although a woman might play with the details of this arrangement, no one thought to upset the centrality of family—a family that owed its existence to the reproductive act of woman. Meaning continued to accrue as women described the quality of the reproductive experience. It made them powerful, massive, and in a way, invincible. But it also exposed them to danger, so that women were fragile as a daisy, delicate as a piece of lace.

Northerners continued to understand. Men went off to their clubs in the evening to escape the female accent in the domestic sphere. Sometimes they feigned a business appointment to shorten Sunday dinner at their mother's, and then they met at the hunt club.[63] Likewise, men recognized female delicacy, gentleness, and weakness—especially its novelty—in the 1850s. One Northerner wrote that while some men praised the businesswoman of yesteryear, he preferred the women of mid-century "who like certain Asian birds nourish themselves on flowers," and who "had a secret intuition of heavenly things . . . and a divine mission to fill."[64] Domesticity came to be seen a divine mission, and often women referred to themselves, like Mme B., as guardian angels; they also encouraged others to make the comparison to things heavenly. In fact, however, women of the Nord operated in the fleshy, sexual, painful, reproductive world. They agonized in childbirth, watched children die, experienced the regular discomforts of being female. In this case also domestic artifacts performed a function—the transformative one—of language. For by naming things, one tames them, or at least makes the first step in bringing nature within the human sphere. From that proceeds classification and ultimately scientific study and, with each procedure, a new sense of mastery. Domestic women everywhere were taking at least the first steps in this process when they engaged in converting natural things to human signs.

The domestic system, however, only took them to a certain point, for they stopped at the level where artifacts have power in themselves, primarily the power to master nature. Had the women of the Nord been asked why they diligently directed the polishing of tables or the concoction of fancy dishes, why they embroidered so fastidiously, why they kept their account books so religiously, they might not have answered. But they surely would have repeated the warnings in books of advice: think what happens to those who neglect their schedules, their polishings, their hems, their manners, their mending. Signs were powerful; women were not.

Language, as a cultural edifice, cannot be solipsistic. On the contrary, it rests on human beings using signs in identical ways to insure communication. Cookbooks, etiquette books, child-care manuals, fashion magazines all developed in the nineteenth century to perform this function. They announced the basic rules and formed a corpus of information about presenting domestic symbols. Here, of course, we enter a treacherous terrain. Are not the rules set by someone out there in the market? Was Worth, for example, not pulling the strings of fashion? Was *La Bonne cuisinière* not directing the use of truffles, or Mathilde Bourdon the gentle nod of the hostess to dismiss her guests? Were bourgeois women not victims, albeit privileged ones, of outside manipulators who alone set the rules and decided the content of domesticity?

I think not. The so-called arbiters of fashion, interior decorating, cooking, child care, and the like certainly made decisions in prewar France. But consider the nature of these supposed transformations they could work in domestic life. Throughout our time span they failed to affect the enduring emphasis on reproduction and nature or the opposition of fragility and mass. This synchronic structure of domesticity was impregnable so long as women's lives remained embedded in nature and reproduction, so long as the contradictions in their position survived. Instead the arbiters played with diachronic aspects of female language and, in fact, worked for the repetition of the perpetual female theme—reproduction. They helped women execute those constant small alterations that said, "I am fresh and fertile"; thus the notion of fashion in any genre of domesticity could only arise at the intersection of reproduction and the market. By announcing the rules, experts created nothing new in itself. Instead, they made for greater homogeneity among women so that the latter might communicate across families, cities, countries, continents, and eventually classes. Mathilde Bourdon could point to a woman's clothing as a mirror of her character and intelligence, and be read throughout France, England, and the United States, only because an acceptance of domestic artifacts as signs preceded her writing.

In another sense, however, only the intensity and homogeneity of signs were new. Women for millennia had announced such physical alterations as coming of age with a change of costume and other rituals. They had used charms, chants, and rites to protect and talk about themselves, to regulate relationships with other human beings and with nature and nature gods. But what did it mean when "modern" women performed similar rituals, when they saw themselves in luxurious draperies or a waxed buffet, when they invested objects and routines with qualities, or even magical powers? To some it meant that women were childlike. Misogynists particularly liked to point to such behavior as indicative of women's trivial-mindedness, of their inability to deal with abstractions, and ultimately of their inferiority. Dismissing the charge of inferiority, we should perhaps think about the childlike aspects of women's mode of communication.[65] For example, language in its most sophisticated form is a logical construct that can be used to deal with contradictions, assert definitions, and ultimately demonstrate truths among human beings. Women's symbolic use of domestic artifacts displayed some of these characteristics of assertion and social communication, but in the long run it fell far short of fulfilling its charge as language. Instead of resolving contradictions, it merely expressed all of them unconsciously and simultaneously. Feelings of power and fragility, the oneness with and fear of nature appeared without comment in the home. There was no logic in the domestic ordering of artifacts to establish priorities among these assertions, to establish the truth of women's condition, or to explore reality. Rather, each woman fused heterogeneous and contradictory elements in an arbitrary way without creating a grammar of domestic signs that could work toward defining the female condition sharply and fruitfully. Neither an inductive nor deductive process of reasoning could result from efforts that were syncretistic and transductive rather than logical.

The absence of abstracting potential in women's symbolic system reduced its expressive power. The language of domestic artifacts limited women in the kinds of statements they could make about themselves; they could not reveal, for example, a complicated intelligence. Through these symbols they expressed merely that they were women and that their condition was complicated. They could not use their system to investigate nature, society, or the world of abstract thought. Instead, their language remained fixed on themselves, and although endowed with some communicative force—one could read a woman by her clothing—it in fact worked with a high degree of solipsism. That is, a woman and her symbols formed a mutual reflection of each other, and only projected outside themselves on occasional moments of social intercourse. Thus little separation existed between the exterior and interior of women, between the subjective and objective worlds. The mind projected its feelings, fears, and desires onto things—fragility into a piece of lace, power into enormous skirts, and the like. This same tendency has been noted in primitive rituals, but also in the solipsistic babbling of infants and children who appear to be communicating, but who in fact perpetually assert their existence through a stream of egocentric speech.

But why should this be so? Why should adult women display such retrograde or infantile states of mind? We can only suggest a return to the starting point in reproduction. Women, by inhabiting a new world constructed exclusively on biology, began repeating in their adult lives the childhood experience or that of other people who lack control over nature. Biological rhythms, physical demands, pain, and insecurity occupied their thoughts the way hunger, wetness, and the struggle for motor competence occupy those of the child. In this situation, physicality and state of mind are difficult to separate sufficiently for there to arise any distinction between subjective and objective worlds. The self is the world; the world is the self; women's mind, reproductive body, and domestic artifacts similarly remained one.

While solipsism produced domestic expressions that many outsiders found comforting or read in a multitude of ways, that expression turned back to tyrannize women. It became their law, a set of rules increasingly codified in cookbooks, the manuals for etiquette and child care, and fashion magazines. The obedience given by women to their own creation likewise arose from the undifferentiated encapsulation of the self in nature. Again, examples from child psychology illustrate the situation of women. The child is dominated by physical forces, most of which consist of his own natural needs, but some of which may include parents or even acts of nature—rain, wind, sun, and the like. He or she invests those forces of whatever kind with extraordinary authority. The same process of finding the power of laws in one's own perceptions—that is, in egocentricity—has been attributed to primitive symbolism, as well. Symbols or rituals invented by the human mind themselves determine human actions, set prohibitions, or provide standards for those who have no notion that they originate in the human mind.[66] In the case of bourgeois women, the symbols that expressed the power of reproduction similarly acted as inflexible guidelines for the fledgling ego. Their safety lay in obeying the so-called arbiters of fashion, etiquette, or decorating; in religiously keeping their account books; or in adhering scrupulously to schedules they, themselves, had drawn up.

In the long run, taffeta-clad ladies represented themselves more than they did their husbands' social position. In all domestic activities they created a female mode of expression born of a tie to nature that was new in the sense of taking them outside the realm of production. Women of earlier generations had expressed themselves differently because, like men, their biology was mixed with other concerns. But the industrial division of labor demanded specialization and brought to women a new closeness with nature. Small innovations can institute major changes in mentality: the industrial worker shares little of the artisan's way of life, though they may appear similar. So too peasants and agricultural day laborers are different breeds. In nineteenth-century France, the portrait of a bourgeois lady conjures up images from other civilizations, historical moments, or stages in life. For all that similarity, however, this lady was neither an old-regime aristocrat nor a child, but rather a bourgeoise, who articulated in a domestic way her dependence, weakness, and importance to an industrial society.

Unconsciously, perhaps, she recognized the insufficiency of such human efforts at transforming the world around her. Domestic rituals did not always succeed in working their magic, nor did they always endow her with strength. Moreover, the domestic language failed to render the full range of human feelings, and with a burst of energy women of the Nord turned to the Church. They placed their destinies in the hands of the supreme authority of an institution whose creed had long promised relief from an imperfect world. In its own way, Catholic doctrine provided a cosmology in perfect harmony with the domestic way of life.

5
Cosmos: Faith versus Reason

In 1879, an out-of-town feminist, after a prolonged stay in the Nord, sketched another portrait of the bourgeoise. This time the lady was dressed in black, with religious medals around her neck and rosary beads moving through her fingers. After morning mass she spent portions of her day reading such spiritual works as the *Lives of the Saints* and the *Imitation of Christ*, and noting her meditations in a diary. For worthy causes she conducted solitary vigils at the parish church; sewed, like Christian women at other moments in history, priestly vestments and altarpieces; took collections at high mass on Sunday. At all times the bourgeoise led her family and servants to the proper execution of their religious duties not only through the example of her own pious conduct but through active persuasion and even cajoling.[1]

The women of the Nord were domestic, even fashionable, but they were also among the most faithful of French Catholics. The superficially opposing portraits should not surprise us, for we have already seen ladies resolve other contradictions. Just as they could be powerful and weak, so they were worldly and spiritual in the same lifetime. But in resolving the contradictions of the flesh and the spirit, they looked to the Church, and in so doing constituted that still extant breed of women, sometimes dressed in black, who fervently worship the Catholic God. Around this religious fervor, which infected women in Spain and Italy as well, the question has always arisen: why did they experience it so deeply when men seemed to be losing their faith? Why women; why not men?

Men had certainly left the Catholic Church in large numbers during the nineteenth century in favor of a quest for the golden calf. In Protestant countries this had not so generally been the case. Doctrine had slowly evolved in favor of secular pursuits; church attendance there was often like receiving a special benediction for the pursuit of wealth. But Catholicism made few concessions to the modern world—though it made some—and thus lost the allegiance of many men. A handful of bourgeois men in the Nord tried to lead a renaissance of faith among their peers and workers; others used the Church's good offices in social welfare projects; but many were lax, and some went to the extreme of abjuring religion altogether. This happened in even the most religious families. Mme Camille Feron-Vrau prayed and proselytized for the conversion of her father-in-law;[2] Mme Julie Van Der Meersch-Behaghel, for that of her husband;[3] and three hundred bourgeois women in the Archiconfrérie des mères chrétiennes of Lille for their sons, husbands, and other male relatives. Even that almost solitary northern French feminist, Mme Julia Bécour, who found so much to criticize in her female contemporaries, saw the men of the Nord as unfortunately indifferent to religion.[4]

In matters of faith there was only a negative agreement among bourgeois men and women: both failed to appreciate the other sex's view of religion. If women prayed for the souls of their men, politicians, businessmen, and intellectuals in the Nord increasingly viewed doctrinaire Catholicism as politically reactionary, hostile to economic progress, and fraught with superstition. In their endeavor to establish a modern and rational social order, they found the persistent support of influential women for an anachronistic cause dangerous. More than that, persistent Catholic fervor invited contempt for women, who were seen as mentally too inferior or blindly fanatical to espouse a more intellectual and less emotional vision of life.

That attitude has passed to succeeding generations of historians, who continue to misunderstand women's religious attachment by interpreting it as evidence of some lack of character or intellect. Despite the contributions of psychoanalysis and anthropology to the study of religion, European Catholic women appear at best as mystified by a manipulating clergy, and at worst as supporters of a creed that allowed them to indulge female bigotry and narrow-mindedness. Although non-Western peoples are permitted their magical or theological interpretation of life, the Catholic woman, especially if a bourgeoise, is not allowed the same choice of creed. Instead of asking why women maintained their piety, most historians utter a few derogatory words before shaking their heads.

Yet justice requires allowing the ladies of the Nord what has never been denied the ancient Greeks or medieval scholastics, not to mention intelligent and respected modern men, especially since women remained preindustrial in their daily lives by reproducing life in the traditional way. In fact, as more acts of production became socialized, the traditional nature of women's lives became enhanced, if only by contrast. A Christian explanation of the universe had long gripped the Western world because of its cogency and coherence, and it would have been stranger for women to reject Catholicism than to embrace it. The acceptance of science and the disposal of religion has built on a security—some have called it hubris—in the face of nature that menstruating, parturient, and menopausal women never had. The mathematical explanation of life proposed by modern science appeared as patent fatuity to the visibly bleeding, swelling, pained women of the nineteenth century. They preferred theology and the pre-Copernican vision of the universe, for reproduction predisposed them to a religious world view.

Space, Time, Matter, Causality, and Action

Religious explanations of the universe have usually envisioned an original chaos.[5] Divine activity served the two-fold purpose of filling the void and of ordering creation. Building on this tradition, Catholicism described God's creation as orderly, although the order became more and more imperfect the closer one came to the earthly center of things. In the context of an imperfect terrestrial organization, it was possible for human beings to bring their own measure of order, and thereby to imitate their god. Thus, when northern French women organized their homes, they created a little universe of order from the random materials of nature, and they too peopled that universe with children—products of their love—as God had done when His goodness and love spilled over to effect the genesis of the universe. Their quest for order suggests less the practical than the sacred. The ability to bring order separated men from beasts, or at least indicated that tiny advance in the chain of being that put the human just below the godly.

The homes of northern French women, who both reproduced and ordered, appears as a microcosm of the pre-Copernican universe. After Newton, the universe became a theoretical construct resting on concepts of infinity and acentricity, with little relevance to a domestic order rooted in perception and circumscribed by walls as clearly visible as the sky. Before Newton, and more immediate to women's experience, was the finite universe, with God inhabiting a fixed and well-defined command post at the outer limits of His creation. Heaven, like home, was as real and spatial as the Elysian Fields or the Happy Hunting Ground. At the center stood the immobile earth—an idea developed from individual experience—as the reference point of all knowledge until astronomy, combined with calculus, interposed a filter between man and the universe. Without a mathematical system to interpret perception and to direct it beyond itself, cosmology was bound to rest on a geocentric, though in fact an egocentric, construction of reality. This egocentric universe coincided by analogy with the arrangement of domestic life, for woman formed the center of a world that she populated, decorated, and ordered.

Translated into social terms, all space was private or familial, attached to an individual woman surrounded by her family. Anything beyond the family or groups of families was foreign. The women of the Nord manifested this sense of the dichotomy between family and outsider with the clarity of the most primitive tribesmen, while their husbands changed such notions of space to correspond to a new mathematical and market-centered experience of the world.[6] That is, while acknowledging the home as an entity, the men of the Nord slowly moved their business away from it and created a space that was public, anonymous, atomistic, and as unbounded as the market or universe itself. Their wives continued the tribal tradition, although they extended it to nonmembers through the agencies of etiquette and charity.

For the women of the Nord, anything beyond the home or collection of homes formed a profane and hostile world, and each endeavored to fill her world with signs of sanctification. They summoned priests to bless each household as it opened. They adorned their walls with crucifixes and filled niches with statuary, especially of the Virgin Mary; many even erected small chapels in their homes. Each morning they greeted their children with holy words; at meals they asked God's blessing; each evening they gathered servants and family members alike for prayer; and before bed they gave each child a special benediction. Observing Lenten fasting and meatless Fridays was a way of life except for those husbands who chose to demonstrate their freethinking. Women hung festoons and banners from balconies and windows on days of holy processions, or even

97

let processions pass through their homes and gardens when local governments forbade their appearance on public streets. The sacred became so connected with family that at times the home seemed sacred of itself, while anything outside its perimeters appeared profane. Just as cleaning could take on the meaning of ordering creation and pre-venting chaos, so other small acts became "religious" as they regulated family life. For example, some women prided themselves on their ability to keep business matters out of family reunions. Others banned "profane" novels from their homes as harmful to the sanctity of the family.[7] In short, religion informed women's attitude toward the space around them.

The women of the Nord ignored modern notions of time. Industry seemed the embodiment of the Newtonian concept of time as uniform, objective, homogenous, measurable, and regular. Factories ran along a rhythm of ceaseless time, accurately measured, in which each minute equaled all the rest; ultimately they dispensed with days or seasons. While this new concept gradually pulled more and more members of society into its orbit, certain groups remained immune, and others felt its compulsion only minimally. Women of the Nord continued such tasks as preparing children for school, instructing servants, meditating or reading instruc-tively, dining, visiting, shopping, and praying. Or they con-nected tasks with seasons: autumn and spring for the grand laundry; summers for canning and making liquors; winters for social gatherings. Women assigned significance to cer-tain natural events such as christening, coming of age, marriage, childbirth, and death. A ritualistic sense of time moved women to set aside certain days such as Saturdays for cleaning and Sundays or Tuesday evenings for receiving the family. Certain hours in the day became ritualized for visiting or letter-writing, and no other time could serve so well.

The repetition, which appears similar to mechanical time but involved quite a different psychology, highlighted events and assigned them meaning. It did not homogenize life. For repetition and ritual symbolized the return to an archetypical moment of renewal most apparent in rituals of the Church, which were adhered to by women with a precision corresponding to the attention they paid to their domestic chores. That precision existed not because events were usual and had to be disposed of efficiently, but because they were significant and deserved scrupulous attention. Each week women in the Nord attended high mass at their parish church, where many industrialists' wives took special charity collections. While the clergy spent great effort to urge men to take Holy Communion at least at Easter, women took the sacrament weekly, and even daily. Women's groups such as the Archiconfrérie des mères chrétiennes sponsored monthly Communion for their hundreds of members. Monthly meetings of the Children of Mary, drawn from the alumnae of the fashionable girls' boarding schools, ritually began with six Hail Marys and six Our Fathers. Ladies in charity groups such as the Dames de St. Vincent de Paul also started their monthly meetings with prayers. Each year all the women's religious and charity organizations remembered their dead members in individual memorial masses. On significant occasions each of the many sodalities scheduled its membership for half-hour stations of prayer in local churches. In May 1889, for example, Mme Léon Delesalle-Humbert was invited to choose a time between 5:30 A.M. and 11:00 P.M. for her adoration of the Blessed Sacrament as a member of the archconfraternity of Notre-Dame de la Treille. As a participant in the organization of the Perpetual Rosary, one prayed each month for a special temporal blessing as well as for spiritual grace: in February for France and for foreign missions; in May for the election of pro-Catholic deputies; in June for the humiliation of the enemies of the Church; in July for the Pope, for the persecuted clergy, for the success of Catholic youth in their school examinations. To the schedule of specific prayers were added wedding and obituary masses, regular retreats and pilgrimages for upper-class women, and special masses sponsored by women's groups. "Madame, the annual ceremony of the benediction of little children will take place Wednesday at exactly three o'clock in the chapel of Sacré-Coeur, 70 bis rue Royale." The fiftieth anniversary of the Society of St. François de Régis, a Red Cross mass for the dead soldiers of the Franco-Prussian War, a retreat for the ladies of the Society of St. Vincent de Paul, a mass for the dead members of the maternal society, a visit by the archbishop to the nursery school society—for all of these a woman such as Gabrielle Delesalle-Humbert was invited "to wear a simple toilette, but bring a well-disposed heart. That will be enough." At home women continued the sacred rituals: daily prayer sessions, grace at meals, observances of Saints' Days, religious festivals, adornment of household statuary. They especially offered thanks and special care to the statue of the Blessed Mother during the month of May.[8]

The accumulation of rituals charged women's lives with meaning by effecting union with a religious moment. Perfect time was God's time, just as perfect space was that of the quintessential celestial spheres. By adhering to God's time, women could do without the meaningless, even chaotic time of earth. The sacred moment that the Church allowed women to recapture as often as they liked was Communion, in which the body and blood of Christ infused women's bodies with holiness as they united themselves with Him at the moment of His sacrifice. From their earliest years, religious women of the Nord eagerly looked to their first Communion, and they remembered it vividly. On the verge of the first experience, young girls already felt the immanence of a holy presence. After being catechized, participating in a pre-Communion retreat, and practicing the sacrament itself, young Germaine Bernard wrote in her diary: "I have been so moved. What will this Sunday be like when there will be a real communion."[9] Many girls on their first Communion made vows intended to last a lifetime, or pledged themselves to convent life. For some the first sacrament never dulled the impact of later sacraments. Mme Camille Feron-Vrau as a girl had written letters about preparations for her first Communion and had felt deeply the presence of Christ, but she received the experience more fully in her later years when "Jesus came" to her in the form of the sacrament several times each week.[10]

Religious rituals returned women to an archetypal moment, a miracle, or a mystery of the human condition. Important events such as marriage recalled the marriage feast of Cana; childbirth, the birth of Christ or even the creation of the world; christening, the baptism of Christ. Signification could extend even to trivial matters as they too became ritualized: cleaning, however gratuitous, recapitulated the banishment of chaos from the universe; preserving fruits at just the right moment harkened back to the time when the earth was provisioned for human beings, and symbolized giving of life in all its sacred aspects. Like space, all of time became attached in some manner to the sacred: hence, the obsession with the twin rituals of home and Church. Ritual of whatever kind meant a connection with God's order and made women concerned with the notion of order itself. Yet order did not seem desirable for purposes of efficiency, which would enable the passage to the next moment in meaningless but productive progression. The punctuality, efficiency, and routine of an older generation of businesswomen and of modern businessmen never paralleled that of the ladies of the Nord. For them order stood as a mirror of God's rich perfection with which they hoped to fill their lives. Exactitude indicated that time was God's, not man's.

In consequence, women in the Nord had a traditional, as opposed to a modern, sense of history. Their concern for the past was motivated by a desire to find repetitive moments of holiness. The great popular writers of the Nord, Josephine de Gaulle and Mathilde Bourdon, poured out biographies of the saints, of queens, or of minor figures whose lives in some sense touched the sacred. Mary, Queen of Scots, was

101

a favorite for her martyrdom, as were Saint Theresa of Avila and Saint Cécile.[11] Little concern for historical fact appears in the works, for they searched only for the moment of sanctity and union with the divine. The stories are boring in their repetition, but consistent in their drive to highlight only human goodness and morality. Women writers, conversely, saw the life of someone like Elizabeth of England as unrelieved evil, embodied in her flight from the Church and her failure to achieve union with the Holy Spirit.[12] Each biography, no matter how similar to all the others in detail, became important for its connection with the divine, which for women in the Nord was the meaning of history. There could be no unique event or progress toward an unfulfillable future, for the past held substance only as it touched the archetypical life of Christ or the sacredness of the universe. Thus, women built their history on romance.

The belief in "immanence" based on the conviction that God or the holy could be called from the heavens to earth or that statues or human events could have intrinsic holy qualities, marked another separation between women and the modern world. From the time that Luther had condemned the Mass for calling God into a world where he could not possibly be, human thought had increasingly posited a universe devoid of quality, be it holy, moral, or aesthetic. For example, although people still lived in a world of color, with the triumph of scientific interpretation color had officially become measurable light rays. God, too, or holiness, was banished from the world, which was left to operate according to natural laws as opposed to holy dictates. In greater numbers men came to view a distinctly secular world ultimately described by mathematics. Matter itself, or any state of being, consisted only of force, density, or volume, while older forms of description such as beauty, goodness, or holiness were relegated to the less and less essential realms of aesthetics, ethics, or theology. At the culmination of this trend, Christ became an historical personage expounding utilitarian ethics.

102

While the men of the Nord lobbied for expansion of scientific faculties in the university,[13] women continued to see manifestations of the holy in matter. Their collection of relics, crosses, religious cards, and holy statuary testified to their belief in the endowment of the physical with qualities. God appeared to them in objects, whether they were Communion wafers or the crosses worn around the neck. Objects contained holiness as well as physical attributes. For this reason, women participated in Communion as often as possible, for the wafer embodied the crucified God as well as a collection of molecules. More than half the families in the Nord named at least one daughter Marie, which could endow her with the blessed qualities of Mary.[14] In this way women of the Nord could bring God into the world or testify to his presence in matter, and again this theological possibility blended with the signification given objects in the home. In domestic life, women still saw objects charged with qualities: household decorations, clothing, and food had qualities apart from the physical. Narcisse Faucheur-Deledicque, in a commemorative note about his wife, wrote that she guarded her wedding dress "like a relic."[15] Other women collected locks of hair, old bouquets, calling cards, and invitations because they had significance. The domestic thus fused with the theological as each system posited a rich and multifaceted reality of signified holiness exactly at the point at which modern science had begun to view them in different ways.

Especially in the social sphere, women's belief in immanence distinguished their activities. Although women gathered around them as many holy objects as possible, they also knew that sin, evil, and poverty existed as part of God's hierarchical order. While women might atone for their own and others' sins and ask for deliverance from further evil, as humans they could not by an act of will extirpate the miasma of evil from the social order. This set the women of the Nord apart from Protestant or positivist reformers, who attempted to fashion a homogenous society and who confidently believed that through the use of psychology, money, and rational planning they could correct what to them was mere malfunctioning of natural law.[16]

Matter, space, and time in the world of the women of the Nord remained, on the one hand, rooted in subjective perception and, on the other, formed part of a theological vision of the world. The same can be said for their views of causality. Rather than accepting immutable scientific principles governing the course of human existence, women in the Nord, in contrast to their husbands, saw God's hand manipulating human destiny. Alfred Motte-Grimonprez, writing of his emotional devastation when his young son died, could not help feeling that, had he called in more competent doctors, somehow the boy might have been saved. He compared his feelings with those of his wife, who did not suffer incapacitating grief because she attributed her son's death to the will of God. "God," wrote Mathilde Bourdon in more than one book, "possesses the absolute and universal control of events in the world."[17] Born of this conviction, pilgrimages of northern French women such as Mme Julie Bommart-Rouzé or Germaine Feron-Vrau became their response to illness, for they knew that God, not doctors, would determine the course of their lives.[18] In response to the deaths of her two brothers and father in the space of a few years, Herminie de la Bassemoûturie wrote in her journal that "God is severely testing us."[19] Bourdon attempted to demonstrate the hand of God in her biographies and novels. She devoted one book to explaining why God had decided that France should suffer the Revolution of 1848, and on a less lofty level she showed business reverses, natural calamities, and personal disasters to be the result of His will.[20] Men of the Nord, however, believed differently. In June of 1848 they went as a unit of the bourgeois national guard to put down the workers' uprising with guns, not prayer. And they arrived early at factories in the morning because they knew that success depended on their own efforts.

Many observers accused bourgeois women in the Nord

of hypocrisy. Fanatical in observing Catholic ritual and ardent in their professions of faith, they seemed cold in the face of human misery.[21] This behavior derived not only from their view of causality, but also from their convictions about human efficacy and action. Women maintained their religious rituals scrupulously because rituals invoked the presence of God and because God welcomed requests to influence events in their favor by awarding them both spiritual and temporal grace. Grace for nineteenth-century Catholic women paralleled knowledge for the "modern" human being, in that both stood as an interpretation of experience. But whereas knowledge allowed for a certain measure of human control over that experience, the grace desired by women of the Nord was only achieved through supplication of the Father and dependence on His, as opposed to their own, judgment. They did not so much work or strive to obtain their ends, as increasingly join together to implore the Heavenly Father to fulfill their wishes.

An example appears in the organization of the Archiconfrérie des mères chrétiennes, founded in Lille in the 1840s and established throughout France and the Catholic world within decades. Mme Louise Josson, wife of a prominent government functionary, started the prayer group for women who, like a friend of hers, were despairing over the defection of their sons and husbands from the Church. Women quickly flocked to combine their efforts and to obtain from the Vatican certain dispensations permitted archconfraternities. In Lille women met monthly to coordinate their prayers and to record both the prayers offered and the grace received. During the only year for which records exist, spiritual and temporal grace was both demanded and awarded. Women testified at these meetings to the efficacy of prayer, and they testified as well in the magazine of the national group.[22] One woman from Lille wrote a characteristic account of her daughter, age eleven, who had been ill simultaneously with bronchitis and pleurisy. Parisian doctors from whom she had sought help had given up on the child, but her mother's prayers effected a recovery. To add to the accumulation of miracles, the death of the girl's infant brother later produced in the still weak child a relapse about which the mother, still in confinement from childbirth, had not been told. "But a mother, can she ever be fooled? Soon I had presentments which made me arrive at the sad truth." Again she launched prayers to God and to the Virgin for her intervention, and again, despite the doctors' pessimism, the girl was spared.[23] This incident of grace accorded in visible form found itself duplicated hundreds of times in the various religious histories of the Nord; a woman childless throughout thirteen years of marriage made fertile; a business saved from impending disaster; a husband returned to the Church; a deathbed recovery effected.[24] Women saw the hand of God responding to their prayers behind these earthly events. Causality was thus linked to the designs of God rather than being attributed to the natural laws of the universe. Prayer, not action guided by scientific understanding, attained desired ends.

Prayer, then, acted in multiple ways in the lives of the women of the Nord as a means of calling upon the divine and as an indication of the power of God in controlling human events. It also stood as a symbol for human weakness: individuals humbled themselves before God and acknowledged their need of Him. This submissive posture paralleled the condition of women in the nineteenth century as a confirmation of the French saying that men forged their destiny while women endured theirs. The maxim seemed to contain more truth in that century. Women submitted to monthly changes in their bodies and endured the pain of childbirth without many options for ending pregnancies or alleviating the dolorous situation in childbirth. They usually watched helplessly as their children perished from even small sicknesses. Prayer acknowledged this reality and heightened the notion of the passive "lot" of women. At first glance, the condition of women hardly differed from the situation in previous centuries. Yet the world in which they lived was making enormous technological strides. Social organization had so metamorphosed within the lifetime of women of the Nord that their families were enjoying increased wealth and power each year. Women, in their insulation from the sources of power, production, and scientific education, witnessed a relative deterioration of their position in the new world. If, for example, the industrial world increasingly determined the values of human life, then the removal of women from that world meant a setback. Or if scientific knowledge had increased longevity on the whole, the persistent exposure of women to the perils of childbirth could only appear a greater danger. The reality presented to nineteenth-century French women was far from inspiring. Prayer accorded with their position of physical impotence.

Theology and Domesticity

While the reproductive life of women inclined them toward a religious as opposed to scientific world view, the doctrine of the Catholic Church addressed itself to many of the themes expressed in domestic symbolism. One part of that doctrine, for example, emphasized human frailty derived from original sin and glorified temporal suffering as a kind of atonement for the fall from grace. The blessed of the Beatitudes are the weak, the poor in heart, the meek, those who mourn or who hunger and thirst after righteousness. In a like manner, the act of salvation consisted of Christ's persecution and agony on the cross—a physical sacrifice to redeem mankind. Because women's weakness sprang from a physical cause, because their reproductivity situated them among the meek and powerless, Catholicism held a special meaning from them. The women of the Nord could and did see their reproductivity as a redemptive act, and Catholicism allowed them, though not explicitly, to take center stage among the blessed of the earth as a result of being female.

107

Bathed in the light shed on the weak, many women of the Nord seemed to search for an increase in suffering and to emphasize that as an important component of their lives. In general, their writings emphasize the particularly female agonies of childbirth, sickness, and betrayal by men. Aside from the novels that we will examine later, letters demonstrate this inclination. In refusing an invitation to meet the Empress Eugénie in 1867, Mme Barrois wrote that she would be suffering too much from the memory of her child's death a year previously to participate in the occasion.[25] Joining in the symbolic expression of weakness, others recorded the pain and agonies endured by the sick for whom they were caring, or they wrote long letters of sympathy to families in which someone was ill: "My very dear lady, . . . I can't tell you the feelings of pain and anguish I felt when . . . I learned of the gravity of Monsieur G.'s illness and of the distressing trials through which your maternal heart has just passed. . . . I have joined with my sympathy . . . my best, my only auxiliary—Prayer, and little confident in my own poor Prayers, I have added those, much more forceful, of those people whom you have always helped so much and who are so grateful. I saw Abbé Papelle who was terribly distressed to learn of Monsieur G.'s sickness . . . and who from that moment has not stopped interceding with the Lord for his speedy and complete recovery."[26] The lives of women in the Nord revolved around suffering and they, in turn, spoke of it at great length. Yet, should suffering fail to arrive, some women sought it out. Germaine Feron-Vrau wore a spiked ornament on her chest to increase her earthly mortification; Mme Gustave Bernard knelt each day on a hard wooden bench for several hours. Other women conspicuously deprived themselves of food, while one abstained from the pleasure of writing in her journal during Lent to create pain that would allow her to merge with the suffering of Christ. Whether naturally inflicted or willfully provoked, suffering was a blessing from God, a sign of His favor.[27] Earthly life was a time of testing, "full of thorns," though not an encounter to be rejected.[28] Through their suffering, the women of the Nord consciously heightened the contrast between themselves—the righteous—and the fat and prospering men who had never "learned to resist the intoxication of power."[29]

In their devotions, the women of the Nord selected those features of Catholicism that emphasized trial and fragility. The church they built in Lille took its name from the Sacred Heart of Jesus, and reflected the increasing absorption of all French women with the bleeding, suffering heart of the Savior.[30] In addition to inflicting hardships on themselves, women worshiped the martyred female saints by noting their feast days in diaries and by pointedly naming their children after them.[31] In the Nord the names Henriette or Clémence almost disappeared in wealthy families in favor of Cécile, Thérèse, Geneviève, and the names of other particularly afflicted women. When the Archiconfrérie des mères chrétiennes was first started, the organization took as its patron saint Joseph, protector of women and children. But he was soon eclipsed by Saint Monica, the burdened and aggrieved mother of Saint Augustine.[32] Above all others, however, rose the figure of Mary, the Mother of Sorrows, to whose shrines the women of the Nord made their many pilgrimages, and on whom they spent their energies, especially during the month of May. Although women never made an explicit comparison between their suffering and that of Christ, they always linked themselves with Mary. God had instructed Mme Camille Feron-Vrau, for example, to take Mary as her model,[33] and Mathilde Bourdon counseled Christian women of all ages and conditions to do the same.[34] Some women of the Nord dressed their children for six or seven years in the colors of the Virgin;[35] the Enfants de Marie of the boarding schools wore and cherished her medal until their deaths;[36] many wrote "Child of Mary" below their signatures on letters.[37] The women of the Nord sought Mary, who above all reflected the image of the burdened, reproductive women. Just as they imprinted their

109

images on the surface of the home, so too, they distributed the statues of the afflicted Mother of God, the persecuted saints, and the suffering heart of Jesus in their homes so that they could worship them.

In adorning and perfecting the reproductive weakness of women, Catholicism served the purpose of all other worldly religions. The other world of Catholicism mirrored and perfected conditions in this world, specifically the condition of the domestic women. Women of the Nord referred to Heaven as "my Father's house" wherein dwelt a holy family of love and peace. God reigned over his realm, but so too did Mary, chosen by God and obedient to His wish that she bear the Christ child. On earth Mary bore her child and suffered as she watched his life sacrificed, but in Heaven Mary ruled by virtue of being the Mother of God. She represented reproductivity triumphant, and served as the model of the *femme forte*, a prototype constantly referred to by the women of the Nord in the midst of their own sufferings.[38] Although for them the crown was technically reserved for the afterlife, in fact the certainty of its existence allowed reproductive women to wear it invisibly in all their undertakings on earth. By imitating Mary, they radiated female power.

Besides providing a twin articulation of power and weakness (found also in domestic symbolism), the figure of Mary gave witness to the possibility of mastering and taming nature. She had conceived a child and remained virginal; parturition did not impair her purity.[39] Women attempted this same miracle when they hid their swollen bodies from public view, when they refused to speak of reproduction or sex, and when they attempted in their clothing to disguise reproductive physical features. They referred to themselves as angels, as if speaking in such a way could do away with physicality. So too when speaking of Mary they emphasized her spiritlike qualities. Mary, wrote Mathilde Bourdon, was so spiritlike even in her lifetime that she hardly needed to eat food. It was all part of a wish that, innocent like Mary, they would bear their children and thus, god-like, rule the natural world instead of being ruled by it. In this way Mary represented a nineteenth-century woman's hope for reproduction and its power without desire or carnal knowledge and with a suspension of the natural law of sanguineous and painful childbirth.

Mary's chastity had another meaning in Catholic doctrine: knowledge of none but God, harmony with His will, and strict obedience. She herself was conceived without original sin, and throughout her life she subordinated herself to God's orders and to the career of her divine son. A parallel obedience existed in the everyday subordination of Northern women to the social order and demands of family, but its implications went beyond such practical exigencies. Their sense of obedience to schedules, the dictates of housecleaning or fashion, or to etiquette, had to do with a symbolic chastity like that of Mary. Every act of obedience to rules prevented outbreaks of sin and chaos or invasions of nature. Women, too, tried to escape sin through adherence to order, whether that of the household or that of the Father.

Such tendencies in behavior do not conform to a simple or simple-minded notion of repressed sexuality.[40] In fact, in a certain sense it constitutes the very opposite. One of the most religious women of the Nord, Mme Camille Feron-Vrau, wrote in her thirties of an encounter with Christ in which he asked that she surrender herself completely to him—not just her mind and soul, but her body and senses as well.[41] Instead of repressing sexuality, religion allowed for its direction toward God the Father. Freud, especially in his essays on female sexuality, interprets this and similar sexual experiences of women. The little girl, because of a recognition that castration has already taken place, can fearlessly throw herself with full sexual energy into the arms of her father.[42] Women could also express that same energy in their religious devotion to a heavenly Father.

Religious fervor, like domestic fervor, released the natural or biological or reproductive side of women, but in a trans-

formative manner. Here again Freud provided insight into
the behavior we witness when he wrote in *The Future of
an Illusion* about the tendency "in an infantile state of help-
lessness" to turn the forces of nature into gods, to replace
pleasure with piety.[43] Women's domestic symbolism expressed the reproductive force of nature, and quickly the
expressive system turned back to become their authority;
they worshiped and obeyed the domestic rules that embodied their own natural force. Having created the world and
peopled it, the Catholic God possessed a similar reproductive
quality. But his physical act of procreation had a spiritual
name that one could worship, just as the reproductive act
of women also had a spiritual name: love. God was so loving
that He created the universe from His own abundant nature.
He so loved the world that He gave His Man-Son to suffer
for human redemption. His love moved the spheres and
united the imperfect universe of beings He had created.
God handed down the law of love: His creatures should love
their neighbors as themselves; yet He felt pain that His own
creation could never meet the standards of His love. The
Catholic faith linked love with genesis, children, agony,
weakness, perfection, and redemption; and the Catholic
women of the Nord associated their own reproductivity with
love, until sexuality collapsed into spirituality, pleasure into
piety. At the confines of the universe dwelt a Being who
was their reflection, repression, ordering principle, and
transformation. He reflected their procreativity, channeled
their sexuality by giving an order to the chaos of the flesh,
and transformed their physicality into spirit. The women of
the Nord threw themselves fearlessly into the arms of this
redemptive Father, and imbued with His strength, they became soldiers in the cause of religion.

The resulting dogmatic militancy prevented the religion
of women from becoming solipsistic and mystical. However
much God might be an incarnation of themselves and their
wishes, or of their desire for omnipotence, they continually
referred to Church doctrine and polity as a point of departure

for their activities. The laws of the Church guided them as they set out to combat the challenge offered by the competing laws of the market or of the democratic state. As commercialism posed an alternative standard, or as democracy sought to substitute the law of man for the laws of God, the women of the Nord became archsupporters of the rule of the Father, be He embodied in the Church itself or in His surrogate, the king.

Theological Politics

During the nineteenth century, women in the Nord and in France generally did rush to the Church. Sodalities, prayer groups, charitable organizations with a religious base, and individual devotions all increased in number. Masses for the dead, supplication for the hard-pressed living, pilgrimages, and retreats for women multiplied. Ritual became a way of life for wealthy women, and many budgeted their time to allow more and more time for God or to serve His institutions through sewing clubs for churches, missions, and the clergy. Women of the Nord held expositions for the Society of St. Elizabeth of Hungary or for the Propagation of the Faith, at which they annually displayed the fruits of their labors. Or they published lists of contributors to the many religious causes.[44] In this way they applied indirect pressure on others of their sex to support the cause that supported them. Mme D. of Roubaix always hastened to fill any application for aid from one of her peers, whether with money or clothing. Any dereliction of duty for the Church would bring censure from other women.[45] Central committees of various organizations discussed whether dead members had been sufficiently scrupulous in their attendance at religious functions or in their performance of religious obligations to receive the customary masses on their deaths.[46] Because women believed that their religious witness had the power to testify to the existence of God, the failure of any one to contribute subtracted from the visibility of God and His ethos in society.

Not only did women in the Nord multiply their secular activities for the Church and increase their religious witness, they also rushed in greater numbers to devote their lives entirely to Christ by joining religious orders. The number of women taking holy vows in the nineteenth century was double that of men, and the Nord was no exception to the national trend.[47] Women such as Eugénie Smet or Mère Eulalie founded orders of international importance, while others such as Marie Wallaert-Brame or Mme Léon Barrois gave their fortunes to the congregations they joined.[48] Only a swelling of devotion, the relative deterioration of the secular woman's position, and the special appeal of the convent can explain this trend. Stories of poverty or the failure to find a husband are less common than those of young women like Marie Toulemonde, from a prominent Roubaisian textile family, who was notably attractive and without financial problems. An elderly Roubaisienne recalled another example: "My great-aunt had a childhood just like anyone else in her day. She was playful, even mischievous. With her beauty and the family's wealth everyone supposed that she would make a brilliant marriage. And then at seventeen she announced to her parents that she wanted to become a nun. You can imagine their heartbreak at the prospect of losing their daughter forever. They asked her to consider her decision for a year; she did. But after that year she was at least as committed as before to life in the convent."[49] The story repeated itself many times in the Nord. Those who chose the religious life seemed like any other child until they announced their decision. In only a few cases, like that of a woman with a leg slightly shorter than the other, were there hints that the decision rested on an inability to find a husband.[50] Moreover, one had to be vigorous for the religious life, as demonstrated by the exclusion of young women such as Louise Charvet and Herminie de la Bassemoûterie on the grounds of poor health.[51] Nor did lack of wealth appear to play a part, for although most nuns came from large families, the orders they entered all demanded substantial dowries. Instead of waiting to test the marriage market, women from the Nord entered convents at approximately age twenty, just when their peers would be setting their feet into the social world that would find them a husband.[52]

Despite the diversity of orders, women in the Nord opted for a limited number of congregations. More than half of them entered teaching orders in the Nord itself. The Mothers of the Sacred Heart, the Bernardines, the Mothers of St. Maur or Ste. Flines or Ste. Union repeatedly received back the young women they had educated. Another quarter chose orders of the opposite type, that is, the cloistered congregations.[53] The Cuvelier and Philippe families saw their daughters become Carmelites, and knew that they would never see them again except through grills of the cloister and veils of the habit. Elisabeth Lefebvre-Faure entered the Chartreuse cloister, and Marie Wallaert-Brame, once widowed, became superior of the Sisters of the Adoration réparatrice du Très Saint Sacrament.[54] Finally, another segment was attracted by orders such as the Dominicans and the order of the Cénacle, where time was divided between contemplation and charitable works.

In the long run the convent provided an attractive alternative to the home—that is, it was a close approximation with none of the disadvantages. Although the position of women suffered a relative decline because of the rising industrial power of men, women in religious orders held positions of respect and power. They ran schools, hospitals, and performed public services that brought them admiration and gratitude, though not always from political authorities. As teachers in orders such as the Bernardines or the Dames du Sacré-Coeur, they could be mothers to their own class of young without any of the pain or anxiety of married life.[55] As nuns, they were the brides of Christ in perpetual union with Him. And the convent, that closed, protected place, offered them shelter and nurtured them so that, unlike their secular peers, they would not have to face the rigors of the profane and lonely modern world.

Just as religious life, either in its secular or congregational form, was drawing women to its fold, the institutional Church in France was suffering from one of those attacks that had periodically plagued its history since the Reformation. During the early nineteenth century, with the restoration of the French monarchy, Catholicism had recouped some of its losses at the hands of the eighteenth-century *philosophes* and revolutionary politicians; yet it never returned to its prerevolutionary position. From within, writers such as Chateaubriand and Lamennais reduced the rigor of the ancient faith, while from without the Church heard a persistent chorus of abuse. Anticlericalists such as Michelet bemoaned the influence of the priest in the family; and republicans, socialists, and even imperialist supporters of Napoleon III challenged the right of the clergy to interfere in politics. The sum of criticism grew in force as French society struggled to become modern and to make use of the Revolution's legacy of liberalism. To modernists, the Church represented all the old political, economic, social, and intellectual values that had to be destroyed if French society was to compete in an industrial world. The verbal attacks were soon to be replaced by political blows at clerical influence in education, social work, and government, so that by the early twentieth century the Catholic Church in France had lost its financial support from the government, and many religious orders had been banished from the country.

The women of the Nord, in this twin context of siege on the Church and their own declining social position, multiplied their religious efforts and combatted the evils of atheism and materialism. Thus the impetus behind the formation of the Archiconfrérie des mères chrétiennes: it offered women the occasion to pray for their sons, husbands, fathers, or other male relatives who had turned from the Church to the side of its enemies. So, too, the multiplication of Church-related organizations for women—innocuous as these prayerful gatherings for supplication and acts of faith might appear—began to fuse noticeably with right-wing politics of the Empire, but more specifically of the Third Republic. Beyond the individual prayers for strayed relatives or the sewing of flags for the Pretender, the Comte de Chambord,[56] women in the Nord worked in groups for the attainment of political ends.

In the years of the Franco-Prussian War, an alumnae group from the Sacré-Coeur boarding school made a dramatic appeal for divine intervention in the public life of France, at a time when the advance of Prussian troops and the Commune in Paris struck most people in the Nord with terror. The department stood on the invasion route of the Germans, and the presence of a large working class threatened revolution in imitation of Paris. In their October 1870 meeting, the Enfants de Marie, with the approval of their Jesuit director, took a solemn vow augmented with constant prayer that if the department of the Nord were spared the twin disaster of invasion and civil war, they would build a church to the Sacred Heart of Jesus. A religious faith in the intervention of God in the affairs of men, coupled with an awareness of the tragic consequences of either event, led them to make this commitment.

Neither communal uprising nor invasion occurred, and the women attributed this blessing to the benevolence of the Heavenly Father. With their customary vigor, the Enfants de Marie launched a fund-raising drive of huge dimensions to build the Church of the Sacred Heart in Lille. The course of church building, however, was not to be smooth, for the city fathers of the postimperial era already had their eyes focused on the Church as an enemy. Proposals for new churches had become suspect as measures for extending clerical power, and ultimately the Enfants de Marie only realized their project through the careful intervention of a handful of powerful Catholic laymen who had the ability to deal with and make compromises with their secularly minded peers. Having finally gained permission for the church to be built, the committee of Catholic men ran into resistance from women over the terms of construction. For the women, faithful to their belief in the intervention of God in the events of 1870-1871, had chiseled into the cornerstone of the new church the contents of their vow beseeching God to spare them the disasters of civil war and invasion. The men, however, maintained that the mention of civil war might appear politically provocative, and demanded that the words be removed. Such political compromise had no place in the faith of women who refused to erase from memory what God had wrought in acknowledgment of their continual prayers. Through their action, women demonstrated how far they remained from both the methods and thought of liberalism: not only was the course of human existence in the hands of God, but supplication and acceptance became proper political tools. Denial in the name of utility amounted to sacrilege. In the long run, the most devout Catholic laymen in the Nord put the politics of this world before God; women could not.[57]

Women, therefore, maintained their prayerful vigils, which attested to the potency of God. Confronting increased attacks on the Church in the 1880s, the organization for the Perpetual Rosary scheduled its members to pray for the survival of a beleaguered Church.[58] In the 1890s, Germaine Feron-Vrau, twenty-three-year-old wife of a thread manufacturer and daughter of sugar refiners, gathered a large group of women to form the League of Prayer in answer to the archbishop's plea for a campaign against the atheistic tendencies of the press. "France," he had proclaimed, "is ravaged by an evil press that ruins faith and morality. This special scandal which outrages God and wounds His Heart should be atoned for by a special crusade of prayers." Each member of the League of Prayer was directed to say a Hail Mary daily and to make special acts of atonement for attacks in newspapers against religion. Mme Feron-Vrau, in her role as director, kept an account of all adherents and their prayers, communions, and special mortifications made on behalf of the league. In 1896, for the national elections, the league launched a subsidiary campaign to help a country "subjected to universal suffrage." Mme Feron-Vrau issued a circular asking, "What Is to Be Done?" She maintained that men must act, agitate, organize, and influence voters. But one had also to remember that without Jesus Christ nothing could be accomplished. She asked everyone to turn toward heaven for guidance, but she looked "principally to Christian women, to girls, to the sick, to religious communities" for help. In this pamphlet, Mme Feron-Vrau articulated the principle that now seemed clearly to guide the relationship of each sex to the temporal world: men must act in it; women must pray for it.[59]

By the early twentieth century, the women of the Nord joined hands with other French women in the general movement not only to combat the atheistic and materialist menace, but to revitalize Catholicism throughout the country. Organized in Paris, the Patriotic League of Frenchwomen attacked godlessness and socialism, and sought, with the aid of such notables as Jacques Piou and Marc Sanguier, a reconversion of communities to a full practice of religion and prayer. Northern women were at first suspicious of the Parisian connection, and maintained their provincial stance of independence. In 1903, the League had one small group in the Nord headed by Mlle Valdelièvre of an industrial family. By 1907, however, Mme Feron-Vrau's name appeared on the masthead of the national magazine, *L'Echo*, as a member of the central committee. In a comparatively short time, the league flourished among Northern women of all classes until it consisted of 150 separate groups containing 35,775 members. Each member prayed for the welfare of France as a Catholic country, and the most zealous proselytized within their communities for the Church and for a strengthening of family values in the face of growing individualism, materialism, and atheism.[60] By the beginning of World War I, then, the focus of women's religious organizations remained the same as it had been when the

119

first Enfants de Marie were formed or when the first Christian mothers met to pray for their children's spiritual health. Yet the industrial society in which they had begun their efforts had metamorphosed and matured. This transformation in the social context shifted the import of women's ritual to a reactionary political position of support for clerical institutions that permitted women to pray.

In some industrial countries politicians and some bourgeois women were able to forge alliances.[61] This was generally not the case in the Nord, where women for the most part redoubled their efforts in the cause of Catholicism. In the arms of the Church they met not rejection but support for a domestic cosmology from priests who seemed to be wooing them to the cause. But women were not dupes of the clergy. They were a natural constituency that priests fortified with their messages and served through directing women's lay organizations, and by officiating at those rites so necessary to the reproductive way of life. The modern world has gone astray, they preached, because men have opted for materialism and even atheism; only women are left to save society for God. At retreats and special services for women's groups, the clergy in the Nord stressed that women were the heart of society, and that the suffering heart, like the bleeding heart of Jesus so important to women, had its value.[62] In this way the Church converted women's political and economic weakness into a crucial factor in human salvation.

For that weakness to achieve conversion, the clergy warned, women needed the Church and its priests. Without Christ's sacrifice, without the Church's sacraments, they would be mired in sin and misery, like women in pagan society. Women heard and repeated the message that "without Christ and his ministers we can do nothing good." They flocked to rallies: at the annual congresses of the Catholics of the Nord, police reports always noted the presence of the clergy, a handful of prominent businessmen, and "three or four hundred women of high society."[63] The clergy encouraged their following, and Church doctrine not only exacted the use of intermediaries but also required guides through the intricacies of its precepts. Walking a tightrope of dualities, women needed priests to keep them from falling into error. Women today, one priest preached at a retreat, are strong in their faith and devotion, but we must make sure that it is an instructed faith.[64] The clergy recognized that without Catholic education, women were often lost in a world of their own religion.

In a certain sense it appears strange that clergymen feared for their women parishioners; signs of religious faith—rituals, relics, and ornamentation—had multiplied in women's lives during the course of the nineteenth century. But critics both within and without the Catholic cause suggested that a hollowness might exist beneath the symbolism. Were Catholicism's doctrinal underpinnings allowed to weaken through neglect of instruction, there might come a time when women's faith would collapse before the force of such industrial values as rationalism, positivism, and individualism. If men had so easily deserted the Church, would not women? Another possibility also presented itself. Women might jettison theology and, while maintaining domestic values and rituals, fashion a secular cult of womanhood. Armed with an exclusively sexual self-righteousness, they might like feminists and reformers in other countries, attempt to force a domestic morality on society. The clergy perhaps sensed both dangers, for throughout the Third Republic they ministered diligently to their natural constituency among the women of the Nord.

Their ministrations were successful and, at least until the First World War, the content of women's lives made women receptive. Drastic changes were occurring in the world around them to redirect the lives and thoughts of their closest male relatives. But in the Nord, women's world view remained traditional because their activities remained "natural." For them, as for peasants and other women, the "old religion" coincided with the "old" way of doing things and the "old" habits of language, thoughts, and fears. Not that they failed to notice the new, industrial environment. On the contrary, they were alarmed at the cataclysms and their possible repercussions on the order they had created in the name of the family and of God. Like people in many traditional environments, they pictured political and social innovations as forms of chaos in drastic need of domestic as well as religious ordering. Far from retreating in the face of chaos, the women of the Nord armed themselves with the weapons of family and faith and set out into the urban world. Their domestic cosmology had a social component that they were determined to uphold.

6

Society: Charity versus Capitalism

In the summer of 1867, Napoleon III and the Empress Eugénie made an official tour of the Nord. At least, official accounts report the emperor's presence. However, when Mme Alexandre Coget of Marquilles described the event to a friend in England, Eugénie alone mattered. As the royal carriage entered the city of Lille, according to the letter, a torrential rain came down. But the empress, concerned that her subjects not be disappointed, ordered the carriage tops rolled back so that she might be seen. In the evening she gracefully instructed Deputy Jules Brame in the art of the dance. And the next morning "en toilette de la plus grande simplicité" she visited the sick in the charity hospitals. "In all minds *without exception* the empress has left the most flattering opinion of her spirit, of her heart, and of her character."[1] Although a portrait of Eugénie, this was the image women carried of themselves when they left home for society.

Gracious society matrons and ladies bountiful: the women of the Nord were both, as well as mothers of large families and servants of the Church. Although the portraits seem incompatible, the centrality of reproduction that informed domestic behavior and Catholicism spilled over to shape both the socialite and the lady of charity. Each image developed from the single focus on reproduction as represented in the family. The women of the Nord saw household and universe as established along procreative lines; they saw order as radiating from the twin poles of home and heaven. In the social sphere, women also believed the family to constitute the primary unit of organization, in contrast to the view of liberal men, who postulated the individual as self-sufficient and prior to any group. From women's belief followed a series of corollaries: they stressed the ties and prerogatives of blood, and emphasized familial concepts of status and place when facing either "high society" or social questions. They approached the chaotic industrial world in which they lived with the same concern for instilling order that dominated their domestic lives. But women's order and their sense of the proper social organization rested on domestic, not industrial principle. It was in the social sphere that the dichotomies produced by a sexual division of labor became most telling.

Women's sociology—if it can be called that—conflicted with the modern or nineteenth-century view of society, a view that began with the Protestant Reformation, grew with the scientific revolution, and became officially installed during the French Revolution. Differing sharply from the older Christian interpretation of the social order espoused by most women, this new vision saw human life as directly set in a natural framework, and as more and more denuded of spiritual quality. Quantity replaced quality as scientists stopped pursuing philosophical questions about the essence of the universe in favor of measuring its mechanical functioning. In a like spirit, men gave up the quest for the essence of man and preferred to investigate his physical place in a material setting. The new and quantifiable attribute of human life became labor, which each individual expended according to his energy—again quantifiable—to amass measurable amounts of property. Thus Locke, whose example directed the investigations of the French, averred the most characteristic act of man to be an animal or natural one as he picked and thereby appropriated berries to nourish himself. Because this first human act was economic, the basic relationship in human life consisted of just this relationship to an economic world of individuals who formed aggregates according to their place in the market. Property or capital—the cash nexus—was the medium that bound them together.

Labor being natural for man, it was equivalent to adherence to the natural laws of the entire universe. The laws of labor or those of the market were quickly seen to be equivalent to the scientific law, and governments were seen to have grown up to insure the proper functioning of the natural law of marketplace society. Less and less did people in the nineteenth century see government as morally purposive, except insofar as the laws of nature embodied in the market and upheld by government were *ipso facto* moral or ethical. Rather, governments should insure the integration of all human beings in the primary social ordering— that of property and work. In this way, utility or that which would insure the proper workings of the market—the proper functioning of which would make men happy—became the standard of behavior for individuals, societies, and governments, because a utilitarian ethic alone could insure that man and society worked harmoniously. In this way function emerged as both ethic and attribute of human life.

The French Revolution had enshrined this type of liberal view and had taken measures toward its proper functioning. By smashing social, political, and economic privilege based on inheritance, it released market forces and gave them freedom to operate. Specifically, the Declaration of the Rights of Man, the Le Chapelier Law, and the Revolutionary and Napoleonic laws of property had worked to this end, while a simultaneous attack on the Church aimed at eradicating an institution whose social preachings had supported an older vision of human society under the *ancien régime*. Yet powerful groups remained committed to a traditional sociology, among them the women of the Nord.

125

To them, human destiny concerned less man's existential than his essential being. Humans, to their minds, differed from animals in their possession of an immortal soul that made life on this earth only one part of the human cycle. Human life was all "becoming," the beginning of a quest for perfection achieved only in another world. In contrast to the liberal view, they saw toil on this earth as indicating an original imperfection or sin implicit in the human condition. Although one accepted the condemnation to labor or, in the case of women, to pain, salvation lay beyond the confines of natural law in the grace of God. God the Creator preceded human beings, and so too, did every other social institution that corresponded to His authority. Humans should obey these God-given authorities as they would obey the authority of God. They should see in secular institutions with power not only correspondences with the Creator, but indications of natural hierarchies. It was along a system of hierarchies that God's authority flowed, and the great chain of being from inanimate nature to perfect spirit was duplicated in inequalities on earth. To the theologically minded women of the Nord, words such as "liberty" and "equality" thrown up by liberal ideologues in explanation of the human condition appeared to be rationales for license and debauchery. More important, however, the new market slogans affronted God's order.

The unifying substance for society was neither labor nor cash, but the love or *caritas* that had engendered the creation, that moved the spheres, and that flowed from God toward humans and was ideally returned to Him in the form of adoration and obedience to His order. Not only should *caritas* flow vertically along the chain of being, it should move horizontally as well among all human beings in "love of neighbor." In this horizontal movement of *caritas* among humans, however, there was room for difference. Those to whom God had given more abundantly had the obligation to return more both to God Himself and to their less fortunate brethren. *Caritas* both as a spiritual binding force and in its tangible form of charity or alms appealed to women's sensibilities. It appealed because as a unifying force, *caritas* was the spiritual equivalent of the blood that bound families and tribes. *Caritas*, as the quality that spilled over to create the universe, also corresponded to the reproductive acts of women peopling a domestic microcosm. Women interpreted those acts as acts of love. Analogies thus linked Catholic theology, a traditional sociology, and the reproductive interests of women. As they ventured into the social arena, these interests were foremost in the minds of the women of the Nord. Armed with the correspondence between their own domestic values and those of their Creator, they tried to stamp society with the code of *caritas* or to rework it in the image of female charity, just as they had done at home. The personification of *caritas* in either the women of high society or the lady bountiful may seem innocuous. In fact, in the political atmosphere of nineteenth-century France, the stage was set for conflict.

Caritas among the Rich

In forming ties among members of their own class, the women of the Nord adhered literally and symbolically to the criteria of blood and family. Because women were bearing more children, families were large and could often satisfy any desire for a varied social life. Mme D. of Lille, born in the 1880s, remembered that her own social connections in her girlhood never passed beyond first cousins. As a child she played only with her nine brothers and sisters who, she maintained, provided her with an abundance of playmates. Once a year her mother permitted each child to invite a special friend from school to dinner.[2] Germaine Feron-Vrau's biography cites the habits of the Bernard family, into which she was born, as following the same pattern. Summers brought enormous family gatherings at the château in Santes; no one, she claimed, was ever bored or lonely with so many companions.[3] A century earlier, Mme Barrois-

Virnot recounted her dinners at her mother's, a visit from a cousin, a trip to see an elderly aunt in the midst of her own busy working schedule.[4] Family ties remained so intense in the Nord that localism prevailed in arranging marriages, and everyone testified that parents avoided "intermarriage" with people from other cities. Families from Roubaix refused proposals from Lille, only a few miles distant, and distinctions remain to this day between the Mottes from Tourcoing and those from Roubaix, despite the fact that the cities are contiguous. Although interurban alliances did occur, some parents reacted like M. and Mme T., who refused to let their daughters move from the parental home into their own for the first year of marriage.[5]

Isolationism could not stand, however, as a consistent policy in the Nord, given the rapidly expanding industrial development. Extension of the market and specialized production brought an interdependence of various segments of the bourgeoisie, both nationally and regionally. Contacts with Paris, Lyon, England, and even the United States multiplied, as did those within the Nord, as businessmen either diversified their holdings or made their enterprises more specialized, thus becoming more reliant on the services of others. Such developments had their social parallel in the proliferation of clubs for men and in a more elaborate social life for all members of the bourgeoisie. Dinner parties, evening gatherings, public balls produced a measure of visible solidarity that also served to mask the fact that businessmen were in direct competition with one another, and that bankruptcies and business failures occurred at an alarming rate.

An industrial world enlisted the services of the home in its endeavor for solidarity, just as it enlisted the consumer power of the home for its own survival. Likewise, many women resisted the call to service, just as they resisted the demands of fashion. The Bernard women, for example, refused to list any visiting hours in the social register, and expressed a preference for complete commitment to the *vie cachée.*[6] Some women who were scheduled to meet the Empress Eugénie, as noted in a prefect's report on wives of important families, avoided social life and stayed instead within the confines of the home.[7] Others, however, "loved society," and as early as the mid-nineteenth century observers had noted the transformation of the bourgeoise who had tended the cashbox for the family business into the "hostess."[8] Alfred Motte-Grimonprez, whose mother had spent most of her days tending her own and her sons' enterprises, wrote detailed accounts of his wife's social activities. In one two-week period in 1873, she gave three dinner parties for a total of 103 guests. On the eve of the first event, Motte wrote, "the house has been cleaned from cellar to attic. The housekeepers, the painters, the glaziers, the upholsterers leave this evening. Our gardeners are worn out. The cooks are arriving. Finally, it is a bustle that makes me laugh. . . . Always I admire the calm and devotion of my dear Léonie."[9] Madame Motte's efforts were matched throughout the Nord by her peers, who held elaborate soirées complete with musical or dramatic programs. While some of these might exclude outsiders, other women invited visiting politicians or business acquaintances. "My mother," recalled an elderly women from Roubaix, "loved large garden parties. I remember meeting generals and deputies and any important person who happened to be in town."[10]

Despite this expansion of the social circle beyond the ties of blood, women, in their symbolic ingenuity, used methods for entertaining that kept their ideology in the foreground. At any of these functions the female dominated, be it in the form of food, fashion, or rules of etiquette. Women saturated the social space with the color and volume of their clothing, their furniture arrangements, and their presence in every detail of the domestic site. Many prided themselves on the fact that at their table business affairs were never mentioned,[11] and this clear exclusion of the industrial world meant that the women set the rules on social occasions. They substituted parlor games they had devised: those of

Mme Barrois-Charvet became the rage in the Nord in the late nineteenth century.[12] Musical evenings proliferated, as well, and in that setting social talents so assiduously developed by northern French women could again dominate.[13] In their early years most women had cultivated skills that would allow them to hold center stage of the social world, and piano playing was primary among them. Gabrielle Humbert, for example, logged thousands of hours of piano lessons in boarding school,[14] and the account book of Mme S. indicates that she continued lessons in solfège long into her married life.[15] Through a multiplicity of acquired social skills women could continue to draw attention to their centrality in the world, and hostesses constructed their gatherings of whatever size around these accomplishments, as opposed to those of the market.

Social gatherings occurred in a highly stylized setting, which focused on the woman and was circumscribed not only by the walls of her personality but also by the rules of etiquette. These rules emanated from the hostess, and although they were standard among hostesses in general, a slight deviation might occur indicating her penchant, say, for a particular number of guests at dinner, for a certain designation of dinner partners. Flowing from her power as arbiter, rules connected each guest around the periphery of the gathering like the rim of a wheel, and further connected them to their hostess in the center. In this way an artificial family was created for the evening through the use of manners. Like other devices in the female world, etiquette contributed to make it run along familial principles by a symbolic ritual initiating outsiders into the home. Recognizing the import of their social activities in creating an artificial family, it was no wonder that many women in the Nord shunned contact with outsiders and preferred the real as opposed to the symbolic family. Within each social occasion lay the possibility that some outsider would betray with an untoward gesture that he or she did not belong. Women learned mechanisms for coping with unexpected displays of "unfamiliarity." The most common was increased preparation for and heightened ritual of any social occasion.[16] Heavy ritual so intensified the atmosphere and absorbed the attention that little room existed for an exotic personality to break the tribal setting. Should the worst occur—spillage, breakage, a rude remark—women knew a hundred gestures for retrieving an evening from the intrusion of disorder. Social life was, nonetheless, composed of such potential disasters, each of which threatened the woman herself because it disrupted a microcosmic order and the symbols with which she identified.

Once a stranger crossed the threshold of a home, he or she entered a world of familial order translated into the code of etiquette. Within each household a hierarchy existed between parents and children, husband and wife, master and servants. Just as court customs in the *ancien régime* showed place, degrees of noble blood, and power, so domestic etiquette served to create a social order duplicating the natural, familial one. The arrangement at a dinner table, for example, indicated the distinction or inferiority of guests. The hostess must know or improvise a hierarchy and signal her recognition through a correct seating arrangement. But so also must the guest acquiesce and display the proper sign of assent. Women learned to be good guests, good surrogate family members, by not doing things that would indicate strangeness. On visits, for example, young women should not play with a fold in the skirt, twirl a parasol, or make other nervous signs of being ill at ease. They knew that in making a visit the most important greeting was made to the hostess, and then a less elaborate one to each guest. Finally, because of her age, she should sit with her eyes focused on the speaker and with a modest, unpresupposing attitude indicative of her position as a young person. All women knew that the arrival of a newcomer formed a sign to rise, cede place, and move to a position farther from the hostess, that is, from the center of the occasion.[17] Perfect familiarity came only through a knowledge of these familial signs embodied in the rules of etiquette. Because any misbehavior upset the arrangement of things or virtually destroyed a universe, it gave rise to a bad reputation.

Reputation, in the female world view, was crucial.[18] How many domestic novels centered on the importance of being correctly regarded by members of a community, but especially by the female arbiters of the wider family symbolized in social life. Reputation was built from the total use of female symbols. In part it could stem from cleverness or originality in the assembling of these symbols. It was more important, however, that a woman order them correctly and that she adhere publicly to that authoritarian set of rules shared by all women in society. Her adherence indicated so many things that it undoubtedly brought tension to all women. Mathilde Bourdon had said, for example, that one could tell immediately the character of a woman from her clothing. One could read a being from external signs. Because a woman existed outside herself, she might interpret an unfavorable outside opinion almost as a statement of nonexistence. Believing in symbolic potency, women clung to domestic rules because they signaled adherence to the entire female cosmology of reproductive and family values. Only a woman who successfully indicated this adherence, who never betrayed the family through the the misplacement of a knife or fork, could belong to this feminine world. Cut from this world through bad reputation, a woman virtually ceased to exist.

Women displayed their belonging through other social institutions such as visiting—a custom that became ritualized in the late nineteenth century, and that acquired more and more rules and less and less substance. Visiting had occurred on a casual basis in the early nineteenth century. Women visited their relatives and friends then with more spontaneity, although less frequently because of their time-consuming involvement in business.[19] By mid-century women had started making visits on "occasions," as Mme S.'s account book indicates. She regularly made trips to see her friends who had just delivered children, for example, and recorded her expenses for "une visite de couche."[20] After the mid-century divide in women's lives, however, the occasions for visiting became specifically enumerated. One "owed" visits to those who had just received a blessing in the form of childbirth, those returning from a honeymoon, the betrothed, or those who had just experienced a particular good fortune. One also owed visits to those who had suffered a reverse of fortune, sickness, or a death in the family. The rituals for such visits included a short conversation of either an exhuberant or a moderate nature, depending on the event that elicited the visit itself. If the recipient of the call were not at home, one left a folded calling card. Rules were also set forth for the dress, bearing, and seating of any visitor.[21]

By the end of the century the custom underwent a new convolution. Women began visiting not because of any particular occasion, but because the visit itself had become an occasion. Now women of the Nord were "at home" once or twice each month, and on those days friends and acquaintances were expected to pay a visit. At the visit a guest arrived, perhaps took a cup of tea, and spoke a few words to the hostess until it was her turn to move down the line of seats on the arrival of a new visitor. An ordinary visit of this type lasted approximately fifteen to twenty minutes, and this enabled a woman to make six or eight visits in an afternoon.[22] These characteristics suggest an evolution of the visit into an important expression of the sum of symbols by which women spoke and ordered their lives. If it had once celebrated or mourned familial events, it now testified to the aggregate of familial symbols maintained by women's activities. But the visit indicated that those symbols extended beyond a single household into the social sphere. Performed with greater frequency, constant visiting was a sign of *caritas* at work in the binding of women, as representatives of the family, into a unity. By demanding daily

133

adherence to domestic rituals and the rules of etiquette, the visit also infused women's social code with vigor.

When confined to the bourgeoisie, that code worked well enough, for the activities all brought a much-desired solidarity for the class as a whole. Men in the Nord generally accepted women's stress on familial values in high society, where blood ties and market ties often meshed. Only occasional difficulties stirred their anger: a woman refusing to receive an important person in her home because he had broken female standards; a hostess rushing to count her rosary beads at the mention of an impious celebrity's name. In general, however, female rituals of social life among the rich posed few dangers to the market, and even worked to strengthen it. Men created solidarity by writing genealogies, forming geographical societies, sponsoring charity balls, and organizing men's clubs; social life in the Nord acted as an important supplement to their business. Like the home, it served an important purpose in buttressing the ruling class. Women's sense of *caritas* as a binding force, and their emphasis on morality in social life reinforced the solidarity of the bourgeoisie, despite the domestic coloration of the ties they wove. It was quite another matter when women attempted to convert their domestic vision to social policy.

Yet this was precisely what the women of the Nord attempted. Not recognizing either the chimerical nature of their power or its limits, they extended their social efforts beyond the bourgeoisie. According to them, not only were the rich bound to one another by actual or symbolic ties of blood, but the poor as well had a familial connection to one another and to the rich. If the individual family revolved around reproductive values, so should the aggregate of families. Women demanded that the social order duplicate their image, just as the home did. Armed with this demand they set out to paint the social surface with female symbols, to infuse it with a familial ethic, and to spread *caritas* throughout a wider world. When they did, the men of the Nord stopped acquiescing. Instead, they displayed a harsh resistance to this challenge to a sexual division of labor.

Nineteenth-century France in its quest to compete in a rapidly changing market world could not afford to support influential groups of women, like those in the Nord, who approached thorny public problems from a familial and theological perspective. Women who saw society as a collection of homes hierarchically organized and bound together by religious principles were out of place and even dangerous in the public arena. With stern moral principles guiding their efforts, women confronted their poorer neighbors and brought them alms, advice, and ultimatums about correct behavior and religious practice. When they did, men fought to put women firmly back in the domestic sphere. The men of the Nord mistrusted their wives in public matters, not because those wives were incompetent and frivolous, but because the more competent and serious they were, the more effective they were in promoting the cause of the anti-liberal and Catholic right.

Caritas for the Poor

The social question in the Nord should have discouraged even an optimist—except that the future of industrial society was at stake. To the informed Frenchman of the nineteenth century, the area bordering Belgium seemed a vast wasteland of urban dreariness and even worse, of disease and potential disorder. Social commentators combed this area to make their investigations and to report conditions under which the poor worked and lived. Local businessmen took more practical measures and constructed housing for their workers, organized insurance, medical, and other plans to benefit them. Municipalities relied on old-regime institutions of urban charity and on the efforts of religious and private philanthropists to come to the rescue of the poor in times of particular economic hardship.[23] But the combination of these methods never seemed adequate for the severe misery of cities such as Lille, Roubaix, Tourcoing, or Douai, all experiencing rapid industrialization and urbanization.

Women in the cities of the Nord had never ignored the misery around them. Like wealthy Roman matrons or the *châtelaine* of the manor, they had served as *dames de charité* and made their individual overtures to the poor even during the old regime.[24] During the nineteenth century they continued these traditions of *noblesse oblige* by visiting those of their neighbors in temporary distress or by holding "days" once a month on which the poor passed through their courtyards to receive money, clothing, or food.[25] Mme Bernard-Roquette of Santes did her newspaper reading while knitting garments for charity, and she trained her children to emulate her by making small savings for the relief of indigents.[26] Such training continued in boarding schools, where girls made their first garment in needlework classes for the poor.

Far from being cloistered, women moved energetically in public. Their physical occupation of the urban world was registered in the bustle of busy hands providing baskets of food for the poor or in the missions to the sick and aggrieved among their husbands' workers. We hear crinolines rustling at bedsides and carriages moving through slums to reach the miserable with words of comfort. This very personal physicality characterized their charitable endeavors and, as in the home and in their entertaining, women charged the world of the poor with their presence and symbolism. In entrusting charity only to her own hands and physical presence at bedsides, as opposed to sponsoring the impersonal workings of a bureaucratic institution, the *dame de charité* struck a public pose identical to the one she maintained at the center of domestic life. Her efforts were always highly visible and manifestly symbolic.

Well into the nineteenth century, male observers, including the city fathers of the Nord, bathed these efforts with romantic language. They saw, as indeed they were supposed to, women bestowing "spiritual" blessings on the urban environment. Most people viewed charity to be gentle as a mother, soft as a petticoat, and insubstantial as a piece of lace. Until the late 1870s, when the presence of women in the public arena began to appear disruptive of liberal ideas for the social order, they praised the delicacy and discretion of female ministrations to the poor. We know too much at this point about the convolutions of the female language not to recognize such an interpretation as a result of a double message read reductively. It was true that charity or *caritas* emitted female connotations. Insofar as *caritas* or God's love had allowed the genesis of the world, it evoked associations with women's procreative power: "charity is a mother."[27] Or in confused moments, when *caritas* and *eros* used the same language, the word "love" could mean a search for the fused ideal of the female and the spiritual. The other half of genesis was order—moral, authoritarian order—just as the home was ordered and tightly structured. So when the women of the Nord structured their charitable work, they did so firmly believing in *caritas*, but believing as well in the authority, order, and morality of domestic life.

These principles underlay the charitable organizations of northern French women, but those organizations also grew from the overwhelming misery of the poor in a rapidly urbanizing area. In 1817, a few women in Lille formed the first coherent female charity, the Société de charité maternelle, or maternal society.[28] This initiative was almost unemulated for several decades until the 1840s and 1850s, when women newly released from their productive activities and newly inspired by a reproductive vision began a flurry of volunteer work that would last until the First World War. By the 1870s most municipalities in the Nord could boast of work-schools and clubs for young working-class girls, day-care centers for infants, kindergartens, organizations to provide linens to poor families, and additional societies to regularize poor visiting—all of them run by bourgeois women.[29] Depending on the population, such societies attracted the efforts of as many as five or six hundred women, while those in small towns were run by as few as two dozen.[30] The large number of women involved set the societies apart from the philanthropic activities of men, which were often as individualistic and dissociated from other men's efforts as factory enterprise itself.[31] The few counterexamples, such as the Association catholique des patrons du Nord, were usually short-lived because inherently distasteful to the male bourgeoisie.

The biggest difference between male and female charity lay in the consistent and almost exclusive concern of women with the familial problems of other women and their children. Unlike their husbands, they never sponsored the construction of working-class housing, the creation of industrial institutes for the technical education of workers, or the arrangement of financial programs such as retirement, insurance, or accident plans. One might see this as a conventional division of labor, but to gloss lightly over the difference in activities ignores the results of the sexual coloring of the social order. For women's concern with women and children had important consequences. Not only did the domestic perspective of women determine their choice, it set the conditions for the reception of charity. Women monitored the behavior of their beneficiaries and revealed in the organization of their societies a firm intention to mold members of their sex into their own image, and thereby to extend, multiply, and strengthen their own domestic standards until they became a social norm.

A glance at the functioning of several charitable societies demonstrates how the women of the Nord combined concern for the poor with a desire to imprint their image on poor women. Their first organized effort centered on improving the conditions under which poor women gave birth to children. Beginning in the mid-nineteenth century, the bourgeoises of Valenciennes, Douai, Le Cateau, Maubeuge, and Dunkerque imitated the women of Lille in founding maternal societies for this purpose.[32] Acting within the parochial divisions of their cities, each active member or *dame patronnesse* assumed responsibility for distributing and soliciting aid. The statutes of most societies regularized assistance according to precise criteria: in Lille this included a layette of twenty-two pieces for the newborn child and a nightgown for its mother; payment of the midwife's fee; and a stipulated sum of money to support the mother's leave from work during the first weeks of her convalescence. Given the enormity of urban poverty in the industrial Nord, the regularization of amounts of charity enabled women to blanket their areas more thoroughly with aid. The extent of poverty also necessitated in some cases strict qualifications for receiving maternal assistance. In Lille, for example, women had to meet certain conditions of need and had to have borne a minimum number of children. In less populous areas or during times of extreme destitution, such as during the Franco-Prussian War, conditions were relaxed.[33]

Laden with the society's offerings, the women volunteers, either singly or in couples, visited the protegée mother recuperating from childbirth. They could then scrutinize the household and offer advice on domestic tasks or personal dilemmas. In Lomme, according to one account, the bourgeoises ransacked working-class quarters from top to bottom in search of signs of neglected female duties.[34] Written into official rules and suggestions of Douai's and Valenciennes' societies was the charge to observe sleeping arrangements. When these arrangements demonstrated that adolescent boys and girls were sharing the same bed, or when other irregularities appeared, the ladies took it upon themselves to procure more beds for the family.[35] More than the monetary relief of poor women was at stake in the work of charity.

That is, an ideological anchor weighted with a specifically female code distinguished these organizations from random largesse or from the later workings of the bureaucratic welfare state. No matter what her state of destitution, each potential recipient had to provide proof of good character,

139

morality, and religious marriage. Though poverty was ne-
gotiable, virtue and religion were not.[36] In this move beyond
the economic imperative, women of the maternal societies
professed to "champion the cause of mothers," and sought
to "watch over their needs, console them, and try to make
them better with constant advice."[37] The maternal cause,
however, was festooned with all the accoutrements of the
home and could not appear naked to outside eyes. The female philanthropists demanded the blessings of the religious sacrament of marriage and the virtue of Mary in a
visible way. If the cause of motherhood (and we should
remember that the *dames patronnesses* were also remind-
ing society of their own motherhood) were to receive public
support, the image of that motherhood must not be blem-
ished by encouragement for the slovenly, unchaste, or wanton women of their cities.

Images, such as those the women of the Nord hoped to
create, did not result from money, sentimental rhetoric, and
efficient organization alone. A union of mothers demanded
participation—visible participation—of rich and poor women.
Toward this end the maternal society's charter stipulated
that no *dame patronnesse* could delegate her function of
visiting poor women in childbirth to anyone but another
member of the society. Any dereliction of this duty would
result in a fine.[38] Instead of using hired personnel or sending
servants to deliver money or layette, the women instead
scorned the coldness and impersonality of bureaucratic
charity, of "charité par procuration."[39] Only some direct sign
of concern could indicate the presence of *caritas* passing
among members of God's creation and binding them to His
authority and order. In sum, the working of the maternal
societies corresponded to the workings of the microcosm of
the home and the macrocosm of the universe. On the social
level, it reflected the image of women, demanded the mastery of reproduction in the maintenance of a chaste presence, ordered the relationship among rich and poor mothers,

and connected them to the moral authority of God through the mechanism of *caritas*.

Concern for family and religion in the social sphere carried itself into other women's charities. In the 1830s, the movement to found kindergartens grew in popularity in France, and in the Nord municipalities and philanthropists began donating funds to start their own.[40] They hoped the *salle d'asile* would serve the purpose of providing rudimentary education for working-class children. In Lille, the largest city in the Nord, the schools had grown to twenty-six by the end of the Second Empire and served more than 6,000 youngsters between the ages of two and six.[41] Although the *salles* received financial support from both national and local governments, in fact organizations of hundreds of bourgeois women, rather than civil employees, oversaw the operation of the entire system.

Supervision of the *salles d'asile* involved immense amounts of work on the part of the *dames patronnesses* of the societies. Not only did they make their own financial contributions to the upkeep of the schools, they also took turns visiting their assigned school each day for the purpose of inspecting the premises and the health of the pupils. During her visit, the *dame patronnesse* was also charged with insuring that the personnel adhered to a minutely detailed curriculum. In addition, using their own resources, neighborhood committees of women provided complete sets of clothing for the students at least once a year. Within this organizational structure, the same standard of personal demonstration of *caritas* prevailed, and fines were exacted from anyone missing her inspection visit or the regular meetings of the society. The *dame patronnesse* was expected to display her concern for the children in the direct supervision of their welfare and in canvassing neighborhoods for prospective students.[42]

The *dame patronnesse* of the kindergarten society saw herself contributing to the development of the useful and independent working-class adult of the future. More important, according to one volunteer, the daily catechizing set by the curriculum and the religious images decorating the classrooms brought the children closer to the goodness of God. In this way, the *salles* might preserve the innocence that had inspired Christ to say "Let the little children come to me," and thus help them overcome the temptations of industrial society. Insisting on the recitation of Hail Marys and Our Fathers and on the performance of religious signs such as genuflection, the women of the Nord saw themselves in the vanguard of the fight against secularism and sin. According to the little legends growing up around the *salles*, members of the working class of all ages learned the lessons of *caritas* through the example set them by their benefactresses.[43]

A third ambitious project of bourgeois women focused on the creation of day-care centers or *crèches*. Between 1845 and 1870, Douai, Roubaix, Le Cateau, and Lille each had some form of nursery for infants, newborn to two years old, of mothers who worked outside the home.[44] Although Parisian initiatives in this field formed the model for the nurseries,[45] none of the industrial wives—Mme Seydoux of Le Cateau, Mme Wallaert-Descamps of Lille, Mme Descat of Roubaix—could have acted without concern for the miserable conditions in which the infants of the working class were often raised when their mothers had to work. High infant mortality rates constantly drew the worried attention of observers in the Nord, and the women philanthropists took one step in alleviating this problem when they undertook the enormous task of building, staffing, and financing their various centers.

Yet concern for infant mortality mingled with other motives, as the case of the four *crèches* in Lille demonstrates. In the 1860s Mme Wallaert-Descamps, the childless matron of a wealthy textile dynasty, began building herself a surrogate family.[46] After several visits to day-care centers in Paris, she opened one of her own for some dozen working-class infants near the family factory in Wazemmes. So successful and satisfying was the venture that she set out to create a network of centers in the city. She began raising funds for the buildings, negotiating with the municipal council for authorization and land, and organizing a committee of women to help her.[47] By 1879, Mme Wallaert had helped construct four *crèches*, staffed them with nuns, and attracted several hundred women for the task of daily and personal supervision and the ongoing job of fund raising.

Realistically acknowledging the fact that poor women often had to work outside the home, the *dames patronnesses* of the *crèches* sought to maintain "the sacred bonds of motherhood" through these institutions. They did this by insisting that all women appear at breaks in the work day to nurse their infants, and by refusing to accept any child who had been weaned before the age of nine months. For the women of the *crèche* society, the visible act of nursing signaled the sacred bond of motherhood. At the same time, the *crèches* turned away illegitimate children, for to accept them would be tantamount to "encouraging sloth and vice" among women.[48] Had the women of the society held a utilitarian standard, had their exclusive goal been simply the prevention of infant mortality, then any child should have been eligible for day-care attention. The women of the Nord, however, championed chaste motherhood in their own image more than they championed social utility.

Another type of organization instituted by wealthy women in the Nord aimed at the twin goal of preventing vice among young unmarried working-class girls and of molding them in the image of their Northern benefactresses. From about mid-century, wealthy women and their daughters launched a succession of *patronages* (recreational groups) and *ouvroirs* (workshops) for the teen-aged girl and the young woman.[49] While the *ouvroirs* provided a healthy, well-supervised working environment, the *patronages* met on Sunday to fill that time unoccupied by employment. Both groups showed the domestic thrust of women's charity. No one hid the attempt of the *patronage* to keep unmarried young women from falling into illicit sexual liaisons. One abbé in the city of Lille preached a fund-raising sermon on precisely that subject.[50] By meeting on Sundays, girls would not fall victim to the seductions of working-class street life. The philanthropists tried to make the *patronages* at least as attractive as cafés, fairs, and other social activities by filling Sunday meetings with games and amusements; and by charging their own daughters with the leadership of the recreational portion of the *patronage*, they incidentally trained another generation of women in the ways of charity. The philanthropists must have had a clear notion of their competition, and must have known as well that virtue was not easy. Otherwise they would not have needed this type of carrot for their protegées.

Short-term chastity was not their only goal. Religious orders assisting the women provided the girls with lessons in sewing, cooking, the keeping of record books on expenditures, and helped them set up accounts for their savings. To supplement the instruction in managing a home, girls also learned at both *patronage* and *ouvroir* the special importance of Catholicism in the life of any woman: that Jesus Christ had instituted the sacrament of marriage to sanctify the sexual union; that His sacrifice on the Cross had rescued women from the state of depravity in which they had lived since Eve's temptation of Adam; that the Church was especially necessary to women for these reasons. The goal of the *patronage* was the religious marriage or entry into a convent of each of its protegées, and thus the further duplication of the kind of domestic universe in which the bourgeois *patronnesses* lived and believed. Any deviation from the path of virtue meant immediate exclusion from the group, but for those who made a suitable marriage the *patronages* furnished a trousseau; for those who entered a convent, a dowry.

These four examples of women's charity in the Nord reiterate a commitment to the family, especially the family centering on woman and her reproductive values. Using a

144

system of rewards, the women of the Nord bound all women
and their offspring into a familial society of alms; or, on a
higher level, of charity; or, on a spiritual level, of *caritas*.
The equivalent meanings become especially significant
with the qualifications women placed on charity. Just as
women would refuse to receive disreputable members of
their own class in the *foyer*, so they refused the poor who
transgressed the family code. Unwed mothers received no
aid from the maternal society; illegitimate children found
no place in the *salles d'asile* or *crèches*; and the fallen young
woman saw the doors of the *patronages* closed before her.
For the bourgeois women of the Nord, the only method of
making reproduction respectable and strong was theological. The transformative powers of the sacraments had to be
called upon to spiritualize the sexual image of woman so
that, in the form of virtue, it might serve as a social code.
And they continued to couple reproduction and chastity; to
fuse family and woman (as if women magically reproduced
alone); to see the social order bound by that intangible *caritas* spread by the visible deeds of women.

Not only did the visible act of charity bind society, its very
existence served as testimonial to an immutable and God-
given social order. Rich and poor both had their place on
God's earth, both had their role to play in charity. Ordained
by God as the responsibility of the privileged, the act of
charity signaled one's place in the social hierarchy and indicated that one was fulfilling His commands. Charity was
thus order, and the sense of order it contained paralleled
the order searched for in the management of a home. Rather
than attempt to remove social differences with a charity that
was money-oriented and that would help the poor attain a
minimum standard of living, women cared little for utilitarian standards. They never devised comprehensive programs to reach every member of society, nor did they want
to remove traces of poverty. Poor infants, said an invitation
to contribute to the *crèche* society, announce "the difference
of condition inherent in humanity."[51] The continued pres-

ence of poverty served as an important indication of structure, which was why women's societies emphasized a temporary helping hand in day care or a basket of delicacies
from a lady bountiful as a holding action until the poor
reached their heavenly destination. This attitude toward the
poor, as we shall see, would stand in marked contrast to the
nineteenth-century thrust toward bureaucratic social welfare programs.

Because charity stood for order, women in the Nord participated as symbols of obedience rather than as salves to
bourgeois bad conscience. Rather than work as efficiently
as possible in a single organization, women sought to multiply signs of obedience by joining as many charitable organizations as possible. Some critics mocked the woman
who was *dame patronnesse* for half a dozen or more different societies and who spent her time attending series of
commemorative Masses for their members.[52] This charge,
however, missed the point. If membership in a dozen societies had become the "fashion," as one observer charged,
the vogue was as meaningful as the notion of fashion itself.
Unstricken by any hostile comments, the women of the
Nord met to sew clothing for children on certain days. They
participated in such rituals as donating a cradle to the *crèche*
when new children were born to their families. Una-
bashedly they received gold medals from the Empress
Eugénie, clothed the *salles d'asile* children in new uniforms
to greet visiting officials, and acted in ways that could only
appear gratuitous to the cause of effective welfare programs.[53] They sponsored charity balls and a biennial bazaar
for the maternal societies, and at such events they made
themselves highly visible in lush clothing and through the
small but carefully worked objects they offered for sale.[54]
The fashionable aspect of the volunteer associations paralleled all speech about women themselves. It allowed society to see that they were acting as women ought, participating in societies that were female, and adhering to an

The Bourgeoise

Ladies of Fashion

Ladies of Fashion

Mathilde Bourdon

The Bourgeois Home

Prize-winning students at the
Bernardine pensionnat

The Pensionnat du Sacré-Coeur of Lille

School Days

The Belle Epoque

En Famille

Mᵐᵉ CAMILLE FERON-VRAU (1839-1913)

Madame PAUL FERON-VRAU
née Germaine Bernard
1869-1927

Religious Leaders

authoritarian order monitored and created by women in accord with a higher order.

In short, charity focused on women just as domestic symbols publicized and reflected a housewife. Women intended no less when they spent their efforts on other poorer women and their offspring. The result was more than just a conflation of the terms woman and charity. It produced personal attention to the *dame patronnesse* in the form of obituary notices on hundreds of charitable women in the Nord. Eugénie Smet, Germaine Bernard, Louise Charvet, Mme Aronio de Romblay, Mme Emile Delesalle, Mme Thiriez-Dupont, Herminie de la Bassemoûturie: the inexhaustible obituaries highlighted not the great works, but the good works of women.[55] The charitable image of women even eclipsed truths that no longer fit; for example, in the funeral oration on Mme Thiriez-Dupont, who had helped forge one of the largest fortunes in the Nord, her eulogizer praised "an existence . . . entirely devoted to the care and well-being of our working class."[56] The obituary of Mme Emile Delesalle, however, is typical of all the rest:

> The poor were the object of her affectionate interest, especially the shameful poor, the fallen people. She sought them out and helped them with perfect discretion which doubled the value of her benevolent interest. To those whom she could approach without fear of bruising their dignity, she brought, along with alms to assure their existence, consolation of the most serious sort—she raised their courage and their hopes. To others, each Sunday, she opened all the doors of her home, above all when her childen were still young. In making them distribute these alms with her, she hoped to initiate them early into the practices of charity.
>
> In the last years of her life the St. Gabriel Orphanage gained her interest. Not only did she accomplish a great deal with her generosity, but she also took on the task of maintaining the clothing of her dear orphans in good

order and in good repair. When she appeared in the courtyard of the establishment at recreation time, all her pro-
tegés surrounded her and lavished her with manifestations of their profound respect and affectionate gratitude.[57]

Despite its banality, the ritualistic appearance of this
obituary and its stereotypical nature should alert us to the
important elements it contains. It certainly focuses on the
works of Mme Delesalle among orphans by muffling the
fact that the committee for the St. Gabriel institution was
composed of hundreds of women.[58] Yet the contradictions
in the obituary do not stop there. For while it emphasizes
the philanthropist's wide-ranging deeds, even public ones,
it strikes an opposite note in mentioning her "perfect discretion." Such an emphasis on discretion is not unique;
other obituaries mentioned the charitable woman's secret
ways. Germaine Feron-Vrau had written in her diary that
"it is true charity that conceals from the protegé his benefactor's identity."[59] And other women kept secret accounts
of every good deed they had performed. Novels, as well,
often built on the suspense of a heroine's secret charity:
would people ever recognize her true goodness when she
herself was so committed to silent actions?[60] This accords,
however, with every detail of women's language in which
they both articulated and hid their meanings. Women's
charity in the Nord was the most public act, fraught with
ritual and undisguised almsgiving, while it remained, optimally, unknown, secret, only apparent in their diaries—or
even better, in their hearts and souls. A repression, which
like every other domestic deed built on a contorted attempt
to act while simultaneously hiding the action, underlay this
convolution. The only factor barring the road to mental
breakdown—and the women in the Nord were more vigorous than languishing—was their extraordinary faith. The
secrets that they kept while acting were known to God.
Their faith in the Father and in His creation and order held
the Catholic system of dualities together and smothered

some of the contradictions in their charitable acts. Because of their faith they could believe in "secret" charity, in purging the sinful from their lists of protegées, and in turning their eyes from the plight of the illegitimate child.

Utility versus *Caritas*

How surprising it must have been when, after decades of accolades for their charitable enterprise, the women of the Nord found themselves more criticized than appreciated. By 1885 municipal governments throughout the Nord had suspended their subsidies to the *crèches* and maternal societies, had set up competing programs for young people, and had so antagonized bourgeois women that they discontinued their work for the *salles d'asile*. The official struggle against their form of charity was not whimsical but rested on broad principles, starting with the conviction among politicians that scientific law, not religious belief, should direct society. The men who took the reins of every level of government after the demise of the Second Empire in 1870 had political minds of a modern cast, and carried with them into office a determination to extirpate those forces that would perpetuate anachronistic social, economic, and political ideas in France from positions of influence.

It is not difficult to see why republicans would dislike the hands of women tampering with the social order. If men represented the cause of industry triumphant, many wealthy women in the Nord looked nostalgically to an agricultural past when manors were presided over by the *châteleine* who ministered to her inferiors. Mathilde Bourdon, the popular writer and lady of charity in Lille, wrote that although one accepted the industrial order as a fact of life, one should combat the misery, immorality, and family disintegration following in its wake through the rejuvenation of traditional institutions.[61] To this end she filled her books with stories of the glorious preindustrial times, of faithful gentleman farmers, or of the heroic efforts of counterrevolutionaries

149

such as the Vendéens.[62] Bourdon, along with many of her contemporaries, thus romanticized the age of monarchs. While she contributed her tales of the saintly deeds of generations of French royalty, other northern French women supported the cause of each new pretender to the throne. Marie Toulemonde dedicated her first poems to the Comte de Chambord.[63] Others, by the score, attended commemorative masses for Louis XVI, Marie Antoinette, and other legitimist martyrs[64]—hardly acts to endear women to republicans. Because their suppport for legitimacy grew naturally from a family ideology, and because royal authority rested in part on an analogy with parental power, they conceived a strong distaste for republics. Democracy for the women of the Nord was merely "the politics of those who cry loudest," while the hundred-year-old slogan "liberté, égalité, fraternité" left them cold.[65] The notion of liberty could only lead human beings to break the laws of God and society, whereas a belief in equality would provoke challenges to an ordained and hierarchical social order. In sum, the political beliefs of northern French women represented just those reactionary ideas republicans had been battling since the French Revolution. Even if reaction was on the wane among men, and if the triumph of a form of political liberalism appeared complete with the installation of the Third Republic in the 1870s, French women, like their peers in other industrial countries, seemed permanently wedded to the past.

Had the women of the Nord kept their opinions safely at home, there would have been no reason to challenge them. Instead, they gained a stranglehold on at least some working-class families—a constituency the republicans sought for themselves. By tying the reception of charity to conformity with their standards, especially to the Catholic faith and politics, female philanthropy with its possible legions of obedient workers posed a threat to the Republic.[66] Each institution they sponsored instilled a domestic message reinforced by theology, so that both aspects of women's charity rightly became a single image in the republican mind: religious kindergartens for legitimate children; religious domestic instruction for virtuous young women; assistance for religiously married mothers; and the care by religious personnel for the legitimate and baptized infant in the *crèche*. To men, each of these charitable acts seemed to entail a new recruit for their enemy—the Church. Republicans also correctly estimated that the price of these alms was adherence to a package of conservative beliefs; thus, destruction of the remnants of an anachronistic but still potent past became an important priority of Third Republic politicians. Women's charity, as one of those remnants, merited an attack.

The first attack was directed against schools in the Nord, most of which, though publicly supported, were run by religious personnel. In some cities anticlericals had succeeded even as early as the late 1860s in removing certain male ordes—*frères ignorantins* they were ungraciously called—and substituting lay teachers. The real onslaught came in the 1870s and 1880s, when city fathers throughout the department not only enforced the Ferry laws, which provided for free, compulsory, and secular education, but made private efforts to purge even kindergartens of religious influence.[67] These acts accomplished, women in the Nord displayed their disapproval by quitting their posts in the *salles d'asile* and by stopping all work they had done in primary schools. Their withdrawal was neither unexpected nor undesired.[68]

Government had developed new plans for public education: public functionaries had already appeared to perform the supervisory tasks of the women's volunteer organizations. Paid personnel inspected schools and controlled the curriculum, though the government erroneously predicted that women would continue to sit quietly at home making the pupils' clothing.[69] They hoped that women would remain mute and out of sight with neither influence nor much responsibility. The women refused the honor.

151

What angered women most was not the elimination of a great deal of responsibility but the purging of the curriculum and the removal of God and His workers from positions of social importance. Instead of remaining quiet, the bourgeoises conspicuously threw the weight of their energy and wealth into the cause of private religious education as alternatives to public and secular schools. In Lille, for example, when city fathers in 1881 refused authorization to a religious order for running a primary school for girls, the Bernard women, wives of important businessmen, opened their homes to the students. The women and their friends provided knitting material as well as towels and handkerchiefs for the 170 children to hem. Each day the parish priest visited the improvised facility to catechize the students.[70]

At this point, centuries of encomia for the generous works wrought by the gentle hands of women were exposed to scorn and rebuke as charity became a political battlefield. A popular newspaper ruthlessly attacked the Bernard women's action as an example of girls being forced to perform "lucrative work" for the Catholic ladies.[71] Yet such public abuse only pushed the women to greater exertions in behalf of their cause. Mme Scrive, from one of the wealthiest and most prominent textile families, donated funds for the sisters of the Enfant-Jésus to open schools.[72] In almost every parish women organized *oeuvres du vestiaire* to provide clothing only for Catholic schoolchildren. By the end of the century, most parishes in the Nord could boast of several Catholic kindergartens and primary schools in addition to various secondary schools and industrial and commercial institutes.[73] A handful of Catholic men contributed to this cause, but the greater work came from the inspecting, provisioning, and proselytizing done by hundreds of devout and wealthy women.

Although of great consequence, laicization of the school system was only a sideswipe at women's charity. The next attacks aimed directly at their organizations. The same impulse to propagate republican institutions moved municipal politicians to rescind public support to women's charity, initially granted because women's societies were so socially useful. Within the changed political climate of the 1880s, government officials on all levels now reconsidered their contributions. The debate raised by the question of women's charity illustrated precisely the sexual difference between views of social welfare.

In the spring of 1883, four short years after it had awarded an annual subsidy for the last of the day-care centers, the government of Lille presented its arguments against the women of the *crèche* society. At the head of the drive to abolish subsidies to women's groups was Councilman Edouard Crépy, whose wife was a prominent participant not only in charitable societies but in such laywomen's groups as the Archiconfrérie des mères chrétiennes. Crépy accused the society of using philanthropy to accommodate religious orders. He had examined the society's accounts and found its costs in excess of what should be necessary to care for infants. He could only deduce that the accounts had been padded for the benefit of the centers' religious personnel. Other councilmen added stories of the society's heavy-handed practices in favor of the Church. They charged that women forced provisioners of the *crèches* to send their children to congregational schools in return for doing business, and that they applied similar pressure to working mothers. The central committee and its employees, according to another councilman, libeled the city fathers for their anticlericalism, instead of acknowledging the financial support the municipal government had awarded the centers. Why do we give this money, he asked, when the people do not know that we are in fact their benefactors? In short, the councilmen sought loyalty in exchange for their money, not the perpetuation of obedience to the ideologically hostile demands of Catholic women.

They also accused nursery schools of spreading disease and of undermining the family. It would be better, some suggested, for municipal bureaucracies to award each mother an individual allocation to keep her at home with her children. Here the council seemed to be articulating a belief in the virtues of family life identical to that of wealthy women. Yet working-class mortality had risen sharply in the Nord, and criticism of day-care centers argued for the efficiency rather than the virtue of the family in matters of child care. In the view of the city fathers, to permit mothers in the factory was equivalent to "homicide" of potential workers—a disaster for an industrial society. The women of the *crèche* society saw nuns as more than adequate substitutes for mothers on a temporary basis, and especially desirable because of the religious imprint they would give each infant. But politicians hammered away with a utilitarian argument.

Coupled with the failure of the *crèches* to protect the lives of infants—a failure that the *dames patronnesses* of the societies demonstrated to be false—a final criticism sealed the fate of all subsidies—local, departmental, and national— to the centers. Officials throughout France found *crèches* run by Catholic women to be "undemocratic" in their discrimination against illegitimate and unbaptized children. Citizens of the republic, they claimed, had the right to expect equal benefits from public money no matter what their marital status or religious beliefs. According to this argument, unwed mothers counted as citizens and deserved as such better treatment at the hands of women philanthropists.[74]

Religious, inefficient, and undemocratic: the charges against the *crèche* society accummulated. City governments took the first steps in the 1880s and cut off subsidies, and departmental and national governments followed suit in the nineties. By that time the sins of Catholic women were legion: they used the wrong baby bottle; *crèches* in the Nord were unsanitary; women philanthropists were haughty and ungracious, but above all persistently "undemocratic" in refusing the illegitimate and unbaptized infant.[75] In Lille as in other Northern cities, men such as Crépy, Scrive, and Cannissié, who voted unanimously against the *crèche* society, who said "we are all anticlericals," had wives, mothers, and sisters on the membership lists of this and other Catholic women's organizations.[76]

For almost identical causes, departmental and local officials terminated annual contributions to maternal societies. At times the debate revealed a light-hearted attitude toward women's efforts. What does it matter, one city councilman of Lille asked, if we remove our subsidy? The ladies will simply hold another bazaar or raise the price of lottery tickets. But the allegation, as it ran along a humorous vein, that ladies bountiful had more than enough money already, only served to introduce more substantial charges. Again politicians claimed that wealthy women were masking their use of public money to support religious orders. The allegation was true insofar as the societies called upon various congregations to perform their bookkeeping functions and receive applications for aid from poor women. Yet the women of the maternal society refused to change their ways in order to keep public subsidies. They were, according to some councilmen, so blinded by religious fanaticism as to refuse all compromise.[77]

This refusal continued when local and departmental officials asked that maternal societies assist unwed and nonreligiously married mothers. In the 1880s each mayor received a letter from the prefect asking him to persuade the women volunteers to change their policy. Throughout the Nord presidents of maternal societies such as Mme Berteau of Maubeuge or Mme Mabille of Valenciennes consistently responded that they could not expand their clientele, that they could not concern themselves with illegitimate or unbaptized children, and that they would forgo all subsidies rather than alter their rules.[78] By the 1890s most women's groups no longer benefited from government funds, and ultimately they had to reduce the scope of their contact with poor women in their cities. The retreat caused little consternation among republican politicians and businessmen in charge of the social order. They nourished their own plans for charity.

The Replacement for *Caritas*

Commonplace in France under the Third Republic, these attacks were accompanied by projects to replace the outmoded organizations with more modern, and of course more republican, facilities for the poor. Local governments courted the loyalty of the poor by instituting bureaucratic welfare. For example, in Lille they reallocated funds from the *crèche* society to a government agency charged with distributing money to poor women who would remain at home to care for their children. This precursor of a national *allocation familiale* aimed at making the working class see in the government and its functionaries a protection in times of trouble. It aimed as well at blanketing areas with assistance through the use of efficient bureaucratic procedures. Local governments also encouraged and even sponsored all sorts of republican organizations that might rally the poor. The 1880s witnessed a proliferation of groups for gymnastics, popular libraries, vacations, lunch programs, stamp collecting, camping, debate, music, and marching. Participants, it was hoped, would notice the concern of the republic for its citizens, and by the same token interpret membership in these small groups devoted to their amusement, edification, and assistance as symbolic of membership in the republic.[79]

There was initially a place in this network for the efforts of wealthy women, a place that most of them refused to occupy. Republicans still professed to want their assistance with schoolchildren, and they created, among other supporting groups for the newly secular schools, a women's auxiliary that seemed to be a revival of the old organization of *dames patronnesses*. Yet this new society of *dames laïques*, stripped of all but the most ornamental functions,

156

appealed to almost no one among the wealthy women of the Nord. Peopled with a few schoolteachers' wives and several spouses of government functionaries, it was defunct by the turn of the century.[80]

Republicans conceived another organization to handle the problem of young children and infants: the Society for the Protection of Young Children. Acting under the aegis of the Roussel Law, a piece of early Third Republic legislation for the inspection of conditions under which poor children were put out to nurse, both local and departmental officials in the Nord assigned public health doctors to visit the children and their guardians. In addition, certain cities and towns encouraged the formation of women's committees to assist the doctors in such an enormous undertaking. Because the clientele consisted of both legitimate and illegitimate children, republicans were apparently fortifying their democratic rhetoric with specific action.[81]

In Lille, the city for which an account remains of the activities of women volunteers, some twenty wealthy women devoted their efforts to visiting both children's guardians and their mothers to check on sanitary conditions and to provide the usual advice on care for the infants. They even "shunned the clerical banner," as one woman wrote, because they knew that they could check baby bottles and the cleanliness of cradles without the advice of priests. For a while the republicans seemed pleased with those efforts. In 1883 the city fathers of Lille eagerly diverted funds to the volunteers and praised their accomplishments at municipal council meetings.[82] This occurred during the heyday of attacks on other women's groups, and the support made the withdrawal of funds and their transferral to a more republican type of charity less suspect. But attitudes of both sexes among the bourgeoisie were still in conflict, and the alliance would not last long.

Catholic women in Lille did not flock by the hundreds to join the Society for the Protection of Young Children as they did to other volunteer organizations. Instead, Julia Bécour, a prominent Lille writer and wife of a leading doctor, complained of the difficulties in recruiting even those twenty women from high society.[83] A bourgeoise who would visit children born in sin was as scarce as an industrialist who would support the *usine chrétienne*. More important, those who did join, like Bécour, still saw their mission as improving the morals and not the material condition of working-class women. Far from being sanguine about extramarital sexual relations, Bécour in both her novels and nonfictional writings saw illegitimate pregnancies as a sign of human degradation. However, rather than avert her gaze from the presence of sin in society, she and her associates sought in their dealings with unwed mothers to prevent another recourse to "vice." The old duality of reproduction and chastity remained intact despite the removal of the organized Church as sponsor.

In addition, women of an apparently more modern and republican mindset maintained their vision of the family as the cornerstone of society and their vision of *caritas* as the social glue binding families of all classes. The presence of vice in society, according to Bécour, was the result of male failure to adhere to morality, the result of male seduction of women, the result of male standards of force as they overpowered those women whom they should have cherished. Men were immoral and scientific—she linked the terms. Their industrial social order created all sorts of misery not only between men and women but between rich and poor. Instead of using the age-old solution of *caritas*, they tried scientific experimentation on the social order and thereby increased social strife. "Only when the love of Christ is present in society," Bécour wrote, "will peace and justice appear on earth and all tensions dissolve in mutual brotherhood."

Republicans, in short, had been deceived: a domestic and traditional *weltanschauung*, not Catholicism alone, was the real enemy of utilitarian social policy. Exhortations to the practice of *caritas*, even women practicing *caritas* itself would not stop an anarchist's bomb or deter a determined working class from attacks on the industrial economy. After a decade of accommodation to the experiment with anticlerical women, republicans in the city of Lille declared women of the Society for the Protection of Young Children "ineffective," and transferred their funds to the municipal welfare program to be administered by bureaucrats.[84]

Julia Bécour made a pronouncement on the republican apostasy. She claimed that the most powerful men in the Nord found themselves untroubled by moral questions. Above all, Bécour complained, they could not see in women an equal except in the home: "they limit [women's] influence to *la vie intime* and keep them in a notoriously inferior position in everything that touches social problems." Writing at the end of the nineteenth century, after observing two decades of attacks on women's charity, Bécour could only conclude that men wanted women out of the social sphere. But notwithstanding real insight, she failed to see that male suspicions grew less from misogyny than from a fundamental disagreement on social policy. *Caritas* belonged to the home and not to the direction of a society based on class rather than family. Only force, scientific management, and the monetary resources of the democratic state had a chance of resolving the problems of people bound together by cash, self-interest, and the market.

Some women defected from the effort to bring the blessings of domestic ideology to their poorer contemporaries after the concerted attacks on their efforts. Instead, they became more committed socialites. For them rounds of social visiting, an attention to fashion and the rules of etiquette, and the scrupulous surveillance of women of the bourgeoisie sufficed to spread the image of women. Despite this withdrawal, a domestic vision of the world did grow among women of the working class. Invited by the agents of advertising, they adopted domesticity and its nonverbal language system, for these women too became more reproductive and less productive by the end of the nineteenth

159

century. Women of the working class, worked during their single years, but once married, they spent themselves and what their budgets would allow on food, fashion, and home decoration, and like wealthy women became advocates of virtue and morality.

Far from quitting the social field, another group of wealthy women in the Nord redoubled their enterprise. After the republican treachery, Julia Bécour proceeded to organize the Society for Abandoned Mothers.[85] In forming a group with such a title she had reached the conclusion that men were to blame for her protegées' predicament, and that specifically men under the influence of modern values were responsible for not only this but for most social problems. Bécour called herself a feminist, but she was joined in her combat against modernity and immorality by conservative Catholic women at the opposite end of the political spectrum. For them a defense of female virtues and of a domestic ideology involved support of a beleaguered Church and the merger of their volunteer activities directly with its own. With the appearance of a secular Red Cross, for example, the women of the Nord took care to call their society Catholic, and as the schools became laicized they championed explicitly parochial institutions.[86] In this uneven battle, however, men had at their disposal all the tools of the French government.

Experience is supposed to bring people to new levels of understanding, but nothing suggests that the women of the Nord, even the most radical, changed their attitudes toward the social order. Operating from a familial base, they continued to perceive society as a collection of families and to insist on adherence to values consistent with such a perception. Despite the social warfare that raged around them, despite the assassination of businessmen in the Nord by anarchists, despite strikes and revolutions, their answer remained more love and morality. The women of the volunteer organizations pleaded, cajoled, bribed, and almost blackmailed people to behave lovingly and morally. When those tactics failed, they turned their eyes toward heaven and hoped that a more loving world awaited their daughters.

III
Passing
the Torch

7
Education: Innocence versus Enlightenment

Mme Bernard of Santes remembered reading in Fénelon that little girls, more than boys, should remain at home for their early training. Accordingly, she kept her daughters there, and with the help of a nun educated them herself while her sons went to school in a nearby town. Her daughter Germaine (b. 1869) remembered walking to mass at seven in the morning and reciting lessons in her mother's presence. The girls sacrificed their desserts so that the savings could go to poverty-stricken neighbors. They helped decorate the church with flowers, and watched their mother's incessant knitting for the poor. In the evening the entire family sat at home doing needlework (the boys also, when they were present) and listened while one read an instructive work to the others. Their day ended with the household gathered for prayer.[1]

In all cases girls first learned charitable and religious ways at their mother's side. Marie Toulemonde accompanied her mother on charity visits, and other children went on pilgrimages sponsored by the many women's groups.[2] They also imbibed a sense of household ritual as they made the morning rounds of cupboards and closets or sat with groups of women and did their own childlike bit of mending. Little girls experienced the same fittings for clothing as their mothers, and even when they later went to boarding school, one of the few people with access to the convent was the seamstress.[3] The lessons learned at home were lessons for womanhood, a womanhood whose imminence was ever-present. Mothers like Mme R. reminded their daughters to learn their lessons well. "If anything happens to me," she warned the eleven-year-old Anne, "I count on you to take my place." To some extent Anne was ready, for in her large family, as in so many others with numerous children, the oldest girls often helped with all the rest.[4]

Except in families like the Bernards, girls sometimes started going to school at four or five. At that age they spent but two or three hours a day with the Soeurs de la Sagesse in Roubaix or the Dames du Sacré-Coeur in Lille. Religion and little domestic skills formed their curriculum, along with the rudiments of reading and writing. Sometimes they made a gift for an "adopted" child in the adjacent schools for the poor, and thus continued their training in the ways of grown women.[5] This relaxed routine continued until pre-adolescence, when a more serious and more complicated preparation for womanhood began.

In the early nineteenth century, preteen-agers began this serious preparation in a variety of ways. Some started regularly attending their mother's rounds of business activities. They learned bookkeeping, the mechanics of production, and sometimes accompanied their parents on sales trips.[6] Their education was based on an apprentice system with a long tradition behind it. Often tutors supplemented these casual, though rigorous, lessons with more formal training in cosmography, the scriptures, arithmetic, writing, mythology, and the like.[7]

An alternative experience consisted of attending a day or boarding school. In the Nord these establishments flourished during the first half of the century. Marie Vrau attended the school of Mlle Brissez, rue de la Barre in Lille.[8] Caroline Lelièvre of Bergues went first to Mme Merwyn's establishment in Dunkerque, and then at the age of fourteen her parents sent her to Mme d'Aubrée's school in Paris. From 1831 to 1835 Caroline put her mind to her studies with increasing success. From "mal" on her early reports, she proceeded to earn three prizes in solfeggio, conduct, and drawing. Thus prepared for womanhood, Caroline was happily married in 1836.[9]

Lay women administered these fashionable schools in the Nord until the convents drove them out of business. Each *pensionnat des desmoiselles* had a precarious existence. Its founder, often widowed or unmarried, could expect her schools to last only as long as she did. In the case of the *pensionnat* started by the Delecourt sisters of Lille, the owners had no successor to inspire confidence in their clientele, so that at their retirement they found themselves with an empty building on their hands.[10] By the 1870s few such schools operated any longer; they had been eclipsed by the convents.

Convents began offering an attractive option to lay education as early as the Restoration. After the state had made peace with the Church, they opened their doors tentatively. The Bernardines (les "oiseaux") started schools in the suburbs of Lille during the second decade of the nineteenth century, and drew their pupils from the daughters of active businesswomen who needed their children safely supervised.[11] Adèle Motte spent some of her teen-aged years there before learning the textile business from her mother.[12] Between 1830 and 1860, other orders arose and began invading the Nord with their schools: Sacré-Coeur started first at Amiens, then with the help of the Comtesse de Grandville opened a *pensionnat* in Lille and another in Dunkerque.[13] The order quickly became one of the most popular in all of France (perhaps even in the Western world) for educating wealthy young women. Douai welcomed the Dames de la Ste. Union;[14] Dunkerque, the Benedictines; and Lille, the Dames de St. Maur, who bought out Mlle Brissez.[15]

The success of these schools was phenomenal, but behind the monopoly they established lay many practical considerations even beyond the institutional support given them by the Church. Religious orders could provide a stable personnel for their schools, which could survive the loss of a headmistress or the old age and illness of its teachers. Because of the growing attractiveness of the religious life to upper-class women, the schools never lacked personnel. Each new sister brought with her a large dowry to contribute to the financial health of the establishment, and the bourgeoisie did not seem to begrudge the heavy tuition and other fees it paid for its daughters to become model women. As the convents became traditions in the Nord, they set up alumnae groups like the Enfants de Marie, and soon had a body of committed laywomen to sustain them financially and even politically when necessary. Yet practical advantages alone did not determine their success. Convents offered the adolescents of the Nord a special indoctrination into the complexities of the domestic life.

The Convent

Catholic adolescence is somehow dark and mysterious, at least according to portraits left by such famous writers as George Sand, Simone de Beauvoir, and Mary McCarthy. Sand writes of stone and cells, of confessions and secrets, and of an atmosphere ripe for teen-aged hysteria. A photograph from the Nord (c. 1880) suggests that these reports may be accurate to some extent. Five students from the Bernardine convent in Esquermes are posing in their long black uniforms. They have won the highest awards for conduct and achievement during the school year, but they look neither festive nor proud of their accomplishments. Instead they have a sober, even frightened look as if the light from the camera were too much for those accustomed to live in darkness; each wears an ascetic coiffure—hair parted in the middle, drawn severely back in a bun.[16]

Another glance at the photograph, however, shows more than darkness and timid faces. The girls have flowers in their hands. They wear corsets and stiff petticoats under their uniforms and large silk bows under their collars. Despite the timid looks, their posture is graceful; the tilt of their heads, composed. One even sits as if she were taking tea and listening to a conversation. In fact, the convent, its darkness included, offered impeccable training in womanhood. The high walls sealing it off from the profane world duplicated the home, as one priest wrote, in a purified form.[17] A closed-off site, it created a microcosm similar to that of the household. Within those walls the nuns were mothers—"ma mère" one addressed them—who led their students through a more advanced version of the domestic curriculum. This included the *arts d'agrément*, lessons in social deportment, and a rich variety of formal coursework in literature, arithmetic, history, religion, and other subjects that would permit girls to become polished matrons.[18] Whatever the field of instruction, convent education directed its students by its very methods toward domestic life.

Girls at Northern boarding schools encountered a strict regime of long workdays and a curriculum of fifteen or more subjects per week. They continued their initiation in domestic skills with constant exercises in fancy needlework, piano playing, drawing, bookkeeping, and sewing for the poor. The nuns lightened what many girls initially found a *corvée* by reading during sewing or knitting classes or by telling their students stories.[19] But it was a hard task. "I think," wrote one student who hated both insects and needlework, that "in Purgatory my punishment will be to knit with caterpillars."[20] Still, these exercises were essential to womanhood.

Lessons in scientific and humanistic areas served the same end of preparing girls to speak the domestic language. They studied literature, history, geography, various sciences, foreign languages, penmanship, and many other subjects. But these studies were not designed to plunge students into the life of the mind. Instead, as one slightly disgruntled alumna of Sacré-Coeur explained, classes were so short (about twenty minutes) and the curriculum so full, "that we could never become engrossed in anything."[21] Insofar as the curriculum was charged with subjects, insofar as each subject received perhaps an hour or two each week, the intent was not to develop a woman's capacity in formal knowledge. Rather, a surface acquaintance with history, literature, two or three foreign languages, or mathematics served as a gloss for the future. Knowledge of another language particularly fell into this category, and it was always clear that women of the bourgeoisie were not aiming at careers in translation or comparative linguistics. To the contrary, a lisping familiarity with English made a woman prettier, or with Italian enabled her to sing with greater charm. And there were prohibitions on language training for women that were part of the common wisdom: be wary of too much Italian, warned Fénelon, for it might lead to forbidden knowledge contained in novels.[22] Latin also remained excluded as the doorway to science, to all formalistic thinking, and to ambition.[23] Had women's education gone beyond the metaphorical, then girls would have received instruction in the scientific composition of textiles or the chemical aspects of cooking and preserving. In Northern France and in every industrial society, for that matter, the needs of the home never demanded that kind of reasoning, and not until the late nineteenth-century drive to rationalize domestic activities and to refunctionalize the home, was it ever suggested. Instead of developing the mind, the convent aimed at polishing the surface and enhancing the external image of women.

In fact, the reflective principle of home life operated in both formal study and in the general atmosphere of the convents. According to the old copy method of education, students would become what they saw, read, or experienced. Such a theory determined the books used in the *pensionnats*.[24] Generation after generation of French women read the letters of Mme de Sévigné, which contained a portrait of the perfect woman: loving mother, with a Catholic education, an observer of society. Through her private letters Mme de Sévigné maintained the ties of family faithfully over the years, and thus could offer to her young students the example of a brilliantly domestic woman. While the heroines of Molière or Fénelon likewise remained in the boarding-school fare, the copy method demanded that works of George Sand and her ilk be ruthlessly suppressed. Sand's heroines consistently chose the road of individualism, and rather than being offered up as portraits of evil to reject, any heroine who stood as an alternative to the accepted one for women had to be banished from students' eyes. For education was to proceed by reflection, not by the investigation or critical rationalism inherent in the scientific method, before whose standards Sand's heroines might have been held in judgment. Thus one learned to be a good adult by reading the *Imitation of Christ* or the *Lives of the Saints*, by studying the Virgin Mary and wearing her medal, by seeing nuns wrapped in their devotion to the Sacred Heart of Jesus, and by reflecting, as did the daughters of Mme Bernard, one's mother.

The walls of the convent allowed the reflective principles of the traditional epistemology embodied in the copy method to work most efficiently, for it could shut out evil influences in a way the home could not. Until a girl reached full womanhood, the convent alone could provide her with pure models and could equally censor pernicious ones. For this reason above all others the convent gained thousands of adherents in the Nord, as the darkness within its walls actually produced the light of the innocent soul, uncontaminated by knowledge of evil, sin, or the ways of an increasingly profane world.

Religious boarding schools in the Nord correctly saw the difference between their system and the new trends in rational education for men. As brochures for prospective students explained, the goal of the convent was not merely instruction, but the formation of a "clearly virtuous young person."[25] Increasingly, young men were intensively instructed in a multitude of subjects, and the goal of their intellectual pursuits focused on unlocking every secret of the universe. To this end nothing was out of bounds for the human mind, which, it was believed, could come to know everything in a factual way. Their curriculum came to entertain every subject that could contribute to the end of complete knowledge. In addition, men received explicit training for their vocations and acquired knowledge directly relevant to their careers. The scientist pursued science; the mathematician, mathematics; the industrialist, economics.

In women's education, on the other hand, a traditional sense of "forbidden knowledge" infused the atmosphere of the convents as the key to forming the virtuous woman. Darkness protected a girl from the search for the inscrutable secrets of God's universe. As Saint Augustine had discussed centuries before, certain knowledge was beyond the capacity of human understanding, and original sin derived from just this quest after God's forbidden secrets. Only the proud or vain endeavored their discovery, while the obedient and wise maintained their purity and innocence. Thus ignorance and darkness meant innocence and true wisdom; but it meant, above all, ignorance of carnal knowledge or of the sexual. At the convent young women, unlike young men, optimally acquired no knowledge of "scientific" pertinence to their adult lives. Had their education rested on the same epistemological base as men's, then girls should have studied hygiene, biology, child care, or sexual techniques. In fact, vocational training for women entailed a considered and complete exclusion of these subjects from the curriculum. How well this traditional epistemology fit the reproductive world of the nineteenth-century woman with all its convolutions! Born to breed for one family, girls maintained through their encapsulation in the convent a physical purity. That was matched by an emphasis on mental and spiritual ignorance or innocence. The entire package was wrapped in a theory of forbidden knowledge, which in the long run equated the physical or carnal with sin.

Instead of encouraging its students to an individualistic search for knowledge, the convent maintained a girl's ego in its undeveloped state. Students learned not individualism, but the priority of the group or family. "We never played individual games," recalled one elderly alumna of the Sacré-Coeur *pensionnat*. "If a nun saw us playing alone in the courtyard at recreation period, she made us rejoin the game of other students."[26] Whether doing flag games or playing ball, each student was required to participate with others and imbibe the spirit of the group, in this case the famous "esprit du Sacré-Coeur." The same purpose stood behind the identical handwriting each student was required to master. Still legendary in France, the handwriting of Sacré-Coeur, which students spent years acquiring to perfection, helped dissipate individualism—or egoism, as it was more often called.

So, too, the dark uniforms—black at the Bernardines, grey at Sacré-Coeur—stood for an absence of self and a lack of personality. Marie Toulemonde, like many others, found this hard to endure, and found particularly difficult the accompanying restrictions on talking. Self-expression of this sort was limited to five times a day. By the time Marie became a nun with the Bernardines she better appreciated her education, to the point of making strict demands on her own students. She continued the tradition of depriving them of rewards when they became too proud of their accomplishments, too egoistic. "A young girl should not want to make herself noticed," she wrote in her journal.[27]

At the same time, girls in the convents were enveloped in a powerful external order that served as a substitute for the definition they might have found for themselves. They received a sense of their station in a corporate order. In much the same fashion as the household or the natural chain of being, the convent had its hierarchy of male confessor, mother superior, her assistants, the teaching nuns, the nuns who performed household duties, and the students arranged by age. Symbols of quality adorned each station to give it meaning. Each class, for example, had its colors, and on prize days certain colored ribbons stood for ranks of excellence in various categories: pieces of ribbon distinguished older from younger students and sashes of blue marked the outstanding, red the second-placed, and green the third-ranked students. These same indications of rank appeared on the costumes of the nuns, and girls learned to behave toward them accordingly. For example, students always wore white gloves to visit the Mother Superior, and acknowledged her with a deeper-than-usual curtsey.[28] The entire system fortified the female emphasis on the external manifestations of order.

Life in the convent was so highly ordered that even today eighty- and even ninety-year-old alumnae can recall perfectly what they did each day. Early rising, mass, breakfast, twenty-five-minute classes punctuated at beginning and end by prayer, meals in silence except for an older student reading for the rest. They remember organized walks along the well-designated paths of the Bernardine convent and the well-regulated visiting days, when they sat in an outer ring of chairs against the walls with their visitors facing them from an inner circle. Before entering buildings or when taking part in processions they ordered themselves by height. In the process they learned that an order beyond themselves and their control, beyond their wants and inaccessible to reason determined the order of their lives. The lesson would serve them well as their bodies went through changes that had no reason, only a certain order and necessity that lay somewhere beyond the self.

Convents prepared girls for the traditional world of the home, which admitted not of reason or inquiry but of adherence. They did this through an emphasis on hierarchies, self-abnegation, and order, and by directing the eyes of their students toward God at the apex of the chain of being, wherein all contradictions found resolution. The Mother Sophie Barat, founder of the order of Sacré-Coeur and its schools for young women, stressed that in her boarding schools Jesus Christ stood at the foundation of all true education. If she taught her students nothing else, she would impart to them respect and obedience to His laws.[29] True to the Mother Barat's wishes, girls in the convents learned that binding all their practical knowledge into a moral whole was the perfect authority and order of God, whom they worshiped at mass in the morning, at the beginning and end of each class, at meals, and on Sundays and feast days. They also worshiped Him in affording perfect obedience to their superiors. Although it may seem strange, we can call this worship a kind of epistemology. One might study things of this earth, but the knowledge thus acquired would be temporal and imperfect. Catholic educators believed that the greatest advantage would fall to those who merged themselves with God's perfection. More than that, to their way of thinking, true knowledge was in fact impossible without faith in the authority of God, for He alone knew the secrets of the universe. As the great progenitor, He stood for the mysteries of new life or of reproduction and sex— mysteries at the heart of the lives of young women.

Girls in the convents learned to substitute love of God and obedience for knowledge—either carnal or intellectual—by directing their energies toward worship of His authority. Innocence became not only synonymous with love of God, but it also represented true knowledge. However, since innocence was the other half of sexuality, and since God was the reproductive force of the universe as a whole, a conflation occurred in the terms innocence, love, and knowledge as a replacement for reproduction. They experienced this conflation and acquired a sense of love of God as true knowledge precisely at the moment when their sexuality was becoming apparent. Rather than demanding a channeling of their libidinal energies into creative activity of an intellectual sort, the theological pedagogy of the *pensionnats* turned adolescent sexuality toward love of the Father in an act that was hardly sublimation but rather a metaphorical heightening of their biological destiny.

175

It is hardly surprising then, that graduates of convents remembered their experience as "the beautiful years,"[30] for during those years they could painlessly press the fullness of their feelings on a being who represented their own reproductive essence. In so doing they acquired true knowledge, which was nothing less than an indulgence of themselves. Upon leaving the convent to enter an adult world, women carried with them a childlike and rapturous commitment to the cause of the Father. They sent their daughters to His schools, joined His alumnae groups, supported His ordained hierarchical social order. In the final analysis it would appear that Freud was right in claiming that women had less superego, not because they acknowledged no authority, but because the authority they worshiped as the source of knowledge was their own reproductive reflection. So educated, young women had received the proper preparation for the reflective system of domesticity.

Innocence Attacked

Almost from their inception in the seventeenth century, rationalist and empiricist epistemologies opened the debate over women's education. Molière, Fénelon, Rousseau, and Condorcet, to name only the most famous, all contributed to a spirited discussion over whether new ways of thinking and instruction were suitable to women. Most recognized that the pursuit of scientific knowledge would somehow push women beyond their traditional horizons, perhaps even into madness. But the questions they raised, albeit implicitly, remained pertinent, and never more so than in the nineteenth century.

Advocates of modernization after the French Revolution understandably judged the traditional education of women, with its implicit valorization of "ignorance," at best an embarrassment and at worst a national disaster. The debate assumed an air of urgency, and even teetered on the edge of reform as it became more apparent, especially in 1860 after the introduction of free-trade policies, that France must live by her economic wits. These economic problems presented themselves at precisely the moment when convents were edging out all other types of educational institutions, and the conjunction was inauspicious for the future. How, it was asked, could France survive when its future leaders received their first lessons from women who relied on the fuzzy concepts spewed out by the nuns? How could France compete when its women possessed no intellectual capacity, and even openly denigrated rational understanding of the world? After the triumph of republicanism in the 1870s, the problem was compounded. Women educated in convents emerged on the political scene carrying clerical banners emblazoned with the symbols of monarchical restoration. In this way they posed a threat to the internal political order. Should they attain their political ends, France would be thrown into civil chaos, with economic and international repercussions. From several points of view, then, the retrograde condition of women's minds suddenly appeared a luxury France could no longer afford. But champions of reform, in their concern for the welfare of the nation, overlooked what Molière and others in his century had seen clearly. Modernization of education might make women unsuited for their reproductive roles and upset a division of labor on which the industrial system depended as much as it relied on rational thought and scientific progress.

In 1867 a modest proposal by Minister of Education Victor Duruy opened a major nationwide attack on the convents.[31] He issued a circular suggesting that municipalities draw upon the talents of male professors in lycées to supplement the education of women. They could offer evening classes to young women of the upper classes to prepare them more thoroughly for their future duties as mothers of the elite. In support of his plan, Duruy contended that the lowliest schoolteacher in France received an education vastly superior to that obtained by the wealthiest women. A dismal

177

future, he said, awaited a nation whose mothers were instructed by nuns whose only qualification for teaching was a religious vow of obedience.

In Paris the proposal gained almost immediate adherence. University and lycée professors hastened to provide young women with instruction in academic fields. Favored by the Empress Eugénie, who sent her two nieces to participate, the courses drew hundreds of students from Parisian society, but that society had been well prepared for the innovation.[32] Within memory Michelet had directly attacked convent education as the preparatory step for the intrusion of the priest in domestic affairs.[33] Jules Simon was further developing the argument in the influential *Revue des deux mondes*. Women's education to Catholic ways, he wrote, had created a schism in French society in which men faced the future and women, the reactionary past. The situation hindered the development of good relationships between husband and wife, and it opposed the development of open-mindedness. Here Simon used phrases that appeared in the war against charitable women in the Nord. Catholicism stood as the antithesis to liberalism by virtue of its authoritarian creed. Women educated in convents had closed minds, whereas liberal men could allow the discussion of any and all subjects on their merits—except, perhaps, Catholicism. Courses such as those proposed by Duruy would open women's minds to this freedom of ideas, and, he implied, draw them toward a patently superior liberal persuasion.[34]

The Nord reverberated with only a muted version of Parisian enthusiasm for the supplementary courses. In Valenciennes and later in Lille, arithmetic, literature, and history were offered at lycées and university to young women of high society to fill the gap in their education.[35] The republican *Progrès du Nord* pushed the program by recalling Simon's arguments: the ignorance of women; the breach in the unity of families caused by women's superstition; the challenge facing the French nation.[36] But bourgeois women were recalcitrant in sending their daughters or attending themselves, and behind their recalcitrance lay the Church, fortifying, as usual, an instinctive female commitment to traditional education.[37]

Early in 1868 Cardinal Régnier, Archbishop of Cambrai, preached a Lenten sermon against Duruy's proposed reform. The courses in Valenciennes, he said, revealed the true nature of what was happening when they opened with an attack on women's ignorance as instilled by Catholic educators.[38] Later that year Monseignor Mermillod came to Lille to a retreat of the alumnae of Sacré-Coeur; he offered another message fortifying the connection between women and religion.[39] Without a Catholic education women would be lost, he said. Finally the Pope sealed the fate of such innovations when he declared his *non licet* to secular education for young girls and for the courses in particular. Out of the controversy, however, came the most important statements supporting Catholic education for women of the nineteenth century: the works of the Bishop of Orleans, Dupanloup, became standard reading for the women of the Nord as they endeavored to hold back the tide of reform and to protect the convents against the inroads of science and secularism. From the heat of battle with Duruy, Dupanloup produced his masterpieces: *La Femme chrétienne et française* (1868) and *La Femme studieuse* (1869).[40] Immediate successes both in France and abroad, these two books were quick to decipher the dangers in so-called innocent reforms. Moreover, Dupanloup placed the struggle for the traditional education of women in the context of a defense of religion as a whole and of the moral tone of society. Far from being a narrow-minded attack on a particular government official, the criticism manifested a broad and human concern for the health of France and especially for the welfare of its women.

For a man on the defensive, Dupanloup was particularly astute in reeling off a list of brilliant women whose religious education had allowed them to contribute to the advance of human understanding. He sounded a bit like a feminist. But instead of turning this list into an argument for change, Dupanloup maintained that the list demonstrated the importance of the status quo. Given the Church's success—a success asserted constantly in both books—what were Duruy's proposed courses if not dangerous and useless experimentation? One could see the danger at hand by turning to the results of the newly secular and rational education men were then receiving. Educated in the modern way, men had conspicuously turned their eyes from heaven toward earth, away from morality and toward materialism. Did not the course of events in the nineteenth century—wars, revolutions, social decay, and the like—give a dismal picture of the fruits of this education? For men morality had become a mere "subject" in the curriculum, as opposed to its being the framework for all knowledge. Fortunately, Dupanloup continued, women at least still received an education bounded by the laws and mysteries of God and by respect for His authority. The moral health of France rested on the continued conventual education of women.

The tone of French life was not Dupanloup's only concern. Women, he maintained, could not live without the authoritarian context of morality, and he turned to ancient history to prove his point. Observing the weak and depraved condition of women in pagan or tribal societies, he drew the lesson that the slow improvement in their social position was derived from the sacrifice of Christ who had redeemed the sexes on an equal basis. Only respect for the laws of God, which assured women both a worldly position and a heavenly salvation, could perpetuate their high status. For only God's law gave the weak consideration on earth and the promise of heaven. Should women succumb, like men, to the temptations of materialism and worldly equality, a return to their primitive debasement awaited.

Dupanloup's books prepared women in the Nord to resist the long siege about to open on their convents. After French defeat at the hands of the Germans in 1870, politicians searched their souls for the cause of such a disaster. Many attributed the German victory to a technological superiority derived from their more modern educational system. In this atmosphere, religious *pensionnats* became more suspect than ever as one source of French weakness. Then came the prolonged depression of the mid-seventies, along with severe threats to republicanism from both right and left. The predictions of earlier reformers seemed to be coming true as the nation suffered on every front. Among the strong measures taken by national and local politicians during this troubled decade was the institution of secular and more scientific schools for upper-class young women.

Politicians in the Nord took action even before the national government. Four years prior to the Camille Sée Law in 1881, which mandated secular secondary schools for young women,[41] the municipal council in Lille opened the doors to the Institut Fénelon.[42] There could be no doubt that the school, with its hefty tuition, its outside professors drawn from the university, and a curriculum almost duplicating that of the convents, was designed to draw students away from the religious *pensionnats*. The city fathers removed religion from the program of study; they chose the most distinguished faculty available; and they discouraged applications for scholarships so that upper-class girls would not run the risk of having a policeman's daughter on the bench next to them. Their long-range goal was nothing less than ending the mental schism between men and women that had developed as the sexual worlds drew apart. Mayor Géry Legrand, who sent his own daughters to Fénelon, spoke for the entire municipal council and perhaps for nineteenth-century Frenchmen in general when he described the city's educational philosophy:

We respect piety, we respect all cults, but we are combatting fanaticism in whatever form it presents itself.

It should not be that an exclusive doctrine seizes the spirit of a woman and establishes between her and men

181

an insuperable barrier. Leave her her convictions whatever they may be; let us respect them, but let us teach her that the beliefs of others have the right to the same respect and the same independence; and the day when woman is formed with this wise spirit of tolerance which goes so well with the sweetness and goodness of her nature, on this day woman will regain in the home the place which belongs to her and to which only education can elevate her.[43]

The point could not be clearer. A division existed in the Nord between reasonable, tolerant men and superstitious, fanatical women. Wedded fanatically to the narrowmindedness of the religious world view, women had lost their sweetness, and their reputation among men had declined from its high point in the earlier part of the century. Men in the Nord believed, along with rational reformers in other industrial countries, that once the light of knowledge penetrated realms of darkness such as the convent, women would come around to their way of thinking. But the "wise spirit of tolerance," as men called their own world view, would be hard to instill in women whose material reality lay not in the liberal marketplace but in the overdetermined world of nature.

Nor did the founders of Fénelon propose changing that situation. They clung to the old finishing-school curriculum without adding Latin—the *sine qua non* for entering any profession. By refusing scholarship students, who were politely directed toward tuitionless schools, they betrayed a commitment to the reproductive life for women. Scholarship students would be upwardly mobile and would show the marketplace value of intellectual achievement. In men's secondary schools scholarships went to talented poor youngsters—like Jean Jaurès—whose accomplishments testified to the marketplace ethic of mobility, like cream rising to the top. Such an example would disrupt the expectation for women that at Fénelon they would receive training for an improved motherhood and for a more harmonious relationship between the sexes. They should imbibe the principles of a modern, competitive world to transmit to their children and to discuss with their husbands without themselves becoming ambitious.

The municipal councilors of Lille, like those in Roubaix and other Northern cities, hoped that a single alteration in the curriculum would make the transformation possible. They removed religion from the Institut (later Lycée) Fénelon's program and replaced it with civics and additional lessons in science. Girls began learning the natural, instead of the theological, laws of the socio-sexual order. The civics text used at the school explained the natural origins of society and governments, of property and patriotism. And it explained too the natural inferiority of women. The author pointed to the reproductive weakness of women and their need for men to guide and protect them. In such a situation women should be patient, gentle, and accepting of their husband's intellectual, physical, and social superiority.[44]

Conspicuously lacking in this explanation was the notion of God's creation and His authority, of the equality of souls and the miraculous transformation of weakness into strength in a heavenly afterlife. And gone too was the opportunity to channel energies toward that God as a means of sustenance in the face of such a gloomy forecast. Republicans omitted the array of female saints and the Blessed Mother to reflect the delicate balance of weakness and strength, curse and sanctification; and they could hardly offer Olympe de Gouges, Flora Tristan, or Louise Michel as substitutes. Instead, the new curriculum pulled out all the props and left its students in the cold world of godless natural law. As a consolation prize, girls leaving Fénelon and other secondary institutions in France could stand in competition for the *brevet*—a diploma that indicated a capability to teach. Because no one expected that they would ever have to teach, the *brevet* symbolized a preparation for *au courant* motherhood from which all traces of superstition and comfort had been removed.

Not surprisingly, given the contradiction in the intent to modernize women's minds while leaving them in a traditional role, the Lycée Fénelon suffered all sorts of disturbances. Mothers of upper-class girls generally refused to send their daughters to the new institution. Its clientele consisted of daughters of government functionaries, of a few girls from the now German Alsace and Lorraine, and of the daughters of smaller businessmen willing to sacrifice tuition for what they thought would be social prestige.[45] Even those students caused problems for the school, as they harassed their teachers and gave them scant respect. Unlike the convents, where nuns came from the same social class as their students, teachers at Fénelon were career women, usually of a much lower social station, who had committed the offense to female sensibilities of using their education to make money. Thus, the official apology for the misbehavior of young women at Fénelon toward their instructors explained the difficulties they had in obeying teachers who were "so clearly their social inferiors."[46] The major problem at Fénelon, however, consisted of resistance to the school's basic philosophy and the founding fathers' anticlerical goals. The exclusion of religion from the curriculum provoked a rebellion among the very people whom the republican fathers had hoped to wean from the Church. Within a decade of its opening, the students initiated a major drive to restore religious instruction at the school. Prominent in the group of rebels was Julie Legrand, daughter of the mayor of Lille, himself the foremost proponent of a modern education of women to the "wise spirit of tolerance."[47]

Resistance to the new schools from outside was just as stout, if not so embarrassing or disheartening, as the internal problems. During the troubled times of the eighties, when the *dames patronnesses* fought for Catholic and female charities, the clergy took up vocal resistance to the Lycée Fénelon and other secular schools for girls in the

Nord. They warned of the dangers to female innocence where classes were conducted by men, and of similar dangers when girls stood in public competition for the *brevet*.[48] Alarmed by changes in the curriculum, critics pointed to the disaster that would ensue from the retreat from moral education. Instead of viewing the universe as a moral whole, girls would learn subject matter, distinct and unconnected. They would see only the atomization of knowledge, and deduce from it the atomization of all creation. Having lost all sense of their place in a hierarchy of ordered functions, future generations would become discontented housekeepers, distraught because the ambitions raised in them by specialized study could never be fulfilled. And having lost sight of their role in God's order, women would fail to provide that complement of charity, consolation, and pardon to the scientific and economic achievements of men.[49] In face of the imminent collapse of social order into an atmosphere of self-interest and force, the Jesuit advisor to the Enfants de Marie drew the conclusion for them: "the devil himself is ruling France."[50]

As for women themselves in the Nord, they had little opportunity for public statements. In the midst of battle, Mme Camille Feron-Vrau made one of the only speeches by a woman in support of women's traditions. At a reunion of alumnae of the Dames de St. Maur, she praised the institution for a Catholic education that had prepared her for life's sorrows, troubles, and struggles, and she urged her listeners to prepare themselves for even greater struggles ahead.[51] More impressive is the record of female activity in upholding the convents. Members of groups such as the Archiconfrérie des mères chrétiennes put aside personal causes and directed all their prayers in favor of the schools.[52] They continued to enroll their daughters in them despite all public disapproval, and they continued their financial and moral support. And when the end came in 1904, they showed how much commitment stood behind their efforts.

In that year the French government exiled many teaching

orders and closed down religious schools, among them most of the *pensionnats* for girls in the Nord.[53] Especially in the case of women's education, the attempt to destroy a traditional world view through persuasion and enlightenment had not succeeded. Not only in the Nord but throughout France as a whole, religious devotion persisted among women to the point of causing such public examples of the sexual dichotomy as that between the socialist leader Jean Jaurès and his wife, who could not be wrenched from her Catholic faith.[54] Nor could the women of the Nord be dissuaded. They appeared publicly to harangue the officials in charge of closing the convents; and sometimes they barricaded themselves in churches about to be inventoried. Like Mme Boselli-Scrive of Lille, they spent their fortunes to buy up convents as quickly as municipal governments put their buildings on the market.[55] As a last act of faith, they sent their money, but more importantly their daughters, into exile with the nuns. Mme L. of Lille told her own story: her mother's grim determination that her daughter go to Belgium to the Mothers of Sacré-Coeur and her father's resignation to his wife's way of thinking.[56] Had they done anything else, the Catholic women of the Nord would have betrayed their domestic and reproductive existence. For them Catholic education worked in the same way as domestic metaphors by reflecting, repressing, ordering, and transforming the contradictions of their universe. At the heart of that education lay the notion of forbidden knowledge, which the closed site of the convent symbolized to perfection. By transforming the sexual into the spiritual love of God, the cult of innocence and virtue sustained the reproductive activities of women. In the opinion of most women in the Nord, republican reforms had extracted the heart of education and substituted nothing of value to pass on to their daughters.

8
The
Domestic
Myth

There is a final portrait of the nineteenth-century woman. In the domestic novel she appears as a beleaguered heroine caught in a whirlwind of intrigue, chaos, and even of evil. Villains harass her, tragedies occur in rapid sequence, and the pattern of her life consists not of domestic routine but of melodrama. Although familiar, this portrait hardly fits the reality we have explored thus far. Only at the end of each story is the harried heroine transformed into a recognizable bourgeoise. At that point chaos disappears, evil is overcome, and the domestic woman emerges with her full array of household activities, religious fervor, and commitment to charity. The intervening disorder and chaos, however, give us fresh food for thought.

Even stranger, this portrait flows from the bourgeois woman's own pen. It is her version of female life, and according to women writers in the Nord, a true one. Mathilde Bourdon of Lille called one of her novels *Real Life*; Julia Bécour subtitled another *A Study of Lille's Customs*. Having so categorized their work, each proceeded to present an impossible reality, a disturbing sequence of events, and an improbable cast of characters. In so doing they and their counterparts in England and the United States left women's writing open to ridicule from critics to whom the domestic novel appeared fatuous. In the meantime, the question of the portrait's relationship to female experience went unexplored.

Behind this first portrait is another: that of the woman writer. Three bourgeois women in the Nord wrote extensively and even gained national and international reputations. Dunkerque-born Josephine de Gaulle (1806-1886), grandmother of Charles de Gaulle, wrote pious short stories, biographies, novels, and eventually edited a literary magazine with her husband. Some of her most popular work went through many editions and was even translated. Most prolific was Mathilde Bourdon (1817-1888), whose work included close to two hundred books of almost every variety—novels, biographies, etiquette and advice books, plays, and religious readings and meditations. Born in Ghent, she migrated to Lille as a bride with her journalist husband. After his early death, she married Hercule Bourdon, a local judge and a former Saint-Simonian. The third author, Julia Bécour (1840-1917) only started writing in her forties, and therefore produced less than Bourdon and de Gaulle. She generally confined her efforts to novels and occasional journalistic writing. Married to a prominent physician, Bécour's feminist and republican political convictions set her apart from most bourgeois women of her day. In all other respects she shared their commitment to the domestic, charitable, and spiritual way of life, and along with Bourdon and de Gaulle advocated domesticity in all her writing.[1] Nonetheless, these were the women who drew the bizarre portrait of the domestic heroine.

One might see the portrait of the domestic heroine as a pure flight of fancy arising from an unbridled female imagination. Perhaps it has no connection with reality. Yet from all the many possible stories that the human imagination can tell, Northern writers (and hundreds like them in France and other industrial countries) drew one and only one picture of nineteenth-century woman: that of the beleaguered heroine who triumphs over forces that would keep her from becoming domestic and good. Details change from work to work: the color of clothing, the number of characters, the age of the heroine, and the setting. Even these differences are minimal in the domestic novel. More important, a common female story regularly appears in the writing of de Gaulle, Bourdon, and Bécour. This distinguishes their work from other nineteenth-century novels, which vary in characterization, plot, and setting. In fact, for all that women's writing adopts the form of the novel, it resembles the repetition of an archetypal myth.[2]

To suggest that the domestic novel might contain a domestic myth is not to fall into a structuralist or Jungian conclusion that women's writing manifests an unchanging female mentality or that the invented heroine is more real than the domestic reality we have explored. Either line of explanation fails because it ignores reality and also because it ignores an important historical fact. Although it was repeated ad infinitum by nineteenth-century women, this is a new story. That century and no other before it produced female writing in quantity. For several thousands years men had speculated on the human condition, had described experience in a number of literary genres, and had set down their observations on the universe, whereas women had remained silent. Then came the flood of narrative from women's pens, including the pens of our Northern writers, and the first attempts by women to tell their own story.

The notion of beginnings—beginnings of narrative—is not trivial, especially when this fact is juxtaposed to the strangeness of the tale. The notion of beginnings takes us back to the earliest narratives we can think of: myths of gods and goddesses, creation stories, and the like. These too are strange to our modern ears, and conflict with our certainty that these myths did not recount real life. Goddesses do not exist; the world was not hatched from an egg, nor the different races from variously cooked loaves of bread. In short, fledgling efforts at narrative often produce the same exotic story we find in the domestic novel.

In addition, the domestic life of women put her in a situation similar to that of the earliest mythteller. The nineteenth-century division of labor had returned her in a sense to a primitive condition, that of being embedded in and controlled by nature. Her existence and ego vis-à-vis the entire social and natural order were as tenuous as that of premodern people confronting the forces of nature without benefit of technology or scientific understanding. In similar situations, early civilizations and modern women began telling the story of their existence. For both groups of people, we are left with the original question: in what sense did the portrait of the beleaguered heroine represent their experience? Or, in what way did the strange array of gods and goddesses develop from that of early tribes?

The most compelling interpretations of the mythical genre affirm their origins in real experience. Myth does not aim at fantasy or invention, but rather describes a believed-in truth. However, myth achieves fantasy because it amalgamates ingredients that in modern explanation are kept distinct. It combines in a single story perceptions of nature, man himself, and human emotions. For example, the story of Apollo assigns him charge of the sun, and in this way conflates man and nature. Nature receives a human form because the mind does not distinguish sufficiently between subject and object to place nature in one category and human beings in another. In consequence, nature is anthropomorphized and universal, or natural events are reduced to a particular humanlike story. A similar particularization or subjectivization occurs in other myths: the creation of the universe is the work of a single, anthropomorphic figure who moves the spheres; or the races come into being because a single baker undercooked and overcooked loaves of bread.

Myth also adds all the emotions stirred in the human psyche by contact with nature. The mythical mind infuses the figure of Apollo with all the awe felt in regarding the sun, and thus converts a force of nature into a god. Society comes to worship the god it has created and to see his story as holy and true. Apollo is thus a fantastic creation but only because his being contains several threads of experience woven into one story. He stands as a single symbol for man, nature, and feeling or spirit.

Modern explanations and stories of human experience differ from mythical ones by separating these threads. For example, the scientist assumes that his perceptual experience of nature is not coterminous with nature itself. He is one thing; nature another. In the case of geometry, the geometrician has so separated himself from the space and shapes he perceives that he can describe nature in the abstract, nonhuman terms of science. And instead of believing in the power of such abstraction, the geometrician understands the system to be man-made and not divine revelation, an exception being the Pythagoreans, who both abstracted spatial relationships and worshiped them. Scientific explanations do not seem bizarre to us because we are used to a clear separation of subject from object and to working with a set of symbols explicitly coterminous with neither.

Modern literature also admits the difference between the author, reality, and a fictional story that exists in its own realm. Characters must act within the realm of natural necessity; plots must proceed according to the laws of probability; there can be no suspension of the laws of nature. Yet although the modern novel disallows miracles and demands conformity with reality, the story is all the while acknowledged to be false, a figment of the author's imagination. It is also secular and open to challenge when either the laws of probability are broken or when the aesthetic of storytelling fails. Thus the novel breaks with mythical tradition by separating the mental territory of the author, the scope of reality, and human interpretations of and reactions to experience.

Not so the domestic novel, which perpetuated mythical forms by fusing perception and reality and by anthropomorphizing the story of the universe in the story of a single heroine. The heroine does represent the bourgeois woman of the nineteenth century, but her portrait, like the portrait of a mythical god or hero, also contains many other ingredients. Just as Apollo's story contains that of nature, so the story of the heroine's environment—the domestic microcosm—collapses into her own saga. The heroine's portrait is blown out of human proportion because it encompasses an external as well as a personal story. That is, a new domestic universe comes into being with the resolution of her problems, just as the story of the seas, the heavens, or the sun progresses within the tale of a particular man-god. This identification of woman with her environment, the tendency to view the domestic universe from an egocentric perspective, should not surprise us, for we have already seen these perspectives at work in the symbolism of the home. Nothing could have been more natural than the bourgeois woman's writing of her story with this fusion of subjective and objective reality.

Women in their domestic life injected the objects around them with many of their reactions to the female condition. Similarly, the author of the domestic novel infused the portrait of her heroine and of other characters with all the feelings of weakness and power inherent in her female and reproductive role. The heroine's story simultaneously reflects the author's reproductive grandeur and her reproductive and social vulnerability. So subjected to authorial oscillations between victimization and victory, the plot took on the air of high melodrama. Instead of taking up the role of narrator, the author imputed motives, manipulated reality to her wishes, and suspended the laws of nature to the point of allowing miracles to occur and devils to appear. It amounted to control by mental fiat like that which women used in the manipulation and ordering of the artifacts of domestic life. For authors and for thousands of female readers, however, the result conformed to real life. Considering the tendency to merge separate threads of reality in domestic life, we can see the truth in this assertion. For critics not participating in this mentality, the female novel remained an absurdity.

In the realm of beginnings, an important step occurs in the mythical story. For all the confusion, myth constitutes the first moment of human self-portraiture. What starts in chaos ends with the triumph of an anthropomorphic god who has transformed chaos into an ordered and tamed universe. This triumph replaces the disorder perceived in nature with the ordering hand of a humanlike ruler, just as the story itself marks the arrangement of myriad perceptions into a coherent narrative. What allows for this ordering, or in classical terms for the triumph of convention over nature, is the newly discovered human character. The god reveals in the course of his struggle to master the universe his strength, courage, wiliness, or wisdom. Human definition comes to consist of those qualities that allow for this triumph and to represent at the end of myth the distinguishing marks of humanity.

I suggest that the domestic novel marks a similar beginning of definition for women. Each story starts with chaos, lawlessness, and struggle. Such a setting indicates both the absence of human—in this case, female—order and the unformed character of a female self. By the end of the story chaos has been transformed into domestic order, and the heroine assumes a finished shape. Like the god or hero, she acquires that shape and definition only through what the Greeks called *agon*. She must confront nature or all that is not human and master it. Being a woman, however, she must also confront and master all that is not woman, namely, man. In the case of the female myth the classical agony is doubled, but in the process female characteristics come sharply into focus. The qualities that allow her triumph become the defining features of an archetypal woman.

The theme of human definition that dominates myth further distinguishes the domestic novel from the novel of the nineteenth century. The latter starts with characters fully formed within an established social context. The story asks: given these characters and the general laws that guide human life, what will happen and how will human beings act? Domestic novels, like myth, reverse the situation. They do not display an interest in how the universe works; no omniscient observer tells a story of a fully defined human species. Instead, myth asks a first, almost childlike question about cosmogony: how did the domestic microcosm (the universe) come to be? Where did woman come from? In general, the answer is that heroine and home were born from chaos and struggle with the forces of evil. Because the struggle is usually successful, all endings are happy. The harmonious household grows from disorder; the portrait of the virtuous heroine dominates all other figures in the domestic landscape. The process by which all this occurs widens our access to a female mentality.

Genesis of the Home

The first pages of a domestic novel plunge us into chaos. In many cases we acquire a sense of disorder because the family lacks one of its members. Most heroines are either orphaned or grow up with only one parent. In Josephine de Gaulle's *Adhémar de Belcastel* the heroine has only her father and the hero's parents are both dead. In Bécour's work few heroes or heroines have a complete family, and the same condition prevails in most of Bourdon's many stories and novels. Occasionally, as in Bécour's *Mariage fabuleux*, a heroine has both parents, but their scatterbrained habits engender disorder nonetheless. The family, then, must be out of joint and succumb to ever deepening layers of chaos for the domestic novel to proceed along its procreative path.

Critics often interpret this situation psychologically by connecting it with oedipal longings for the death of parents. But we can also associate the orphaned condition of the heroine with general lawlessness. On the death of a parent, familial law disintegrates and leaves all survivors without a sense of order. When parental law disappears, and as household regulations fall into abeyance, no one knows how to behave. In Bourdon's *Les Belles années* the young heroine's lack of a mother means that she will grow up stubborn, spoiled, undisciplined, and ultimately prone to disaster. Or in *Blidie* by Julia Bécour the heroine's orphaned condition subjects her to laws of another family that fails to accord her justice. From the failure of justice ensue Blidie's continuing misfortune and, ultimately, her death.

When family members are missing, characters lack an orientation in the domestic universe. But the situation is even more serious, for it weakens or even destroys self-definition. In the home one received definition from other family members. "Father" was the sum of relationships to others; he was "not-child or -mother." So too, mother, son, daughter, brother, sister—all categories grew from relations and also from hierarchies of status. For the heroine, the loss of a parent entailed at least a partial loss of definition. She often began to behave in "uncharacteristic" ways and to disintegrate as a potentially virtuous woman. But any member of the family can feel this loss of definition, and thus leave the domestic unit weakened and ripe for further disaster.

The domestic cosmos thus coming apart, strangers can easily enter to complete the wreckage. Consider the case of Bourdon's *Léontine*, in which the heroine has left the parental home to set up her own. Before she can complete the arrangement and establish law, a false friend, Flavie, invades her house and destroys the beginnings of a domestic universe. This antagonist is all disorder and without domestic discipline: "I wake up late, dress up a little, take a bit of a walk and stroll through the stores."[3] Such chaotic inclinations accompany her to distribute themselves in a physical way throughout the heroine's environment. She introduces Léontine to her novels, concerts, and worldly amusements to the end of turning the heroine from her own domestic pursuits. Ultimately Léontine loses her child and develops an unhappy, potentially disastrous relationship with her husband. When meals are not on time or servants poorly supervised, then children fall ill, bankruptcies occur, and the home disintegrates. Both heroine and home, or heroine and the possibility of creating a home through marriage, collapse simultaneously because to the mythically oriented mind of the author they are fused entities.

Not unexpectedly, men are especially responsible for bringing chaos. Sometimes, like Hubert in *Fée Mab*, they do not understand domestic order and morality. Their intrusion into the life of the home causes its decay until they imbibe its law and make it their own. Before that, everything is thrown out of joint, particularly the character of the heroine. Most male figures, however, carry with them not merely a temporary "unfamiliarity," but represent all that is nonfamilial and foreign to domestic order. In all of Bécour's novels, and most expressively in Bourdon's *Femme et mari*, men bear the mark of materialism, individualism, rationalism, and secularism. Their pursuit of the golden calf of money, their quest for scientific knowledge, or their devotion to positivism estranges them from the family circle. While that estrangement causes chaos to the extent that it unbalances the arrangement of the domestic cosmos, each male principle has a particular embodiment that ruins life in the home. For example, the hero's adherence to the materialist slogan "money must roll"[4] in *Femme et mari* dispatches him and his family to Paris in search of greater fortune. Stability and harmony quickly disappear as movement of this male type renders life chaotic. Or Morcauf, the rationalist tutor in *Blidie*, instructs his pupils according to Lockean epistemological principles, a technique that ends in disaster. According to his student Lucie's explanation of her selfish deeds, she only did what her sense impressions passing along her nerve endings directed. From girlish misbehavior Lucie proceeds to make an unfortunate marriage, while even greater misfortune awaits Blidie, Morcauf's other student. For women and the household, nature in its scientific form and as a guide to life meant disorder and imperfection.

Scientific knowledge or the quest for money were but examples of how male principles could decompose the arrangement of elements in the domestic universe. In contrast to the free motion, acentricity, and atomization of the industrial male's universe, the domestic world had to move like the heavenly spheres, without conflict; in fact, this amounted to no movement at all, but rather the stasis of corporate society wherein fixed position was the rule. Accordingly, the resolution of all domestic novels depended on achieving just this moment of stasis, of harmony, of a utopian return to a world without a future. Unlike romantic heroes, the domestic heroine does not plunge into any disorienting quest. Rather, outsiders disrupt the domestic universe. As action proceeds around her, she only struggles to achieve a quiescent state or to exist until the return of order.

Before this can happen, the forces disturbing domestic tranquillity must become fully immanent. Evil steps in where chaos and lawlessness reside to usurp control of the world. Here again the domestic novel moves along a mythical course, for most myths entail a cosmic struggle between the forces of good and evil, and they demand a victory for the righteous as preliminary to the advent of a new creation and the establishment of law. Thus, as the story progresses, we realize that the stranger or foreigner is not just disordering. He or she carries, in fact, a destructive power that, because of its "otherness," its disjuncture with domestic law as it formerly existed, receives the name "Evil." Evil takes a material and forceful form in specific characters. Just as unwaxed furniture, unpleasant smells, or ants and cockroaches suggest qualities and possess symbolic force, so too a character in the story materializes perceptions and fears. In Bécour's *Une heure d'oubli* Adèle Vilner transports with every ounce of her flesh the sign of evil, and her be-

havior works from the first moment we meet her to unfold
the fullness of her stigma. Evil reveals itself in her negligées
and inappropriate dress, in her behavior, and in her wanton
and sensual conversation. More than this, Adèle's evil is
physically powerful, for she has the ability to transmit the
miasma to others and to spread its influence to the innocent.
Her seduction of the hero and its necessary close physical
contact infects him also with evil. This infection has nothing
to do with psychology or theories of the mind and its influence on behavior. No sense of characterization directs the
actions of individuals in the story. Instead, evil and good as
self-contained and potent qualities pass throughout the
scenario to settle in characters and determine their deeds.
Each character is but an obvious projection of the author's
mind as she attempts to sort out what is good and female
from the undifferentiated elements around her. Only in this
ruthless fashion can the household take shape.

Amidst chaos and uncertainty two polar forces—good and
evil, sacred and profane, or female and "other"—distribute
themselves as a preliminary to the great conflict for control
of the formless domestic world. As the characters draw
themselves up in battle formation, no room exists for sub-
plots. Minor figures have not the luxury of a life of their
own, as they do in the standard nineteenth-century novel.
Rather, they exist only to align themselves on either side
in an ascending order of goodness and a descending order
of evil. In Bécour's *Une heure d'oubli* the central figures,
Jeanne the heroine and Jean the hero, constitute the prey
of either side. On the fringes of the forces of good are arrayed
Max, the heroine's children, and finally, as the leading
champion of virtue, Lucienne, the heroine's wise and elderly
confidante. The heroine's brother-in-law Durouble, through
his inherited interest in a factory and his indifference to
morality, is topmost—that is least important—on the ladder
of evil; below him the heroine's sister Clothilde actively
pursues material distinction and performs undomestic acts.

She has been infected by the most powerful antagonist, Adèle Vilner, who approximates the devil.

The battle ensues as each character acts or makes a pronouncement that demonstrates the force of one side or the other. The doctor Max functions solely to utter pious pronouncements that accrue to the side of righteousness: "the family is still that which is best in the world."[5] Or he castigates women whose clothes are overadorned with jewelry. His counterpart on the other side, Durouble, makes statements of indifference to behavior, morality, and the like; these count for the enemy. He buttresses his statements by overindulging the whims of his wife, Clothilde. The most efficacious signs of power derive from those characters who actually possess the wherewithal to transfer good or evil from themselves to another character. Adèle Vilner contaminates the hero with her sensuality and seals his estrangement from the heroine: a triumph for the antagonists of the home. Lucienne, in her wisdom, inspires her pupil at the moment of betrayal to patience and reconciliation for the sake of her family. Lucienne's success in calming Jeanne demonstrates the strength of virtue. Like the multiplication of signs in the home to reflect the presence of woman, the cosmic battle in the domestic novel turns upon the ability to muster signs of virtue or of the female, arrange them in proper order, and thereby establish their efficacy.

The unfolding of this type of tale depends not, like the modern novel, on the development of a consistent characterization subject to the laws of personality or psychology, but rather on the invocation of ritual patterns. The author, like the woman in her home, must compose characters and events to produce an effect of virtue. She assigns each a weight, and this type of authorial attribution can be as bewildering to the uninitiated as the insistence that a chair have a specific position and no other in a salon. If the domestic novel appeared formulaic and stereotypical, it was for good reason. Only through imputation and ritualistic arrangement did the woman writer display her force. This demonstration prevented the triumph of virtue from being either allegorical or completely ethical, for it ultimately represented only the efficacy of the magician. Thus the final moment in every domestic novel when evil succumbed to good issued from a type of thaumaturgy generative of a new creation.

The mythical mind has always demanded that a sacrifice precede creation either as a purgative or fertilizing act. In Bécour's *Une heure d'oubli* the heroine's husband has succumbed to the seductions of Adèle Vilner and consequently dies from the evil that has invaded his body. But his death purges the family circle of its taint and permits its reconstitution along female principles. Similarly, the death of St. Clair in de Gaulle's *Adhémar de Belcastel* removes the evil force from the scenario so that the creation of the Belcastel household can peacefully occur. Although Bourdon's works contain many cleansing deaths—of Lucien, for example, who had fled the family for naval adventures, or of Adrien, who had become infected with scientific knowledge—her stories also use a fall into poverty as a sign that materialism has been chased from the family hearth. None of these deaths results from germs, no misfortune occurs logically. Each testifies to the presence of evil and to the subsequent reduction of its force, all through authorial removal of the tainted individual.

Innocents also meet death in the domestic novel, but instead of making a purgative withdrawal, they remain as fructifying symbols for the new familial creation. Creation takes place in memory of them and because of their deaths. Blidie's death causes all characters in the novel to regroup as they meditate upon the principle of virtue she embodied. Her memory guides them, refreshes them, and ultimately permits a reconciliation of hitherto estranged elements in the home. Or in Bourdon's *Antoinette Lemire* the death of little Charles prompts the heroine to return home "full of serious thoughts on the immense misfortunes which follow all disorder." Although the noble mystery of death appears drowned in bathos, the event testifies to death's potency as a generative force and constitutes the transfigurative moment when good replaces evil.

Nonetheless, death is robbed of its transcendent mystery insofar as it serves as a mere mechanism of exchange: a death for a new creation. With this type of exchange we find another example of the formulaic, alchemistic, and mythical character of the domestic novel. Kenneth Burke has suggested that the creation of the universe serves as the prototypical act of magic, and this suggestion helps in understanding many generalizations about the domestic novel. Magic works only according to formulas; therefore what critics have branded as mindless stereotype is in fact a *sine qua non* of the genre. Without the ritualistic element, the domestic novel would no longer be itself or be attractive and believable to its readers. As Cassirer notes, the question why is not relevant to the mythical mind. Rather it demands sequential ordering: in this case familial rebirth demands a prior sacrificial death—be it purificatory, expiatory, or fructifying.

However, all characters must recognize the sacrifice for it to be efficacious. Recognition and belief performed as a common act is the beginning of cult and of family. As the characters in *Blidie* gather around the heroine's grave, they suddenly see her virtue, and its visible power forms the basis of law. The heroine's virtue becomes the ordering principle for family reconstitution and for the new domestic cosmos. Husbands and wives return to each other; lovers marry on the basis of a recognized domestic law of virtue contained in the sacrificial death. This act of acquiescence to law and virtue, this belief in the potency of death, parallels the acquiescence to a woman's rules of etiquette or the admiration of her costume, which affirms her power and even her existence. In the domestic world recognition of female reproductive potency as its own kind of law forms

201

a creed for the birth of the family. A symbolic potency alone eliminates nonfemale values such as materialism, rationality, or individualism from the domestic environment. Such at least was the myth of female power and the law.

At the end of each novel, then, a new family arises from the chaos that had dominated the story, and the act of creation follows two patterns. In many of Bourdon's stories an old family is reborn in a new and chastized form. For example, *Femme et mari* depicts a family's quest for fortune—that is, for male values—that disorders the family and invites disordering strangers into the household. By the end they have lost most of their fortune and one of their children. But the sacrifice has transformed them: the husband finally sees the importance of familial, not financial, order, and even returns to the Church. His wife, without the heavy social obligations of a financier's wife, can devote herself to him and to their remaining child. The dissolved family reappears in a manner similar to the reconstruction of a decomposed picture. Each element takes its proper place and we are left with a motionless portrait. Another ending involves the family created through a new marriage. This occurs through a similar act of recognition: the hero and heroine recognize each other as a perfect match and can join the familial cult. Their marriage also produces or reproduces the domestic universe.

The themes of disorder and lawlessness, the confrontation of polar forces, a redemptive act, and the birth of a new familial universe lend the domestic novel the tone of a creation myth. At the creation every element receives its place in a universe after a disorderly confrontation between the forces of good and evil. People are sacrificed, punished, and transfigured into characters acquiescing to law and moral standards. Thus it is that the mythical mind explains the beginnings of human society. The female novel did no less in imagining the origins of domestic order. Its most significant accomplishment, however, was the creation of woman.

The Birth of the Heroine

In the twentieth century, a variety of methodologies exists to help us speculate on human life. Through this array of methodologies we ask questions about the human confrontation with nature, about human evolution over time, about the individual psyche in relation to the need for social order, about human dignity in the face of the permanent tragedy of death. For all its permutations and speculation, our Western interpretation of the human predicament ultimately rests on the mythical accomplishment of Mediterranean civilization, which first decisively separated out an ethical human figure from the various forms of being. The domestic novel continues this tendency to sketch out a human figure, but it shifts its energy to the definition of female being, and especially to separating woman from the natural world with which she had historically been so closely identified.

At the beginning of each story the heroine appears in her unformed state, and this incompleteness is stressed in several ways. Mathilde Bourdon's *Real Life* opens on this note: "Two more months and my education will be finished."[6] Many heroines are pointedly adolescent, with neither the physical maturity nor spiritual wisdom of an adult. Sometimes the author emphasizes the physical frailty of the heroine as a way of making us aware that she must evolve into a strong and visible person. Each novel has the task of coloring a portrait of woman, of filling in her outline, of distinguishing her from the surrounding landscape. This last distinction is the crucial one in myth, for in its domestic variant it establishes categories for what is female being and what is "other." Although we see in the heroine the potential for her becoming a woman, as an adolescent she still possesses too much of the purely animal, too little of the ethically female.

Like the young untamed animal, the young heroine acts according to her impulses and fancies. Her desires know no bounds. In Bourdon's stories protagonists initially want worldly distinction: they crave intellectual achievement, sometimes fortune or clothing, at other times a handsome suitor. Bécour's heroines search for love—an uncontrolled, physical, and animal passion. Either focus of desire is at odds with a suitable female definition, for instead of leading the heroine toward strength and wholeness, it produces her breakdown as a character. As long as heroines eschew the female or fail to find its values, they suffer a chaotic existence like that of Laure in de Gaulle's *Marie et Laure*. For her, the best advice comes from the advocate of good: "think of how to curb your spirit, which is always too inclined to escape the limits assigned you."[7] In learning order and restricting natural and disorderly impulses, the heroine's task settles on the difficult job of self-control. Such a task involves more than mindless adherence to a set of do's and don'ts. It demands "learning the limits" in the sense of understanding the boundaries of female definition. Beyond that lies a fall into formlessness and worse.

The path toward becoming a defined woman as opposed to remaining subsumed in natural instincts and appetites appears blocked for the heroine. Not only is she young and vulnerable, she has usually lost a parent who represents her one guide, support, or ally in the venture. To the extent that parents personify law, and especially the mother—who administers domestic law—the heroine flounders without a sense of order or value. In Bourdon's religiously oriented novels, the heroine usually lacks her mother, whose absence deprives her daughter of a strong commitment to Catholic doctrine as an orderly and defining set of principles. Antoinine Damirault in *Les Belles années* finds herself in precisely this situation and must attend the convent her mother had attended before she can acquire the protection of Catholic or maternal law. Or in de Gaulle's *Adhémar de Belcastel* Blanche receives an education in "filial devotion" from her father,[8] but without her mother's religious and female instruction and example, her worldly virtues have no spiritual fortification. This lacuna in the heroine's life caused by the twin absence of parent and law has a physical component to the extent that it leaves her open to the penetration of evil. Could Blanche, for example, but wear the medal of the Virgin, as her mother would have insisted, she would possess a ready-made defense. Had other heroines their mothers, such protectors would block the invasion of outside forces.

Instead, the heroine oscillates between order and disorder in a chaotic continuum that parallels and even determines the confusion in the story of the family. Léontine wanders in two worlds: one of children and domestic duty; the other of theater, social events, and worldly pleasures. All the while preferring the quiet life around the hearth, Claire Duperron in Bourdon's *Femme et mari* plays the society matron to please her husband. Julia Bécour's heroines, endowed with a measure of virtue, nonetheless cast their eyes on unworthy men and become enemies of the female self. Elfa, Blidie, Georgette, Lucie, and Jeanne all sense an incongruence in their relationships with men, but none of them possesses sufficient strength or social independence to choose the path toward womanhood.

The problem of personal authority and strength looms large in the domestic novel. The heroine's inchoate subjectivity is emphasized in her submission to a multitude of unworthy advisors. Her adolescence, her tutelage, or her submission to a materialist husband or fiancé cause her troubles and indicate her situation. Léontine had no inclinations to move in social circles until her husband introduced her to novels and ridiculed her faith. As his wife, she followed his lead. Nor did Claire Duperron want to entertain scores of strangers daily, but her husband's ambition demanded such loyalty on her part. Any surrender of self to the wishes of others entailed or marked a lack of definition— opposite to the goal of the heroine's strivings. Until she can establish herself, free herself from tutelage, and confirm her heroic stature she, like the mythical hero, remains the prey of antifemale forces.

In the meantime the unfortunate consequences of the heroine's lack of full character unfold through the agency of all that is "other," or more conveniently, through the agents of evil. In the hands of male tutors, misguided husbands, foolish fathers or friends, she is the victim not of neutral, but of evil forces. While the mythical process of female definition is going on, anything antifemale is *ipso facto* evil and tends to absorb the fledgling female personality. Blidie, for example, falls under the influence of Justin, and succumbing both to his promises and her passion, she sleeps with him. This act destroys her subjectivity as she hands herself over both to nature and to a man instead of resisting these hostile forces. This total collapse of character completed, Blidie dies. Fortunately, most heroines meet these external foes more successfully.

Blidie's plight illustrates the extreme test in store for the heroine. Each must meet all enticements of "otherness" or evil with increasing resistance, or at least temporize until the other is proved wrong. Specifically, heroines must first meet the temptations offered them by men. Husbands, fathers, fiancés, almost any male acquaintance can personify all that is foreign to the home: materialism, rationalism, and sensualism. These qualities, although they are disordering, stand in a secondary position to what the male mainly represents: power and authority rivaling that of the heroine in the domestic realm. Initially, René masters Léontine, Maxime controls Claire, Justin enchants Blidie, and Evariste influences Lucie. The list is endless of heroes whose domination of the heroine derives not so much from the cogency of their principles: Blidie, Léontine, Claire, and Lucie articulate more or less forcefully their distaste for male values. Rather, men are able to impose their views on others and to act as agents, whereas heroines, before the resolution of a story, possess no such agency and lack control of their own world. With men at the helm, the story descends into evil, and a succession of misfortunes ensues. Bankruptcies, deaths, and prolonged illness all testify to the chaos caused

by male direction of the domestic cosmos. Only the clear
establishment of female authority in the form of a clearly
defined and independent heroine can restore health, law,
and prosperity.

The appearance of this female subjectivity develops
through consistent assertion of virtue in counterpoint to
male misdirection. Virtue steadfastly maintained eventually
brings the hero to submission, a submission evident either
in his begging the heroine's forgiveness or in his request
for her hand in marriage. The request is tantamount to an
abjuration not only of materialism or atheism, but of the
authority on which masculinity depended. In consequence,
the hero looks to the heroine as the source of all strength
and leadership. Maxime turns from his quest for money,
and instead of governing his wife looks to her direction with
"absolute confidence." She becomes the "faithful anchor
which supports him; he consulted her in all matters."[9]
Claire, like most heroines, has incorporated male powers to
gain control of the domestic world. From this establishment
of sovereignty subsequent domestic order flows because the
center of the universe has been established in the heroine's
character.

Before this apotheosis occurs the heroine confronts another force of evil and disorder. Throughout their lives
women no less than men have struggled against the power
of nature, and that struggle permeates the domestic novel.
At every turn nature, in the guise of death, illness, and
disorder invaded the household, as well as the female myth.
But nature was particularly threatening in its reproductive
form, which not only threatened the woman's life, but her
definition as an ethical or human, as opposed to an animal,
being. In the household women employed the corsets, clothing, cleaning rituals, and other conventional signs to tame
the reproductive component of their being. Before she could
appear safely defined, a similar task faced the domestic heroine. She was compelled, like the god or romantic hero, to
meet and best the natural foe.

Here the domestic novel acquires a further convolution, for the reproductive foe can be none other than a woman. The heroine must "control" her sexual impulses, an ongoing struggle more often than not suggested in a range of temptations substituted for the sexual act itself. Only in Blidie does the sexual impulse appear with all its evil potential. But this was unusual; most authors could not posit a woman both dead and a heroine. Instead, for the full threat of the sexual or natural to unfold without destroying the heroine, the mythical mind of the author separated the heroine into two characters illustrative of the polarity within the persona of a single woman. Most heroines have a double who embodies one aspect or another of sensuousness. Even titles indicate the bifurcation of a single woman and the element of opposition: *Marie et Laure, Les Deux belles-mères, L'Ainée et la cadette.* For emphasis, the heroine and her double are often sisters, or children born on the same day, unrelated girls raised by the same woman, or the closest of childhood friends. From an initial commonality, their paths soon diverge as one aims for righteousness, the other for pleasure. Some stories, like Bourdon's *Femme et mari*, allow the double a position parallel with that of the heroine: Andrée is not only Claire's cousin, she serves as governess to the children, develops an intimacy with the heroine's husband, and thus duplicates each of Claire's roles.

The presence of a double allows the full consequences of nature, or the antifemale, to appear without precluding the heroine's eventual triumph. Permitted to observe the actions of the antiheroine, the heroine herself draws lessons passively about all she should not do. Yet she suffers the effects of her double's evil deeds as if they were her own: children die; husbands go astray; she herself may be infected with traces of the antiheroine's stigma, which serves notice not only of the potency of nature and reproduction, but of its presence in every woman. It is this sexual or instinctual woman over whom the heroine must prevail in order to receive her definition. Just as Neptune mastered

208

the seas, incorporated their power, but became in the process a man-god and therefore "not-nature," so the domestic woman must best the embodiment of nature in the antiheroine, incorporate her sexuality in a spiritualized form, and thus mark the difference between herself and the unrelieved being in nature. Specifically, Claire Duperron watches Andrée's eclipse, reclaims her influence over the children and her husband, and thus becomes a kind of goddess in the family. Or Léontine recognizes, while she observes the voluptuous figure of her double, Flavie, wither like a faded flower, that she must suppress adulterous, animal thoughts. The demise of nature allows Léontine to assert her own feminine control over her husband René and to revive his attention to their family. In both cases the heroine's triumph over nature in its antifemale form amounts to an assertion of a female as opposed to animal side of reproductivity.

Like all domestic heroines, these women have become household goddesses with a particular ethical characteristic. It is the triumph of female "virtue" that has righted the domestic cosmos and restored the harmonious rule of law. The absence of this particular feminine quality to move the spheres had caused chaos and invited evil in the first place. The reappearance of virtue at the end of the novel, a virtue not passive but potent, makes clear the composition of the female self. This quality has subdued the male while simultaneously flowering as the distinguishing characteristic of woman. Virtue consistently maintained alone prevents woman from succumbing to men, from giving herself, losing herself and her autonomy. Virtue is thus antimale, or the essence of womanhood. As such it has a close connection with the bio-sexual definition of woman as reproductive. Virtue constitutes reproduction spiritualized, the biological side of woman lifted from the animal world and made distinctly human. When the heroine bests the animallike antiheroine, she has accomplished the mythical feat of defeating nature and incorporating its power in a new form. In the process, female character acquires a conventional and human definition, replacing, though stemming from, the biological: woman is virtuous. This endowment of the female portrait with ethical or human as opposed to animal or biological shape was the consistent message of the domestic novel.

The moment when the heroine comes to dominate both men and nature amounts to a passage from amorphous adolescence to complete womanhood. Once prey to nature in the form of her own instinct, to the manipulations of nature in the guise of another woman, and to the antifemale in the form of masculine authority, she henceforth stands as a powerful subject and sovereign. Strength and subjectivity replace impotence and objectification. Such a transformation is never smooth; instead it contains all the agonies of death—the death throes of the frail and vulnerable adolescent as preliminary to the birth of woman. Obviously the heroine cannot suffer her own physical death, so a child or woman must serve as her substitute. Bourdon's heroines lose children or siblings, and yet endure an agony that is their own. Parents also take their child's place as an indication that the dying adolescent heroine embodies the infirmities of the aged. In Josephine de Gaulle's *Adhémar de Belcastel* Blanche, at the instant of her transmutation into the dutiful wife, enacts a vigil at the deathbed of her father. More severe, Bécour robs her female protagonists of fiancés and husbands who often share the heroine's name—such as Jeanne and Jean in *Une heure d'oubli*. Such deaths leave them prostrate with grief and pain, stricken as if with a mortal wound, but ready for metamorphosis.

This type of substitution was natural to the mythical mind of the nineteenth-century woman. In the reflective ordering of the domestic universe any activity, event, or tragedy in the household was but her mirror. Dirt implied the condition of her soul; children's misbehavior incriminated her; and both would fill her with horror as she identified with them. Any event, whether universal or trite, had a personal reading. In observing the death of children, siblings, or other relatives, the heroine thus experienced her own fate. She read her destiny in the state of the environment, in the physical context of her life. Chaotic conditions, images of death evoked in the heroine the utmost pain as she reduced all life to an expression of herself. This fusion of objective death, perception of its horror, and the incorporative mind of the domestically oriented author produced the agonies of the heroine.

Freudian theory suggests an alternative, but clearly parallel, reading of this suffering heroine as a continuous expression of oedipal crisis. To the extent that death brings impotence, the death witnessed by the heroine implies her own lack of power. Thus, when Léontine visits the sick and helpless Flavie, formerly so sexually enchanting, she is moved by the potential similarity of her own condition. An oedipal vision suddenly fills the heroine's mind, inspires her with sorrow born of identification with the dying character, and fixes her determination on correct behavior, on adherence to law. Antoinette Lemire draws a personal lesson from the death of little Charles, whose fate might be said to embody her own castration. The lesson was simply this: women were rendered impotent as a result, in Antoinette Lemire's words, "of any disorder." As a corrective, she represses the source of disorder in her natural self and begins her course as an enforcer of law and virtue.

Psychoanalytic theory further buttresses the mythical parallel by proposing that the creation of this superego in women has specificity. Whereas boys, in the absence of the father from the home, build a principled and universal concern for law, girls fix on law as derivative from their individual mothers. In women's novels, the adolescent heroine often seeks a retrieval of law in the discovery of her particular mother's traces. Bourdon's Antoinine Damirault has lost her mother and therefore her way. Misguided by her father and grandmother, she grows up spoiled and uncontrollable. Her grandmother's death fixes the girl's future: Antoinine must go to the convent. Horrified at her own misdeeds and sin, which she perhaps connects with her grandmother's death, she finds her dead mother's spiritual journal, which suddenly offers a model for correct behavior. Once corrected and converted to obedience to her mother's female law, Antoinine joins her father in a happy reconciliation, for she is now prepared to direct the family.

Thus the apocalyptic moment signaling the rite of passage is filled with death, horror, and similar indications of the painfulness in the transition to womanhood. It can also devolve from a trance or amnesia, such as that experienced by the heroine of *Fée Mab*. Or in Bécour's *Une heure d'oubli* the heroine smashes porcelain, screams imprecations, rends her wedding garments, and generally falls into frenzy before she "comes to herself" and is metamorphosed into a wise and virtuous woman. In a melodramatic way such mysterious scenes conform to an equally mysterious development of woman; they recall the darkness aroused by black magic, mystical writhings, and the like in preparation for the advent of a bright, miraculous change.

The heroine's plunge into darkness results in her apotheosis. From the struggle with men, sexual women, and her own animal instincts she emerges fully defined. The accomplishment is announced not by the heroine herself, but by other characters in the story. Maxime admits to his wife, "Claire, you are good and I did not recognize it."[10] This new recognition constitutes the moment when the female persona that had formerly blended into nature has become distinct. She has precipitated out from nature to establish her claim to being human. Moreover, her human force becomes apparent as she proceeds to act upon the universe in a human way, and particularly upon the characters in the domestic sphere. With Hubert in *Fée Mab*, Mab is now an agent who can produce in him "a new and exquisite impression." She converts his "brutal" sensualism into "an intense joy in loving, a refined pleasure in caring."[11] Other characters return to the Church in accord with the heroine's wishes, while still others adopt the example of domestic virtue she sets. Female objectification, an adolescent condition, has been exchanged for subjectivity. Instead of being one among many manipulated beings, the heroine possesses full powers—even, one might say, the powers of a goddess at the center of the universe. And as such everyone recognizes her.

If the nineteenth century produced a cult of true womanhood—and I believe it did—the domestic novel played an important role in its development. The characters in the novel literally come to "worship" the female heroine who in a symbolic way died, sacrificed herself for them. The genre gave women a heroine whose female qualities had the power to establish human order, just as the detective or cowboy story continued the mythical tradition of heroes whose masculinity had a similar efficacy. But whereas the courage, loyalty, and strength of the mythical male had a long past, the domestic heroine was new and as yet one-dimensional. Her portrait had only the shadings of reproduction spiritualized through the act of suffering and tribulation. Nonetheless, the attribution of heroic stature to women opened many doors. It especially opened the door to feminism—a feminism that could only arise with the belief in the essential subjectivity or ethical character of the female sex. Newly united by a belief in female heroism, united by the cult of virtue triumphant over suffering and death, feminists proceeded to endow the female portrait with further human dimension and to claim a share of power for the newly recognized humanity of womanhood.

9
Woman's Mentality versus Liberal Consciousness

The original question—what is a bourgeois woman?—returns for an answer. In the case of the Nord, she was a woman whose life proceeded within the context of industrial society. In her lifetime she witnessed the historical events of nineteenth-century France: its economic progress, its political quarrels, and its social problems. In one sense she was a creature of this society because she married for economic reasons, reproduced children who would inherit responsibility for the capitalist order, and accepted as her duty a specialized female function and none other. But if these activities made her a child of bourgeois society, in other ways she bore little resemblance to her parent.

As a result of her reproductive experience, the bourgeois woman became the last bastion of a preindustrial, traditional, or premodern world view. She continued to express her tie to nature and its attendant weakness and power through primitive signs and rituals. She maintained a tribal sense of family and blood, and extended that interpretation to society at large. Her view of the universe and the microcosmic home was egocentric and pre-Copernican, while her interpretation of human experience rested on religious foundations. Believing in essential mysteries, the futility of scientific knowledge, and the complementary tension between virtue and sin in an imperfect social order, the bourgeois woman continued an outdated holistic vision into the fragmented atmosphere of the nineteenth century.

This is the bright surface of her portrait; the underside was darker. The bourgeois woman's undifferentiated ego lay embedded in the environment, the objective world of domestic magic that came to be her authority. Childlike, she conceded her autonomy to codes, to rituals, and to the dictates of whatever forces appeared larger than she. Science, rationality, and the values of liberal society passed her by as she maintained a reactionary posture. Corporate politics appealed to her because they emphasized the hierarchic, tribal, blood-cult, antiindividualistic quality of the home. Her Ligue patriotique would feed into the Action française; and she would be ripe for the authoritarianism of "Famille, Patrie, Travail," or any similar slogan that could swallow up while enhancing her small self.

Only one other system offered an alternative. The women of the Nord might have opted for the cult of womanhood divorced from the sanctions of Church and monarchy—that is, she might have opted for feminism. In the domestic novel several Northern women had contributed to the development of a self-constructed woman—a heroine the recognition of whose suffering had restored universal harmony. In many countries the aura of this mythical figure nourished women's claims to a wider role: women had suffered throughout history and only their recognition by the market world would end wars and social injustice. Most of all, the domestic novel recast women's reproductivity into the ethical form of virtue, and thereby took them out of the animal world with full human characteristics that would allow for their participation in society. Once women had grafted this reproductive motif onto the liberal ideology of representation, then they were armed with a political cause. But in the Nord, where Catholic tradition already encouraged women to be the *femme forte* and guaranteed them an eth-

215

ical shape (at least in the afterlife), the feminist alternative failed to gather momentum.

It failed because of a corporate past that comforted women and explained the contradictions in their domestic present. Feminism also had difficulties everywhere in France, and suffered periodic eclipses in Protestant countries because of an enduring conflict between the liberal world view and that of the home and women. From the beginning, liberal consciousness with its emphasis on abstract harmonies of marketplace, democratic political systems, and social interaction had been disbelieved by some. Right and left, albeit for different reasons, condemned its slogans of equality, justice, and its overarching commitment to free enterprise as either misguided or insincere. Women, like those in the Nord, joined this chorus of criticism when they said that the marketplace ignored the human side of life. Feminists also took a stance against the market. Hoping to participate in the liberal order, they nonetheless believed that women would somehow transform it, perhaps into their own creation. However, every time they attained a self-appointed goal (such as suffrage) that promised a utopian future, things turned sour.

Feminism declined whenever it forgot an essential female quarrel with the industrial order by accepting too many favors from liberal politicians. It diminished, too, when the rush to gain influence engendered attempts to wipe out the reproductive past that had fostered women's claim to influence in the first place. Disinterest in or suppression of the story of women like those in the Nord in favor of less reproductive and family-oriented women drained feminism of numerical support. But more important, such ignorance of the historical grounding of women's lives diminished the vitality of the feminist critique. The story of the reproductive past is unpleasant for its revelation of women's primitivism and antirationalism. But it is crucial when demonstrating the solid commitment of women to things human, their cogent critique of the marketplace, and a unanimous de-

216

termination to claim a share for women in shaping the social order.

When Simone de Beauvoir breathed new life into twentieth-century feminism, she did so by looking in the first place at the facts of reproductive experience—including its narrowness and limitations. She examined the intersection of biology and culture in a way that exposed the mechanisms producing the domestic woman, her fragile ego, and her allegiance to the cause of surrogate fathers. *The Second Sex* did not constitute a "backlash" against the cause of women, as many today categorize attempts to uncover the biological foundations of female life. Profoundly illuminating and politically forceful, the work of this bourgeois French woman instead drove others to revitalize their social critique. In this respect the story of women, like those in the Nord, does not close doors on feminism but rather gives us important access to female mentality.

Appendix
Tables

All information for this fertility study of more than three hundred women in the Nord comes from genealogies listed in the bibliography. Two criteria were used in selecting the sample: first, the father and husband had to be an industrialist, financier, large landholder, or important wholesaler; second, the genealogy had to include children who died within a few days of birth. The reader will note that the number in the sample will vary within the same age cohort because information was missing—for example, the age of the husband. The cohorts were determined by the woman's birthday. Approximately two-fifths of the women were from Lille, with the rest fairly evenly divided between Dunkerque, Roubaix, Tourcoing, Douai, and Valenciennes. There was a scattering of rural women, mostly the wives of important sugar refiners. The only interurban difference, and one that the sample was too small to test, was the generally lower fertility of women in Dunkerque. Their husbands were more often in commerce than in industry, and an interprofessional comparison might make an interesting study.

Table 2 reveals the fairly constant age of marriage for women and the decreasing age of marriage for men. As fortunes in the Nord became more stable, men apparently could take on the economic burdens of a family at a lower age. For women the pattern remained constant, and probably biologically determined. Only the last age cohort, that which came of marriageable age during the First World War, shows a significantly higher age of marriage. Sometimes women in this cohort were older than the men they married.

Table 4 shows a generally rising family size. This is clear even though the last two age cohorts show a downward movement. However, the last two age cohorts' fertility was sharply affected by World War I. Families of women in the 1879-1888 cohort were interrupted by the presence of an occupying army; often industrialists were taken to Germany as hostages; and the men of the Nord were away with the army. Individual women show continued childbearing until 1914, then an interruption until approximately 1920, when they have one more child. Had fertility continued during the war, families might have been larger by as many as three. The same is true of women in the 1889-1900 cohort, who began reproducing several years later than usual, and whose fertility may also have been affected by the depression of the 1930s and another invasion of the Nord. Data on this group, however, is hard to come by because some of the important genealogies were written between 1920 and 1945.

Finally, these appendices are only a supplement to the text. The aggregate figures they contain do not recapture the texture of individual lives, of certain mothers watching the deaths of child after child, of many others giving birth to eight and more children, of bio-sexual rhythms beyond those of childbirth, and the like.

Table 1

Business Interests of Fathers and Husbands of Women Born into or Marrying into the Scrive Family, 1835-1914

Maiden Name	Date of Marriage	Business of Father	Business of Husband
Marie Bigo	1835	linen	linen, mines
Emélie Briansiaux	1836	linen	linen
Laure Scrive	1837	linen	cotton
Sophie Briansiaux	1841	linen	linen, cards
Pauline Debuchy	1843	weaving	linen
Marie Wallaert	1845	cotton	linen, finance
Clémence Debuchy	1849	weaving	linen, trade
Caroline Scrive	1855	linen, mines	cotton, mines
Emilie Scrive	1859	linen	linen, trade
Louise Scrive	1861	linen	notary
Henriette Scrive	1863	linen	linen (commerce)
Mathilde Loyer	1866	cotton	cotton
Marie Scrive	1867	linen, finance	finance
Delphine Prévost	1869	linen	linen, paper
Nelly Viseur	1872	linen	linen
Valérie Gloxin	1872	trade	linen
Lucy Scrive	1874	linen, trade	notary
Marie Dumon	1877	wood, trade	linen
Adrienne Bonte	1878	cotton	linen, diverse
Marie-Louise Dujardin	1884	notary	linen
Naomi Scrive	1886	linen	wool
Antoinette Ozenfant	1887	trade	doctor
Emilie Dujardin	1888	notary	notary
Nelly Scrive	1894	linen	brewing
Nelly Roussel	1895	notary	notary
Henriette Boutry	1896	cotton	linen

Table 1 (*cont.*)

Maiden Name	Date of Marriage	Business of Father	Business of Husband
Madeleine Roussel	1899	notary	insurance
Germaine Bigo	1900	diverse	cotton
Marguerite Lecat	1902	metallurgy	linen
Eugénie Scrive	1903	diverse	industrialist
Geneviève Scrive	1903	linen, diverse	insurance
Geneviève Delesalle	1904	textiles	electrical prod.
Claire Roussel	1904	notary	notary
Thérèse Roussel	1904	notary	doctor
Antoinette Scrive	1907	linen	banking
Emilie Faucheur	1907	linen	linen
Marie Thiriez	1907	cotton	weaving
Louise Scrive	1909	diverse, politics	industrialist
Germaine Scrive	1909	diverse, politics	industrialist
Jenny Mabille de Poncheville	1911	notary	notary
Ghislaine Mabille de Poncheville	1914	notary	textiles

Table 2

Median Age at Marriage (whole years)
1789-1925

Age Cohort	Women		Men	
	Sample	Age	Sample	Age
1780-1798	28	20.0	28	29.0
1799-1808	19	21.0	19	27.0
1809-1818	29	22.0	27	28.0
1819-1828	34	21.0	35	28.0
1829-1838	22	20.0	22	26.0
1839-1848	43	21.0	40	26.0
1849-1858	24	20.5	24	26.0
1859-1868	36	21.0	32	26.5
1869-1878	24	21.0	24	28.0
1879-1888	45	21.0	45	25.0
1889-1900	28	23.0	28	26.0

Table 3

Interval from Marriage to Birth of First Child (whole months)

Age Cohort	Sample	Median Interval
1780-1798	28	12.5
1799-1808	19	11
1809-1818	26	12.5
1819-1828	34	12.5
1829-1838	22	11.0
1839-1848	41	12.0
1849-1858	24	11.0
1859-1868	36	11.5
1869-1878	19	11.0
1879-1888	45	11.0
1889-1900	28	10.5

Table 4

Family Size and Infant Mortality

Age Cohort	Live Births			Deaths of Children under Twenty Years	Average Final Family Size
	No. of Families	*Births*	*Average Births*		
1780-1798	28	132	4.7	25	3.7
1799-1808	19	130	6.8	43	4.5
1809-1818	29	135	4.6	32	3.5
1819-1828	34	192	5.6	32	4.7
1829-1838	22	103	4.6	27	3.4
1839-1848	40	219	5.4	41	4.4
1849-1858	24	152	6.3	18	5.5
1859-1868	34	189	5.5	33	4.7
1869-1878	24	126	7.3	16	6.6
1879-1888	45	308	6.8	21	6.5
1889-1900	23	140	6.0	8	5.5

Table 5

Age and Fertility

Age Cohort	Number in Sample	Women's Median Age at Birth of:		Percent Families Completed before Mother is:	
		First Child	Last Child	30 Years	35 Years
1780-1798	28	21.5	32.5	28	60
1799-1808	19	22.0	36.0	15	42
1809-1818	29	23.0	32.0	37	72
1819-1828	34	22.0	36.0	30	45
1829-1838	22	21.5	32.5	18	77
1839-1848	40	22.0	32.0	25	72
1849-1858	24	21.5	35.0	20	45
1859-1868	36	22.0	32.5	47	66
1869-1878	19	22.0	37.0	10	31
1879-1888	45	22.0	37.0	13	33
1889-1900	23	23.5	36.0	0	34

Acknowledgments
and Sources

The reader has probably noticed the heavy dependence of this book on personal interviews. When I first started doing research on the women of the Nord it seemed that my information might be confined to a line here and a line there about women. However, several scholars—Jean Lambert, Pierre Pierrard, the late Claude Bellanger, Father Hughes Beylard, Chantal de Tourtier Bonazzi, and Louis Trénard—suggested that some families in the Nord might be willing to talk about their mothers' lives. I would like to thank them for this, and for other valuable suggestions. Families in the Nord are known to be "closed" to outsiders as a result of their nineteenth-century business practices. I found this not to be the case. Several dozen men and women were eager to assist me in various ways, and some of them spent days showing me letters and photographs and describing what they could remember of domestic life. One woman was (in the mid-1970s) in her nineties; others in their seventies and eighties. Yet their memories of childhood and young womanhood were vital and precise. Some shared these recollections on the condition that they be used anonymously. I have chosen to use all in this way and to change the initials of all informants to make for uniformity and to insure privacy. They can be thanked here for their extraordinary hospitality and help: the late Mme Elisabeth de Durand, M. and Mme Yves de Durand, Mme Crespel, Mme Pierre Delesalle, Mme Joseph Butrille, Mme Desmarquest, Mme Edmond Nogez, Mme Lucie, Mme Tourret, Mme G. Villié, Mother Mullier, Mother Verley, Mme Motte-Dubar, M. and Mme Antoine Giard, M. and Mme Watine-Motte, M. and Mme Sion-Lepoutre, Mme Prouvost-Franchomme, Mme E. Leblanc, Mme R. Barrois, Mme Ghislaine Rastouil, M. Marcel Decroix, Mme T. Saint-Léger.

The bibliography for this book depends heavily on sources for the economic and social history of the Nord, and especially for the men of the Nord. Sometimes these works contain that line here and there about women. In general, however, I used these sources because the history of women can not be written without an understanding of the milieu in which they lived, in this case the industrial and political structure of the Nord in the nineteenth century. My teachers at the University of Rochester first insisted on such an approach, and I want to thank them here. Eugene D. Genovese, even after he had more than filled the requisites of a dedicated teacher, took time to read and criticize the manuscript. Christopher Lasch's continuing quarrel with my interpretation of domestic novels forced me to think about them in a different way, and I hope he will be pleased with the outcome. Sanford Elwitt, however, has endured this project longer than anyone both in his capacity as severe critic and as a painstaking and loyal teacher. He has read this work in many forms, but as all his students know, his friendship and commitment to scholarship always prevent him from not having time to help in their efforts.

From the beginning Robert J. Smith encouraged my work on the women of the Nord and took time from his own research on French education to help with any number of problems. It was my good fortune that Joan W. Scott devoted special attention to finding the ambiguities, errors, and other signs of muddled thinking and to giving suggestions for the manuscript's improvement. My friends, William R. Leach and Carole Gottlieb Vopat, contributed their ideas on history, literature, writing, and feminism. And a list of people need thanks for varieties of help: Françoise and Eugene McCreary, Angela H. Zophy, Nell Lasch, Louise Tilly, Ellen Sewell, Richard Rosenberg, Woodroe·Dunn and Barbara Allemand. Terry Koehler, Marge Shawaluk, Linda Lasko, and Maureen Funk helped prepare the manuscript.

228

Gail Filion and Margaret Case of Princton University Press encouraged me to strengthen the manuscript and contributed their own editorial talent to its final form.

Patience, John, and Patrick deserve thanks for fun and forbearance. And finally my husband, Donald R. Kelley, put aside his prejudice against "ticky-tacky social history" and domesticity long enough to read the manuscript once. He then made me read St. Augustine, Newton, Cassirer, and rewrite.

Abbreviations

ADN	Archives départementales du Nord
AMD	Archives municipales de Douai
AML	Archives municipales de Lille
AMR	Archives municipales de Roubaix
AN	Archives nationales
APSCL	Archives du Pensionnat du Sacré-Coeur de Lille
ASJPC	Archives de la Société de Jésus de la Province de Champagne
BML	Bibliothèque municipale de Lille
LCMPV	*Ville de Lille. Conseil Municipal. Procès-verbaux*

Notes

One. Introduction

[1] "Is Female to Male as Nature Is to Culture?" in Michelle Rosaldo, ed., *Woman, Culture and Society* (Stanford, Cal.: Stanford University Press, 1974), pp. 67-86.

[2] New York: Knopf, 1977.

[3] To Mathilde Bourdon "liberty" meant licence and had no Lockean virtues whatsoever: *Nouveaux conseils aux jeunes filles et jeunes femmes* (Paris: Blériot, 1897), p. 34.

[4] Barbara Welter's series of articles on this topic generated a spate of writings touching on the cult of womanhood or domesticity. Her suggestive theories have been adopted and expanded most notably in Ann Douglas' *Feminization of American Culture*; in Nancy Cott's *The Bonds of Womanhood* (New Haven: Yale University Press, 1977); and in Mary Ryan's *Womanhood in America* (New York: New Viewpoints, 1975).

[5] Among the most important twentieth-century sources from which I have derived insights are Freud, Piaget, and Cassirer, who have explored problems of myth and the relationship of subject and object in a modern cultural context; more recent writings by certain anthropologists (Geertz, Dumont, Eliade, Evdokimov, and occasionally Lévi-Strauss); literary critics (Burke, Frye, Barthes, and Lukacs); and historians of science and philosophy (Lovejoy, Koyré, Lenoble, Burtt, and if he may be so classified, Foucault).

[6] Angela Howard Zophy's "For the Improvement of My Sex: Sarah Josepha Hale's Editorship of *Godey's Lady's Book*, 1837-1877" (Ph.D. dissertation, Ohio State University, 1978) illustrates this point. Though writing during the abolitionist campaign, the ordeal of the union in the 1850s, the Civil War, and Reconstruction, Hale took virtually no notice of events beyond the domestic world: this has been a constant characteristic of women's magazines.

[7] I am indebted to William R. Leach for letting me read drafts of his *True Love and Perfect Union* (N.Y.: Basic Books, 1980) on the ideology of the American feminist movement, in which he asserts the coherence of that ideology and its dependence on the rationalist, secular, and individualist tradition in modern political theory.

[8] Quoted in R.W.B. Lewis, *Edith Wharton: A Biography* (New York: Harper and Row, 1975), p. 413.

Two. The Nord and Its Men

[1] References to the economic and social history of the Nord are drawn from the following sources: F.-P. Codaccioni, *Lille, 1850-1914, contribution à une étude des structures sociales* (Lille: Service de reproduction des thèses de l'université, 1971); Claude Fohlen, *L'Industrie textile au temps du Second Empire* (Paris: Plon, 1956); Bertrand Gille, *Recherches sur la formation de la grande entreprise capitaliste (1815-1848)* (Paris: S.E.V.P.E.N., 1959); Marcel Gillet, *Les Charbonnages du Nord de la France au XIXe siècle* (Paris: Mouton, 1973); Bertrand Gille, *La Banque en France au XIXe siècle* (Paris: Droz, 1970); A. Hamon, *Les Maîtres de la France*, 3 vols. (Paris: Editions sociales internationales, 1936-1937); Jacques Laloux, *Le Rôle des banques locales et régionales du Nord de la France dans le développement industriel et commercial* (Paris: Giard, 1924); Jean Lambert-Dansette, *Quelques familles du patronat textile de Lille-Armentières 1789-1914* (Lille: Raoust, 1954); André Lasserre, *La Situation des ouvriers de l'industrie textile dans la région lilloise sous la Monarchie de Juillet* (Lausanne: Nouvelle Bibliothèque de droit et de jurisprudence, 1952); Pierre Pierrard, *Lille et les lillois* (Paris: Bloud et Gay, 1967); Pierre Pierrard, *La Vie ouvrière à Lille sous le Second Empire* (Paris: Bloud et Gay, 1965); *Lille et la région du Nord en 1909*, 2 vols. (Lille: L. Danel, 1909); Alexandre de Saint-Léger, *Les Mines d'Anzin et d'Aniche pendant la Révolution*, 4 vols. (Paris: Leroux, 1935-1938); A.-J. Tudesque, "La Bourgeoisie du Nord au milieu de la Monarchie de Juillet," *Revue du Nord* 46 (October-December 1959), 277-285; Amaury de Warenghien, "Histoire des origines de la fabrication du sucre dans le département du Nord et de l'école expérimentale de chimie pour la fabrication du sucre de bettraves," *Mémoires de la société nationale d'agriculture, sciences et arts centrale du département du Nord*, 3e série 12 (1909-1910), 215-627; Alexandre de Saint-Léger, *Notre pays à travers les âges* (Lille: Robbe, 1913). I have also consulted the periodicals listed in the bibliography and published by nineteenth-century scientific, historical, and geographical societies of Dunkerque, Lille, Roubaix, Valenciennes, Cambrai, Douai, and Avesnes. These are rich sources of information on the development of business and agriculture, especially in the seventeenth, eighteenth, and nineteenth centuries.

[2] Descriptions of industrial poverty have become commonplace. For the Nord, see Jean Baptiste Dupont, *Topographie historique, statistique et médicale de l'arrondisement de Lille* (Paris: Delarue, 1833); Louis Villermé, *Tableau de l'état physique et moral des ouvriers employés dans les manufactures de coton, de laine et de soie* (Paris: Renouard, 1840); Jules Simon, *L'Ouvrière* (Paris: Hachette, 1862); Emile Zola, *Germinal*, translated by Leonard Tancock (Harmondsworth: Penguin, 1974). The most recent description for Lille can be found in Pierrard, *La Vie ouvrière*, pp.

79-263. Assassinations are mentioned in Henri Rollet, *L'Action sociale des catholiques en France (1871-1914)* (Paris: Boivin, 1947), pp. 296-297.

[3] My sources for the development and mentality of the Northern bourgeois man are especially the genealogies and family histories found in the "Genealogy" section of the bibliography. Lambert-Dansette's *Quelques familles du patronat* is especially helpful. See also Jacques Ameye, *Tourcoing ma ville* (Tourcoing: La Brouette, 1968); Jacques Toulemonde, *Naissance d'une métropole: Roubaix et Tourcoing au XIXᵉ siècle* (Roubaix: Frère, 1964); *Fleur bleue*, April 1951-June 1952, special issues devoted to pioneers in the linen industry; Anne-Marie Vahe, "La Bourgeoisie douaisienne au temps du Second Empire," D.E.S. thesis, Université de Lille, 1959; Danielle Dassonneville, "Le Patronat lillois de 1815 à 1870," maîtrise d'histoire, Université de Lille, 1971; Michel Legein, "La Bourgeoisie à Dunkerque 1800-1886," thesis, Université de Lille, 1975; M. Camier, "Cambrai sous la Monarchie de Juillet," thesis, Université de Lille, 1956; Henry-Louis Dubly, *Le Caducée et le carquois* (Lille: Mercure de Flandre, 1926); Henry-Louis Dubly, *Eugène Mathon, 1860-1935* (Paris: M. Blondin, 1946); Narcisse Faucheur-Deledicque, *Mon histoire: à mes chers enfants et petits-enfants* (Lille: Danel, 1886); *Lettres d'Alfred Motte-Grimonprez, 1827-1887*, 3 vols. (Paris, 1952); Pierre Legrand, *Le Bourgeois de Lille* (Lille: Lefebvre-Ducrocq, 1851); [Jules Scrive-Loyer] *Portraits bourgeois contemporains* (Lille, 1886).

[4] Faucheur-Deledicque, *Mon histoire*, p. 369.

[5] Louis Baunard, *Les Deux frères. Cinquante années de l'action catholique à Lille. Philibert Vrau, Camille Feron-Vrau 1829-1908* (Paris: La Bonne Presse, 1910), p. 84.

[6] Toulemonde, *Naissance d'une métropole*, p. 174.

[7] See, for example, the letters of Motte-Bossut to his wife while she is at various northern vacation spots and he remains in Roubaix. Gaston Motte, *Motte-Bossut. Une époque, 1817-1883. Lettres de famille* (n.p., n.d.), passim.

[8] *Lettres*, especially his letters to Joseph Gillet in Lyon, passim.

[9] This interpretation may be found in Fohlen, *L'Industrie textile*, and especially in David Landes, "Religion and Enterprise: The Case of the French Textile Industry," in Edward Carter II, Robert Forster, and Joseph N. Moody, eds., *Enterprise and Entrepreneurs in Nineteenth- and Twentieth-Century France* (Baltimore: Johns Hopkins University Press, 1976), pp. 41-86. Landes' interpretation, if not carefully read, would seem to establish the male bourgeoisie of the Nord as overwhelmingly family-oriented and severely religious. I am attempting to show the different use of the terms religious and family-oriented by male and female members of the bourgeoisie. However, I disagree with his emphasis on the *usine chrétienne*, which all evidence shows was dead before the turn of the century, and which never received heavy support from big industry.

[10] On the success and problems of the various members of the Motte family, see Gaston Motte, *Les Motte, Etude de la descendance Motte-Clarisse, 1750-1950* (Roubaix: Verschave, 1952), and *Lettres d'Alfred Motte-Grimonprez, passim.*

[11] For a fictionalized picture of Northern families battling each other to the point of bankruptcy, see Jean Cossart [René Joscat], *Le Cran aux oeufs* (Paris: Gallimard, 1934). The story involves the struggle between two brothers-in-law for control of family fortunes. In the process, dowries come into question, siblings work for deathbed control of wills and stocks, and rumors are started concerning the financial prospects of the respective firms to cut off credit. One minor point in the story shows the disdain of these businessmen for social programs of the Church. Finally, Cossart's novel is in no sense antibusiness; the firms are happily consolidated under the leadership of the "best" entrepreneur. The entire work is dedicated to "La générale Morgon," formerly Mme Mahieu-Ferry, who ran one of the textile firms in Armentières. Cossart was manager of this factory.

[12] The opposition to free trade by Northern businessmen is well known. For the alliances they formed despite other political differences, see Robert Schnerb, *Rouher et le Second Empire* (Paris: Colin, 1949), p. 228.

[13] *The Making of the Third Republic* (Baton Rouge: Louisiana State University Press, 1975).

[14] The police gave particular attention in their surveillance to right-wing businessmen, and the same few names of men are mentioned repeatedly, in contrast to the hundreds of women involved; see for example, ADN M 154/13-15, Politique. For a brief history of the political quarrels, see Pierrard, *Lille et les lillois.*

[15] On the *patronages* for young working men, see Pierrard, *La Vie ouvrière*, pp. 386-392; and on Kolb-Bernard, see Louis Baunard, *Kolb-Bernard, sénateur du Nord, 1798-1888* (Paris: Poussielgue, 1899).

[16] For a general history of the Christian factory movement and the association of Catholic businessmen, see Rollet, *L'Action sociale des catholiques*; and Robert Talmy, *Une forme du catholicisme social en France: L'Association catholique des patrons du Nord, 1884-1895* (Lille: Morel et Corduant, 1962). For an account of the Christian factory in one firm, see Paul Feron-Vrau, *Quarante ans d'action catholique* (Paris: Imprimerie Paul Feron-Vrau, 1921); Paul Feron-Vrau, *Centenaire de la maison Ph. Vrau et Cie* (Lille: La Croix du Nord, 1919); Baunard, *Les Deux frères.*

[17] The problem with this interpretation is that it fails to distinguish between social welfare programs instituted by men who happen to be Catholic and who use Catholic personnel, and those with a Catholic sociology at their base. The latter only involved a small number of businessmen. The origins of this confusion perhaps derive from Georges Duveau, *La Vie ouvrière en France sous le Second Empire* (Paris: Gallimard, 1946) and Fohlen, *L'Industrie textile.*

234

[18] Pierrard, *La Vie ouvrière*, pp. 383-417.

[19] Talmy, *Une forme du catholicisme social*, p. 176.

[20] Ibid., p. 43, mentions the concern of the founders of the association with the de-Christianization of the *patronat*, especially as it affected workers. Sympathetic to this project, both Talmy and Rollet emphasize its lack of attraction to most industrialists. This indifference forced the founders to move down the social ladder in their search for members, and to bring in small *commerçants*.

[21] Quoted in Rollet, *L'Action sociale des catholiques*, I, 313.

[22] Quoted in Talmy, *Une forme du catholicisme social*, p. 82. Talmy adds that in Lille the religious aspect of the Christian factory always came second to its concern with social welfare.

[23] Toulemonde, *Naissance d'une métropole*, p. 172; Lambert, *Quelques familles*, pp. 750-751. Lambert mentions that interest in religion seems to grow by the end of the nineteenth century. But this appearance can be attributed to the high visibility of the Catholic businessmen, who were few in number, and especially to the increasing religious activities of women. Toulemonde gives no evidence of this growth, and merely says that the bourgeoisie of the nineteenth century, though Catholic on the whole, was not interested in religious matters.

[24] See his *Le Bourgeois de Lille* and *La Femme du bourgeois de Lille* (Lille: Lefebvre-Ducrocq, 1852).

[25] C. J. Destombes, *Vie de son Eminence le Cardinal Régnier Archevêque de Cambrai* (Lille: Lefort, 1885), II, 453.

[26] Toulemonde, *Naissance d'une métropole*, p. 172. My findings in genealogies confirm Toulemonde's statement about the lack of male vocations in the nineteenth century. See also Chapter Five; and for the general trend of women in contrast to men in entering religious orders see Claude Langlois, "Les Effectifs des congrégations féminines aux XIXe siècle. De l'enquête statistique à l'histoire quantitative," *Revue d'histoire de l'église en France* 60 (January-June 1974), 39-64.

[27] Legrand, *La Femme du bourgeois de Lille*, p. 21.

[28] Quoted in E.-O. Lami, *Voyages pittoresques et techniques en France et à l'étranger* (Paris: Jouvet et Cie., 1892), p. 309.

[29] Quoted in Henry-Louis Dubly, *Vers un ordre économique et sociale. Eugène Mathon, 1860-1935* (Paris: Blondin, 1946), p. 174.

[30] Quoted in Lami, *Voyages pittoresques et techniques*, p. 310.

[31] As benefactress of the Jesuits, Mme Bigo-Danel's name is found among other places in BML Fonds Humbert, carton 10.

[32] The praise for Napoleon as benefactor of industry may be found on his statue in the old bourse of Lille. Erected in the early 1850s, this monument highlights only the scientific and industrial contributions of the emperor.

[33] Interview with M. G., grandson of the deputy.

[34] The practical aspects of geographic discovery are emphasized in most works of the society. This quotation appears in the society's history contained in *Lille en 1909*, I, 697.

[35] Nothing better describes this elusiveness than Cossart's *Le Cran aux oeufs*.

[36] On the evolution of Scrive enterprise and residence, see Marcel Scrive, *Antoine Scrive-Labbe et sa descendance* (Angers: Editions de l'ouest, 1945), pp. 12-18.

[37] Pierre Valdelièvre, *Les Heures émues* (Paris: Beffroi, 1912), pp. 89-92. Scrive-Loyer, in his *Portraits bourgeois contemporains*, said that men of the Nord, who are all "positifs," only liked music for its utility. He added that they scorned musicians in general because they could make more money managing factories, and only appreciated them because they provided a necessary repose from business cares.

Three. The Productive Life of Women

[1] A few examples of this recognition may be found in Toulemonde, *Naissance d'une métropole*; Lambert-Dansette, *Quelques familles*; the various genealogies and collections of letters edited by Gaston Motte; and Faucheur's *Mon histoire*. Faucheur's mention of his women acquaintances in banking is particularly helpful, for information on these women is usually only found in archival sources.

[2] *Lettres d'Alfred Motte-Grimonprez*, letter to Joseph Gillet, 17 February 1871, II, 297-298.

[3] V.-J. Etienne Jouy, *L'Hermite en province* (Paris: Pillet, 1826), IX, 354.

[4] For the De Clercq legend, see J. Lambert-Dansette, "La Bourse des valeurs de Lille et l'essor des charbonnages au dix-neuvième siècle," in *Charbon et sciences humaines* (Paris: Mouton, 1966), p. 207; and Gillet, *Les Charbonnages du Nord*, 45-46, 53-54, and passim. Among others, Edouard Grar, *Histoire de la recherche, de la découverte et de l'exploitation de la houille dans le Hainaut français, dans la Flandre française et dans l'Artois* (Valenciennes: Prignet, 1847-1851), vols. I-III; and Saint-Léger, *Les Mines d'Anzin et d'Aniche* list women stockholders. For metallurgy, see *Denain-Anzin, livre d'or de la société* (Paris, 1949), p. 33, as an example.

[5] The best information on textile development appears in the following: Lambert-Dansette, *Quelques familles*; Lasserre, *Situation des ouvriers de l'industrie textile dans la région lilloise*; Th. Leuridan, *Histoire de la fabrique de Roubaix* (Roubaix: Vve. Béghin, 1864); Léonce Bajart, *L'Industrie des tulles et dentelles en France* (n.p., n.d.); S. Ferguson, *Histoire du tulle et des dentelles mécaniques en Angleterre et en France* (Paris: E. Lacroix, 1862); Fohlen, *L'Industrie textile*; J. Houdoy, *La Filature du coton dans le Nord de la France* (Paris: A. Rousseau, 1903); *Lille*

et la région du Nord; and various articles in *Revue du Nord*. One should also look at Ravet-Anceau, *Annuaire de commerce, de l'industrie, et d'administration* (Lille: Danel, 1852 and thereafter); and Christophe Dieudonné, *Statistique du département du Nord*, 3 vols. (Douai: Marlier, 1804).

[6] See *Feuille de Roubaix* (found in the Bibliothèque municipale de Roubaix), August 2, 1828; the Charvet genealogy also contains a brief description of the home business of Mme Augustine Defrenne-Prouvost in Roubaix: Pierre Daudruy-Dubois, *La Famille Charvet* (Fécamp: Durand, 1964), II, 16 n.11. Another summary but typical house plan is found in Paul Parent, *L'Architecture civile à Lille au XVIIe siècle* (Lille: Raoust, 1925), p. 23. A good description of the Scrive buildings is found in Scrive, *Antoine Scrive-Labbe et sa descendance*, pp. 23-27.

[7] See the story of the business of Jean-Baptiste and Pauline Motte-Brédart, as an example, in Motte, *Les Motte*, p. 35.

[8] Motte, *Motte-Bossut. Lettres de famille*, p. 214.

[9] T. Leuridan, "Alexandre Decrême," *Mémoires de la Société d'émulation de Roubaix* (Roubaix: Alfred Reboux, 1888), X, 338. Other information on Decrême appears in ADN M 557/5 "Expositions universelles des produits de l'industrie," which shows the Prefect Dieudonné's interest in the progress of their business.

[10] Toulemonde, *Naissance d'une métropole*, pp. 170, 177-180.

[11] Faucheur-Deledicque, *Mon histoire*, pp. 369-379.

[12] Baunard, *Les Deux frères*, pp. 2, 83-84, 87; and H. Masquelier, *Une apôtre de la ligue patriotique des françaises: Madame Paul Feron-Vrau, née Germaine Bernard, 1869-1927* (Paris: Maison de la Bonne Presse, 1931), p. 63.

[13] Motte, *Les Motte*, p. 67.

[14] E. Gennevoise, *Notes généalogiques. La famille Lorthois de Tourcoing. 1600-1910* (Lille: Lefebvre-Ducrocq, n.d.), p. v.

[15] See *La Cordée du patriarche* (newspaper of the Dubois family), March 1957; and Henri Bernard-Maître and Pierre Daudruy, *La Famille Dubois* (Fécamp: Durand, 1924), I, 161. The latter work also contains information about the business activity of her sister-in-law, Mme Sabine Dubois-Serret, whose family founded the Hauts-Fourneaux et Aciéries de Denain (today part of USINOR), and of her aunt, Mme Bracq-Dubois. The Motte history notes that Adèle Dazin-Motte also made business trips.

[16] One may find these and other examples of women involved in labor disputes in AMR F II ge 4, Conseil des Prud'hommes, Contestations 1837-1841. Later in the century Mme Casse of Lille went bankrupt following a series of labor disturbances at her factory. According to accounts, these disturbances arose because of her unfair practices and severity with workers. See BML Fonds Humbert, Biographie, carton 3, and Fonds Quarré-Reybourbon, 2/C. In addition, ADN M 613/1, Contraventions lists firms cited for failure to adhere to the law of 1841 restricting child labor. Among

them are firms headed by women, and some in which women played a substantial role in management.

[17] On Mme Mahieu-Ferry, see "Les Pionniers industriels français du lin," *Fleur bleue* 16 (September 1951), 49-60; and Lambert-Dansette, *Quelques familles*, p. 598.

[18] See F. Kuhlmann, *Exposition des produits de l'industrie. Rapport du jury départemental du Nord* (Lille: L. Danel, 1844), pp. 167-169. The story of Mme Lefebvre's success is also told in *Peignage Amédée Prouvost et Cie. 1851-1951* (Roubaix, 1951), unpaginated, while an anecdote from her early life is recounted by Eugène Motte, "Discours de Monsieur Eugène Motte prononcé le 4 septembre 1927," in *Lettres d'Alfred Motte-Grimonprez*, I, xvi.

[19] Kuhlmann, *Exposition 1844*.

[20] Dubly, *Le Caducée et le carquois*, passim.

[21] Ibid., letter from Mme Barrois to M. Barrois, 18 November 1790, pp. 334-335.

[22] *La Cordée du patriarche*, March 1957; Bernard-Maître and Daudruy, *La Famille Dubois*, I, 89, 161.

[23] Motte, *Motte-Bossut. Lettres de famille*, p. 11.

[24] On Louise Dazin, see Toulemonde, *Naissance d'une métropole*, pp. 181-183.

[25] Dubly, *Le Cauducée et le carquois*, letter from Mme Barrois to her husband, 19 September 1790, pp. 227-228.

[26] Baunard, *Les Deux frères*, pp. 83-84.

[27] Motte, *Les Motte*, p. 54.

[28] Toulemonde, *Naissance d'une métropole*, p. 170

[29] *Lettres d'Alfred Motte-Grimonprez*, letter from Pauline Motte-Brédart to Alfred Motte, 21 January 1945, I, 79. The theme of economy runs through Mme Motte-Brédart's letters to her son, as it did through the letters of Mme Motte-Clarisse to her son Jean-Baptiste Motte-Brédart.

[30] Dubly, *Le Caducée et le carquois*, letter from Mme Barrois to her husband, 19 July 1790, p. 59. Gaston Motte reports this same indifference to clothing in Mme Motte-Brédart, *Les Motte*, p. 38.

[31] See the book on accounting practices by the Lille author, E. Brun-Lavainne [H. Prévault], *Traité de la tenue des livres* (Lille: Lefort, 1835). Brun-Lavainne, before he became a popular local writer, spent his early years working for some of the local businesses. One can see examples of this practice in the Arthaud account books, AML, Fonds Gentil-Descamps, carton 80/3058-3061, in which business expenditures stand side by side with laundry bills.

[32] Baunard, *Les Deux frères*, p. 84.

[33] *Lettres d'Alfred Motte-Grimonprez*, II, 298.

[34] Legrand, *La Femme du bourgeois de Lille*.

[35] Motte, *Les Motte*, p. 37.

[36] Toulemonde, *Naissance d'une métropole*, p. 181.

[37] Albert G. J. Cuvelier-Verley, *Généalogie de la famille Cuvelier d'Oresmieux 1535-1927* (Lille: Société d'études de la province de Cambrai, 1927), pp. 21-22.

[38] Dubly, *Le Caducée et le carquois*, passim.

[39] A copy of this balance sheet may be found in Motte, *Motte-Bossut. Lettres de famille*, p. 214. Gaston Motte reports that although Mme Motte-Brédart respected the traditions of the Church, she was broad-minded about religion.

[40] Legrand, *La Femme du bourgeois de Lille*, pp. 5-15. Ange Descamps, *Lille, un coup d'oeil sur son agrandissement, ses institutions, ses industries* (Lille, L. Danel, 1878), p. 37, reports the same transformation.

[41] Masquelier, *Mme Paul Feron-Vrau*, pp. 30-31; and Anatole de Ségur, *Paul Marie Charles Bernard, 1840-1874* (Paris: Tolra, 1875).

[42] Information generously provided by Mme Antoine Motte-Dubar. Mme Dujardin's dossier for the Legion d'honneur is too recent for communication. The plant she managed was the largest manufacturer of engines in France.

[43] Information provided by Mme Jacques Prouvost-Franchomme, Adjointe au Maire de Roubaix, from her unpublished paper "La Femme à travers l'histoire de Roubaix."

[44] See "Les Pionniers industriels français du lin," *Fleur bleue* 16 (September 1951), 49-60. The reference to running the business with a "firm hand" probably dates from her strong stand in the 1904 strike, cited in Lambert-Dansette, *Quelques familles*, p. 598.

[45] Dubly, *Le Caducée et le carquois*, letter from Mme Barrois to her husband, n.d. (November 1790), p. 312.

[46] See A. Trelcat, *La Famille Despret* (Lille: Société d'études de la province de Cambrai, 1929), as well as various editions of the *Annuaire statistique du département du Nord* (Douai, 1826 and thereafter).

[47] Alexandre Faidherbe, "L'Organisation du travail d'après M. Le Play," *Mémoires de la Société d'émulation de Roubaix* 9 (1870-1871), p. 84.

[48] See Chapter Eight.

[49] Baunard, *Les Deux frères*, I, 247-248.

[50] See Motte, *Les Motte*, pp. 55, 61, 79, 86, 91, and passim.

[51] On Mme Briansiaux-Bigo, see Bonnie Smith, "Women of the Lille Bourgeoisie," Ph.D. dissertation, University of Rochester, 1976, pp. 151-237. Information on Mme Descat was generously provided by Mme Jacques Prouvost-Franchomme. On her work in the *crèches* of Roubaix, see ADN X 58/8, Crèches; and AMR M IIe (1-2), Crèches de St. Joseph, de la rue des Viviers, Ste. Elisabeth de Lannoy.

[52] See this argument presented in Edward Shorter, *The Making of the Modern Family* (New York: Basic Books, 1975).

Four. Domesticity: The Rhetoric of Reproduction

[1] This description is based on a picture of Mme Auguste Scrive-Wallaert found in BML Fonds Humbert, biographie, carton 20.

[2] As did the family of Mme Bernard-Roquette, according to the description in Masquelier, *Mme Paul Feron-Vrau,* p. 26.

[3] Women and consumerism is also an old theme found in such various sources as J. K. Galbraith, *Economics and the Public Purpose* (Boston: Houghton Mifflin, 1973) and other Galbraith books; or "A Redstocking Sister," "Consumerism and Women," in Vivian Gornick and Barbara K. Moran, *Woman in Sexist Society* (New York: Basic Books, 1971). Any of these market-oriented treatments fails to capture the symbolic aspects of the household, in an attempt to make women's activities "rational" in terms of market definitions.

[4] Thorstein Veblen, *Theory of the Leisure Class* (Boston: Houghton Mifflin, 1973).

[5] The term derives from Marx's critique of political economy and forms the basis for social-scientific inquiry. I am grateful to the work of Daniel E. Little for explaining its principles, in his "Marx's *Capital*: A Study in the Philosophy of Social Science," Ph.D. dissertation, Harvard University, 1977.

[6] Regionalism in marriages is well known. I have observed it, though I have not calculated the exact figures, in the two hundred cases that form the basis of the fertility tables. Lambert-Dansette mentions it in his *Quelques familles,* p. 649, and says that families even avoided alliances with families in neighboring cities. Mme D. described how upset her family was when she received a proposal from a young man from the Midi, although his family had already intermarried with another in the Nord. And her son, born from this marriage, is certain that there was always a prejudice against the offspring because they were not pure Northerners. See also Fernand Motte, *Souvenirs personnels d'un demi-siècle de vie et de pensée, 1886-1942* (Lille: S.J.L.I.C., n.d.), p. 26, who describes how surprised the rest of the family was when his sister married into the Gillet family of Lyon. This family had close business and personal ties with all the Mottes, as demonstrated in the letters of Alfred Motte-Grimonprez, grandfather of the bride.

[7] Information provided by Mme R. in several interviews, June and July 1976. Mme R. is the family historian and archivist for a large Northern family whose many intraregional alliances make her an expert in the local customs. She spent many hours answering my questions about marriage practices and the daily life of women, and provided access to letters, all of which are cited anonymously in the text, according to our agreement.

[8] Ibid.

[9] The prejudice against marriages for love was repeated again and again

by my sources. One woman said that the only nonarranged marriage she had ever heard of was that of her parents. By the time they were married the husband was already one of the most successful businessmen in the Nord, a self-made man without family. Her own marriage was arranged, and of the two possibilities, she preferred the latter. "What do children know about marriage?" she said. Because the system has broken down, according to her, Northern wealth and family ties have been dissipated, wasted on movie stars and strangers.

[10] See especially her *Souvenir d'une mère* (Paris: Blériot, 1886) in which the heroine endures a lifetime of misfortune for falling in love as an adolescent with a young man slated, by her parents, to become her brother-in-law.

[11] This unhappy family scandal is told in Jacques Foucart, *Jules Brame* (n.p., 1964), pp. 69-76. Jules Brame's own account appears at the end of the work, pp. 306 ff.

[12] See Chapter Three and Dubly, *Le Caducée et le carquois*, passim.

[13] Masquelier, *Mme Paul Feron-Vrau*, pp. 35 ff. on the arrangements for the marriage. The rest of the book gives an account of the Feron-Vrau's activities on behalf of the Church.

[14] Letters of Marie D. to her aunt, Mme B., 25 July 1897, contained in *Archives du Batut* (a privately published collection of letters and memorabilia kindly communicated to me by Mme R.).

[15] Letter from Auguste Duhamel to Caroline Lelièvre (July?) 1836, quoted in Madeleine Isoré, "Bourgeoises de Bergues en 1830," *Mémoires de la Société dunkerquoise* 64 (1927-1928), 262.

[16] See, for example, the letters of Motte-Bossut to his children in Gaston Motte, *Motte-Bossut, un homme, une famille, une firme* (Tourcoing: Frère, 1944). Mme R. indicated that her family letters are filled with expressions of concern for speedy pregnancies.

[17] Genealogies demonstrate this *fin de siècle* movement into allied fields. See especially Scrive, *Antoine Scrive-Labbe et sa descendance*.

[18] The Bernard family reunions are legendary in the Nord. See Adolphe Théry, *Les Bernard: une famille d'industriels qui passe en 20 ans de 489 à 983 membres* (Paris: Spes, 1929); and Henri Bernard-Maître, *Généalogie de la famille Bernard* (Paris: L. Durand et fils, 1952).

[19] Anatole de Ségur, *Vie de l'Abbé Bernard* (Paris: Bray et Retaux, 1883), p. 62, a statement attributed to the Abbé's mother.

[20] This is the charge of M. G., who took many hours from his business to share with me his enormous knowledge of Northern history. M. G. warned me about the accuracy of his information because his family was not really Northern, having arrived in the area as recently as several hundred years ago from Normandy.

[21] "Plan d'éducation d'une mère chrétienne," in Ségur, *Vie de l'Abbé Bernard*, pp. 426-430. Internal evidence suggests that this document was

241

written by Mme Henri Bernard in the late 1850s shortly before her death at the age of forty, after the birth of her eleventh child.

²² In sorting out her family's papers and letters, Mme R. discovered how absorbed women were with the problem of children's illness. Although women did not always care for the sick child themselves, in their letters they traded information about remedies they had found successful—vin de Bordeaux, veal stock, and the like. Ségur's *Paul-Marie Charles Bernard*, p. 65 describes Mme Bernard applying leeches to her mortally ill young husband. A handy book, *Le Necessaire des dames* (Lille: Castiaux, n.d.), attributed to Simon Blocquel but perhaps the work of his Lille wife, contains a long section on home remedies. The use of these remedies appears in a valuable source, "Comptabilité ménagère d'une famille lilloise très connue, dont le chef fût commandant des canonniers. Curieux document commencé en 1843 et qui s'arrête en 1858, donnant des détails intéressants sur les dépenses d'une maison bourgeoise aux XIXᵉ siècle," BML Mss. 1158 (hereafter cited as "Comptabilité ménagère"). Internal evidence suggests this to be the account book of Mme Clémence St. Leger, who, according to BML Fonds Humbert, biographie, carton 20, was a pious woman. Her husband, Victor St. Leger, was a prominent politician, known for his liberalism and for his sense of order. His motto, "travail et probité," informed his practices as a highly successful industrialist and financier. Mme St. Leger's account book provides crucial information on women's lives because she accounted for her expenses in the most minute way by indicating the purpose for which she hired a cab or made a visit, at which store she made a purchase, and exactly what sums she spent on herself, family, and servants. In the area of illnesses and medication, she made many entries for specific drugs at the pharmacy. One can also find Mme Humbert's pharmaceutical receipts in BML Fonds Humbert.

²³ *De dix-huit à vingt ans. Journal d'une jeune fille* (Paris: A.-L. Guyot, n.d.), p. 45.

²⁴ See "Comptabilité ménagère" for examples of the delicacies purchased by a woman from Lille. For similar practices in Douai, see Adrien Demont, *Souvenances. Promenades à travers ma vie* (Arras: Nouvelle société anonyme du Pas de Calais, 1927), p. 147. Jean Lambert mentions in his *Quelques familles*, p. 719, the "repas soigné et prolongé" of some Armentières families, and elsewhere he mentions the indications of huge expenditures made by the Scrive families at Meerts. For weddings, anniversaries, and galas, Northern families outdid themselves, at least according to menus found in Gérard Hannezo, *Histoire d'une famille du Nord. Les Barrois* (n.p., n.d.).

²⁵ See "Comptabilité ménagère," for furniture purchasing—large purchases in 1843 followed by recovering and refurbishing later on. The additions of Mme S. throughout fifteen years are noted in her account book. Mme R. mentioned in one interview similar practices in her family.

The seasonal rearrangement of furniture is explained in Demont, *Souve-nances*, p. 85. See also *Le Necessaire des dames*, passim, for housecleaning practices.

[26] Women and needlework is a constant theme in literature on the Nord, and was mentioned by almost every woman I interviewed. Mme M. and Mme R. both explained the practice of making girls' clothing at home even though boys' was purchased. Mme R. told me about the special sack that women often carried for holding mending. Demont, in his *Souvenances*, p. 89, says that he was so used to the grey socks knit by his grandmother that one day in a store he was shocked to see some in other colors. The "Comptabilité ménagère" shows Mme S. constantly purchasing yarn for knitting, hiring a seamstress for the day to help her with sewing projects, and buying material to make new chair coverings and small rugs.

[27] At social gatherings, according to Demont, *Souvenances*, p. 148, young married women did "un petit ouvrage d'agrément," while the older women played cards. There was always decorative needlework to be done for the Church and often put on public display by the Société de Ste. Elisabeth de Hongrie. On fancywork for the many charity bazaars in the various cities, see, for example, Henri Thomas, *Herminie de la Bassemoûturie* (Tournai: Casterman, 1867), p. 383, on her homemade contributions to the Ste. Enfance lottery at Cysoing. See also Chapters Five and Six for other organizations to which women contributed their needlework. On symbolism in needlework, or a practical guide to its use, see Simon Bloc-quel, *Nouvelle sémiographie. Langage allégorique, emblématique ou sym-bolique des fleurs et des fruits, des animaux, des couleurs, etc. Ouvrage dedié aux dames* (Lille: Blocquel-Castiaux, 1857). Finally, Mathilde Bour-don of Lille counseled women always to have needlework handy, especially when they were house guests, and to sit at parties at the worktable doing needlework; see her *Aux jeunes personnes. Politesse et savoir-vivre* (Paris: Lethielleux, 1864), pp. 59, 86-89.

[28] E. des Buttes noted the tendency in a public speech in the Nord, "Les Réclames, les romans et les journaux des modes," *Assemblée générale des Catholiques du Nord et du Pas de Calais tenue à Lille du 22 au 26 novembre 1882* (Lille: Lefebvre-Ducrocq, 1883), pp. 467-476. And Mathilde Bourdon was so upset by the trend that she wrote a play in which a sewing machine was the villain: *La Machine à coudre* (Lille: J. Lefort, 1869).

[29] The growing love of clothing and fashion appears in many sources, among them the two works cited above, as well as Motte, *Souvenirs*, p. 19, in which he mentions not only his mother's passion for clothing but also her concern for his sister's toilette, p. 22; "Comptabilité ménagère," which details Mme S.'s expenditures—and lavish they were—on jewelry, hats, and dresses; in genealogies that show, especially for the post-1850 generation, elegantly and fashionably dressed women; in the novels of Bourdon and Bécour, which often consists of diatribes against overly

adorned women, but which also describe elegant costumes on their heroines; and from the local society newspaper, *La Vie lilloise*, which focused its attention on female dress at parties, weddings, and public events. Mme R. gave me the estimate of six or eight new dresses each year, and also confirmed the frequent refurbishing.

[30] *Politesse et savoir-vivre*, p. 172.

[31] APSCL, "Conseila, 1868-1882. Comte-rendu des séances. Enfants de Marie du Sacré-Coeur," meeting of 28 November 1877. Mother Superior Verley generously assisted me in using this material. She also provided other information about conver.: life, and arranged several invaluable interviews with alumnae who had attended the boarding school before the war. These women also patiently described for me their mother's lives.

[32] Pictures are scattered throughout the genealogies listed in the bibliography. Others may be found in BML Fonds Humbert, Biographie; the frontispiece to Masquelier, *Mme Paul Feron-Vrau*; the frontispiece to Baunard, *Mme Camille Feron-Vrau*; and family pictures communicated to me by Mme W. of Roubaix and by Mme D.

[33] APSCL, "Conseila. Enfants de Marie," Meeting of 28 November 1877. This advice seems to have worked. François Chon in his *Promenades lilloises* (Lille: L. Danel, 1888), p. 118, mentions that local bourgeoises no longer think they have to have all their clothes from Paris. Instead they are supporting local dressmakers. This, however, did not mean that Lille's women were any less interested in fashion. Rather, according to Chon, seamstresses for upper-class women were working harder than ever. This information agrees with that given me by Mme M., 18 and 25 March 1975, about her mother, who loved fashion and high society, but who limited her purchase of clothing from Paris to one garment per year. The rest were made at home.

[34] *La Vie lilloise* 24 (2 February 1902).

[35] See "Comptabilité ménagère," for Mme S.'s expenditures on clothing and jewelry.

[36] Letter of 3 November 1883, quoted in *Dame St.-Albéric Toulemonde, religieuse d'Esquermes, O. C. Sur les deux ailes de la simplicité et de la pureté* (Paris: Desclée, de Brouwer, 1940), p. 62. I wish to thank Father Hugues Beylard, S.J., archivist of the Province of Champagne for finding this as well as other obscure biographies of women of the Nord.

[37] See "Comptabilité ménagère," for Mme S.'s expenditures on clothing and jewelry.

[38] The goal of thrift with charm is mentioned by Mathilde Bourdon in her *Nouveaux conseils aux jeunes filles et aux jeunes femmes*, p. 133. I know it is unwise to challenge the received tradition that all members of the bourgeoisie are concerned with thrift or by challenging the current interpretations of domestic economy. Among the women of the Nord, however, I have found not one piece of evidence to suggest that women of the

post-1850 generation had any more than a symbolic interest in keeping their account books. Their expenditures demonstrate, and their grandchildren and children testify to, an absolute disregard for thrift.

[39] Motte, *Souvenirs personnels*, p. 19.

[40] See "Comptabilité ménagère."

[41] A regular question asked in interviews concerned the number of servants in the household. In no case did any source indicate that her parents had fewer than three live-in servants. Jean Lambert in his *Quelques familles*, p. 711, says that in Armentières women contented themselves with fewer servants and often did their own cooking. I interviewed no women from Armentières, where, as Lambert says, the bourgeoisie was less well established. He cities Elise Dansette of that city as an exception, with six servants; for other cities—Roubaix, Tourcoing, Lille, and Douai—this seems to have been normal.

[42] Letter from Mme B. to her mother, Mme R., 18 August 1870, *Archives du Batut*. I am grateful to Mme R. for alerting me to this aspect of bourgeois life, and especially to the search for the one-time offender for wet-nursing. Letters recommending and requesting servants can also be found in BML Fonds Humbert, Biographie, carton 9, which contains a letter from the Comte d'Hespel to Mme Humbert recommending Louise Vandepente and his new wife. These two sources are among many demonstrating the standards set by the bourgeoisie in their search for high-quality servants.

[43] See especially Mathilde Bourdon's *Le Divorce* (Paris: C. Dillet, 1865), in which Gabrielle's home life is threatened because she lets one of her maids talk to a young peasant. The scrutiny of servants, however, is a constant theme in Bourdon's work.

[44] Information about the Oeuvre des servantes was provided by Father Hugues Beylard, S.J. from ASJPC, "Diaire de la maison des pères Jésuites de Lille." The organization met monthly from the 1850s, but I have no information about its founding, its membership, or about when the organization expired.

[45] Information received in interviews. Mme S. of Tourcoing said that her parents paid for servants' children to attend school. "Comptabilité ménagère" indicates that Mme S. paid for her maid's mother's funeral, for her clothes, bought her presents, and financed her small excursions.

[46] This explains one striking change in household design. Servants in the nineteenth century stopped sleeping in chambers adjoining their employers and were moved to their own floor.

[47] One may easily acquire a sense of the changes in women's fashion from *Godey's Lady's Book*, from the *Journal des Modes*; see also C. W. Cunnington and Phillis Cunnington, *English Women's Clothing in the Nineteenth Century* (Boston: Plays, 1970); Phillis Cunnington, *Costume in Pictures, 1750-1850* (London: Faber and Faber, 1970), which is good on male fashion; Henriette Vanier, *La Mode et ses métiers, frivolités et*

245

luttes des classes 1830-1870 (Paris: Armand Colin, 1960). Pictures in genealogies and those shown me by interviewees show that the women of the Nord adhered to changes in fashion and that their husbands upheld the unchanging bourgeois uniform of the dark suit.

[48] Mme S.'s account book shows her purchasing all these small objects either for needlework, dinner parties, or for her table. Bourdon's *Politesse et savoir-vivre*, p. 53, lists some of these signs and signals, and Demont's *Souvenances* tells how his mother gave commands with "un petit signe de tête," p. 146. For other indications of delicacy in meals, see menus in *Archives du Batut*, in Hannezo, *Les Barrois*, or in Demont, *Souvenances*.

[49] Virginie Demont-Breton, *Les Maisons que j'ai connues* (Paris: Plon, 1926-1930), I, 222, describes her future mother-in-law's parade of her treasures: porcelain from the Empire and from Japan, Marie Antoinette's snuffbox, "un nid d'amour de Sèvres." Demont himself describes his parents' home in Douai with its massive furniture and its artificial fruit, vases of flowers, clocks, and the like all preserved under glass globes: *Souvenances*, p. 86. Julia Bécour also talks extensively in her novels about interiors with their plants, precious books, *objets d'art*, and magazines.

[50] One of my informants, Mme S., suggested that many women were lax in this, as in most matters of child care.

[51] Many of my informants mentioned the family gardener, a staff member missing from pre-1850 literature. See also Motte, *Souvenirs*, p. 27 and the *Lettres d'Alfred Motte-Grimonprez*, II, 323, for other examples. Artificial flowers, according to Isoré, "Bourgeoises de Bergues en 1830," p. 249, were the rage in the Nord. For instructions in making them, Northern women could consult the work of one of their own, Mme Simon Blocquel, *L'Art de confectionner des fleurs artificielles* (Lille: Blocquel, n.d.).

[52] This information comes from Mme R. during interviews in June and July 1976. It is confirmed, for example, in Demont-Breton, *Les Maisons que j'ai connues*, I, 82-83, in which she says that women might know how to make "un Polonais—une galette sèche à la cannelle et aux amandes." According to Mme R., the loss of a cook was a family tragedy during the nineteenth century because women did not know how to cook. Mathilde Bourdon suggests that women at least know the principles of making preserves and that they give some surveillance to the general activities of the kitchen, *Nouveaux conseils*, p. 133.

As the servant problem intensified after the war, some girls from the upper class were sent to cooking school because their mothers had no skills and could not teach them. This information comes from Mme S. of Tourcoing, who herself attended one of these *écoles ménagères*.

[53] See "Comptabilité ménagère" for examples of the use of flowers. Women also used flowers, real or artificial, to decorate statues of Mary or church altars (see Chapter Five).

[54] Specifically, the Ligue patriotique des françaises (see Chapter Five).

[55] The stories of a mother's initiation of her daughter were told by Mme R. She also mentioned that even in post-World War II France women did not speak of miscarriages, but rather took to their beds and said they were ill.

A divorce case of some notoriety in the Nord also exposed women's general ignorance in sexual matters. In the course of this case a woman had to testify that she went to her sister, after two years of an unconsummated marriage, and asked why she had not become pregnant. See *Causes célèbres du Nord et du Pas-de-Calais. Demande en séparation de corps de Mlle Josephine Paeile contre F. Paul Callau, son pseudo-mari* (Douai: Lucien Crépin, 1884); and Cour d'appel de Douai, *Mémoire à consulter pour Mme Josephine Paeile, épouse de M. Paul Callau, contre M. Paul Callau, son mari, neg. à Lille.* Both pamphets are found in BML Fonds Lefebvre, carton 14.

Sending girls to boarding school protected them from viewing pregnant women, as did the practice of sending them away from home when their mothers or other women relatives became visibly pregnant. They remained away until a telegram notified them of the birth. See Demont-Breton, *Les Maisons que j'ai connues*, p. 190. Those women who brought up the matter of their sexual knowledge during inteviews admitted to having absolutely no awareness of sexual matters until they were married. Part of the criticism of women's education at the end of the nineteenth century derived from this ignorance; it was felt that they should learn at least a few principles of biology.

[56] Mme D. said that she and her siblings always showered with their clothes on. Demont, *Souvenances*, pp. 189-190 talks of a movement led by women in Douai to have the genitals removed from statues and replaced by plaster leaves.

[57] On the exterior cleanliness in the Nord see Chon, *Promenades lilloises*, p. 73; and Comte de Pimodan, *Simples souvenirs, 1859-1907* (Paris: Plon, 1908), p. 341.

[58] Bourdon, *Nouveaux conseils*, pp. 133-136.

[59] Interview with Mme L., Paris, 17 May 1976. Mme R. confirmed this belief in interviews during June and July 1976. She mentioned that her mother told her she wouldn't be sick so often if she wore a corset.

[60] Mathilde Bourdon opens her book on etiquette with a critique of laissez-faire in the home. She says that people tend to think of the home as a place to relax, a place where they can say anything and abandon manners; *Politesse et savoir-vivre*, pp. 8, 122-123. Bourdon's emphasis on order and rules suggests that the notion of home as haven was contrary to all female convictions.

[61] As did the *Echo des modes de Lille, Journal de la société élégante du département du Nord* I (May 1858), 16.

[62] The discussion in this section on language comes from reading in the

field of linguistics. That all sorts of behavior may be communicative has long been understood by anthropologists. For historians who want to begin considering such possibilities one starting place is Ted Polhemus, ed., *The Body Reader: Social Aspects of the Human Body* (New York: Pantheon, 1978); or Roland Barthes, *Système de la mode* (Paris: Seuil, 1967).

[63] The number of extrabusiness activities for men in the Nord was enormous in the nineteenth century, and it seems from much of my evidence that men spent little time at home. For example, Adrien Demont mentions that his father regularly went to his club in Douai from 6 P.M. to 10 P.M., *Souvenances*, p. 99, and that his uncle did the same, p. 123; Louis Dépret, *Silhouettes de villes* (Paris: Hachette, 1874), p. 179, says that in Lille members of more than one club would sometimes visit several in the same evening. Toulemonde, *Naissance d'une métropole*, p. 173, mentions the escape from Sunday dinners through such excuses as migraine headaches or urgent business, followed by a reunion at the Hippodrome. Lambert, *Quelques familles*, 731-734, notes the societies to which men belonged and their regular sporting life.

[64] Elie Brun-Lavainne, "Les Femmes célèbres de la Flandre," *Echo de la littérature et des modes* I (1859), p. 66.

[65] For this discussion I am basing my argument on the works of Jean Piaget. For a summary of Piaget's work, see Howard Gardner, *The Quest for Mind* (London: Quartet, 1976), pp. 51-110. This summary does not cover all the points in this discussion.

[66] This interpretation derives from readings in Piaget, Freud, and Cassirer's *Philosophy of Symbolic Forms* (New Haven: Yale University Press, 1953-1957), especially volumes I and II on myth and language, respectively.

Five. Cosmos: Faith versus Reason

[1] Marguerite Poradowska, *Le Mariage du fils Grandsire* (Paris: Hachette, 1894). Poradowska was the niece of Edouard Gachet of Lille; see BML Fonds Humbert, Biographie, carton 12.

[2] Baunard, *Mme Camille Feron-Vrau*, p. 13. Mme Feron-Vrau, during her betrothal, also castigated her future husband for being so lax in religious matters. Feron-Vrau later became a leader in Catholic politics, and we can perhaps assume that much of his work was the result of her efforts.

[3] Felix de Backer, *Vie de Mme Van Der Meersch (Julie Behaghel)* (Paris: Le Coffre fils, 1876), p. 278.

[4] Though anticlerical and republican—an unusual position for a bourgeois woman—Bécour was nonetheless religious. She saw most men in the Nord as "positif," committed to science, money, and with no spiritual life whatsoever. See Chapters Six and Eight, in which she figures prominently.

⁵ I have been influenced in this discussion of the religious mind and its attitudes toward space, time, matter, causality, and action by the works of Mircea Eliade, Robert Lenoble, especially his *Histoire de l'idée de nature* (Paris: Albin Michel, 1969), Arthur O. Lovejoy, E. A. Burtt, and A. Koyré.

⁶ Various essays on tribal attitudes toward strangers may be found in V. F. Calverton, *The Making of Man* (New York: Modern Library, 1931) and *The Making of Society* (New York: Modern Library, 1937).

⁷ In this and other chapters in the book, the problem of documentation is intractable. Instead of citing every source that mentions festooned windows or crucifixes, every woman who did not let novels into the house, and the like, I will generally give only one example, as in the preceding chapter, and direct the reader to the genealogies in the bibliography, to biographies already cited, and to the following additional sources: *A la mémoire de Madame Delannoy-Desnoulez, Présidente de la conférence de la Société de Saint Vincent de Paul, du patronage des jeunes filles et de la salle d'asile de Sainte Catherine* (Lille: Imprimerie de St. Augustin, n.d.); *Centenaire des enfants de Marie du Sacré-Coeur* (Lille: SILIC, 1932); Mme Eugène Delahaye-Théry, *Les Cahiers noirs* (Rennes: Éditions de "la province," 1934); Mme J. Leclercq-Huet et al., *Les Richesses éducatrices du foyer chrétien* (Lille: Giard, 1921), in which Mme Leclercq describes her attitudes toward her home and children; *Louise Charvet, enfant de Marie 1848-1877. Simples souvenirs dédiés à sa famille* (Lille: J. Lefort, 1877); *Madame Théodore Aronio de Romblay. Pieux souvenir* (Lille: L. Danel, n.d.); *Notice sur Mlle Julie Flamen* (Lille: Ducolombier, 1876); *La Violette du Louvencourt* (Dunkerque: Lorenzo, 1860); one may also look at obituaries in *Annales de l'archiconfrérie des mères chrétiennes*; and on the freethinking of husbands, Pierre Legrand, *Le Bourgeois de Lille*, some of which is repeated in his *La Femme du bourgeois de Lille*.

⁸ A list of women taking collections appears in the diocesan newspaper *La Semaine religieuse du Diocèse de Cambrai*. On the Archiconfrérie des mères chrétiennes see T. Ratisbonne, *Nouveau manuel des mères chrétiennes* (Paris: Poussielgue, 1866); Louise Josson, *Rapport fait à l'archiconfrérie des mères chrétiennes. Assemblée générale de Notre-Dame de Sion. Le 5 février 1864* (Paris: L'Archiconfrérie, 1864); and Louise Josson, *Rapport fait à l'archiconfrérie des mères chrétiennes dans la chapelle de Notre-Dame de Sion* (Paris: Olmer, 1859); *Annales de l'archiconfrérie des mères chrétiennes*; and for the Lille chapter, ASJPC, "Diaire de l'archiconfrérie des mères chrétiennes," Mss. G. 11. 379 (hereafter cited "Diaire AMC"), used with the kind permission of Le Père Hugues Beylard, archivist. On the Enfants de Marie, I relied heavily on APSCL, "Conseila, 1868-1882. Compte-rendu des séances. Enfants de Marie du Sacré-Coeur," with the kind permission of La Mère Supérieure Verley.

For the Society of St. Vincent de Paul, see F. Chon, *Notice historique sur la Société de St. Vincent de Paul à Lille* (Lille: Lefort, 1883) and Paul

Delemer, *Noces d'or de la conférence de St. Vincent de Paul de Saint-André à Lille* (Lille: H. Morel, 1908). Police reports in ADN M 222/376 and M 222/527 also give membership lists and accounts of the organization. Fonds Humbert, BML, Cartons 5, 7, 36, 43-44 provide information on the Perpetual Rosary as well as on other ceremonies in which Mme Humbert, her daughters, and daughters-in-law participated.

[9] Masquelier, *Mme Paul Feron-Vrau*, p. 27, quoting her diary.

[10] Baunard, *Mme Camille Feron-Vrau*, p. 6, quoting her diary.

[11] See, for example, de Gaulle's *Histoire de saint Joseph, patron de l'Eglise catholique, sa vie et son culte* (Lille: Lefort, 1874); *Le Libérateur de l'Irlande, ou Vie de Daniel O'Connell* (Lille: Lefort, 1851); *Vie de général Drouot* (Lille: Lefort, 1848); or Bourdon's *Etudes historiques. Marie Tudor et Elizabeth, reines d'Angleterre* (Paris: Putois-Cretté, 1868); *Histoire de Marie Stuart* (Paris: S. Victor, 1853); *Saint Thomas de Cantorbéry* (Lille: Lefort, 1852); *Sainte Jeanne de Valois, fondateur des Annonciades* (Lille: Lefort, 1851).

[12] See Bourdon, *Marie Tudor et Elizabeth.*

[13] On the interest of Northern men in science and on their activities to further its development, see Lambert, *Quelques familles*, pp. 729-732; *Lille en 1909*, I; the yearly reports of the Catholiques du Nord et du Pas de Calais; the papers presented in the proceedings of various scientific societies, and the legion of books written by Northern men. I have not found a single work on science by a Northern woman.

[14] This I found by looking at the names of all daughters of women in the fertility study.

[15] Faucheur-Deledicque, *Mon histoire*, p. 361.

[16] As shown, for example, in the works of Michel Foucault in his work on the treatment of the insane, the sick, and the criminal; or for the United States see Robert Wiebe, *The Search for Order* (New York: Hill and Wang, 1969); or David Rothman, *The Discovery of the Asylum* (Boston: Little, Brown, 1971).

[17] Mathilde Bourdon, *Le Pouvoir de la prière* (Lille: Lefort 1857), p. 21.

[18] Théodore Bommart, *Généalogie de la famille Bommart de Douai* (Lille: Danel, 1893), II, 81-84; Masquelier, *Mme Paul Feron-Vrau*, p. 104.

[19] Thomas, *Herminie de la Bassemoûturie*, p. 287, quoting her diary.

[20] *De la confiance en Dieu dans les calamités publiques* (Lille: Lefort, 1849), and her novels.

[21] Julia Bécour, for example, brought this charge obliquely in her novel *Une heure d'oubli* (Lille: Ch. Tallandier et Gaujac, 1891); and the stringent rules of charity outlined in Chapter Six were often construed as signs of indifference.

[22] ASJPC, "Diaire AMC." When I showed interest in the archiconfrérie, Father Beylard combed the Society of Jesus archives and prepared a paper

on the founding of the order, now Ms. G 11.380 "L'Association des mères chrétiennes à Lille et les Pères Jésuites," 1975.

[23] *Annales de l'archiconfrérie des mères chrétiennes*, I (1865-1868), 153-154.

[24] Other miracles of this order may be found in Mathilde Bourdon, *Histoire de Notre-Dame de la Treille* (Lille: Reboux, 1852).

[25] ADN M 141/31, letter from Mme Barrois to Mme la Préfète, 13 August 1867.

[26] Letter from Mme C. Tilloy to Mme Emile Humbert, 27 June 1875, found in BML Fonds Humbert, carton 23, Biographie.

[27] Examples of self-inflicted pain appear in *Fidèles pour la vie à Jésus et Marie* (Lille: Béhague, 1889), a booklet about alumnae of the Sacré-Coeur pensionnat; in Masquelier's *Mme Paul Feron-Vrau*; and in Thomas, *Herminie de la Bassemoûturie*.

[28] Thomas, *Herminie de la Bassemoûturie*, pp. 118-119, quoting her diary. Our lot in life, she wrote, is "suffering and tears."

[29] Bourdon, *Le Pouvoir de la prière*, p. 21.

[30] Many women in interviews stressed their mothers' special devotion to the cult of the Sacred Heart.

[31] For examples of diaries dated according to saints' days, see *Sacerdoce d'une mère* (which I believe to be the diary of Henriette Becquart-Dewavrin [1876-1941]); and Delahaye-Théry, *Les Cahiers noirs*; or the biography of Herminie de la Bassemoûturie.

[32] ASJPC, "Diaire AMC."

[33] Mme Camille Feron-Vrau noted in her diary on 28 August 1876 that Jesus had told her, "Mary is your Mother; she will be your model." Quoted in *Une âme réparatrice. Madame Marie-Lucie Vrau, veuve de Monsieur Camille Feron-Vrau, 1839-1913* (Lille: Desclée, de Brouwer, 1914), p. 1.

[34] For example, in her *Journée chrétienne de la jeune fille* (Paris: Putois-Cretté, 1867), p. 71 and throughout her *Mois des serviteurs de Marie* (Paris: Putois-Cretté, 1863).

[35] For example, Mme Louis Cortyl, mentioned in de Backer, *Vie de Mme Van Der Meersch*, p. 271.

[36] Mme D., born in 1884, showed me her Enfants de Marie medal, which she kept with her at all times. She said that it was the most precious treasure of her life.

[37] See the letters of Mme B. in *Archives du Batut* in which "Enfant de Marie" or "E de M" always follows her signature.

[38] The notion of the "femme forte" does not seem to have a similar place in Protestant culture. In the Catholic Nord, however, women received praise for being strong. See, for example, such documents as a funeral card of Mme Pauline Fauchille-Prévost, 20 November 1902 which uses Biblical passages on the "femme forte" to describe Mme Fauchille-Prévost

during her lifetime (kindly communicated to me by her grandson, M. Marcel Decroix).

[39] I derive this interpretation of Mary's attractiveness to women from the commentaries of Bourdon. In addition, Marina Warner's *Alone of All Her Sex* (New York: Knopf, 1976) is helpful.

[40] Peter Cominos' "Innocent Femina Sensualis in Unconscious Conflict," in Martha Vicinus, ed., *Suffer and Be Still* (Bloomington: Indiana University Press, 1972) emphasizes this aspect of women's sexuality. I think there is more to be said for a strictly Freudian interpretation like that of Juliet Mitchell in her *Psychoanalysis and Feminism* (New York: Vintage, 1974).

[41] Baunard, *Mme Camille Feron-Vrau*, p. 23, quoting her diary of October 1872.

[42] Sigmund Freud, "Female Sexuality," in *The Standard Edition of the Complete Psychological Works of Sigmund Freud*, translated by James Strachey (London: Hogarth Press, 1953-1974), XXI, 225-243; and "The Dissolution of the Oedipus Complex," XIX, 173-179.

[43] Ibid., XXI, 17, 49.

[44] The Enfants de Marie sodality starts in various convents in the 1840s; the Archiconfrérie des mères chrétiennes, in 1849-1850 in Lille, and subsequently in other cities. Its numbers grew, in Lille, from a handful of women to more than 250 by 1875; see *L'Archiconfrérie des mères chrétiennes* (Lille: Lefort, 1875), a booklet found in BML Fonds Humbert, carton 36. On the various religiously oriented charity groups, see Chapter Six. The organization for the Perpetual Rosary was most active after 1870, and, as discussed below, the Ligue de la prière was started in the 1890s. Yves-Marie Hilaire's *Une chrétienté au XIXe siècle. La Vie religieuse des populations du diocèse d'Arras (1840-1914)*, 2 vols. (Villeneuve d'Ascq: Université de Lille III, 1977), cites a parallel movement toward the Church among women in the Pas de Calais. Hilaire's contention that this movement included women of all classes, and that the dichotomy existed between the sexes on every level, suggests that much work needs to be done on the faith and religious fervor of women in general. For lists of women's contributions to such organizations as the Oeuvre de Ste. Elisabeth de Hongrie, see *La Semaine religieuse de Cambrai*, from vol. I, 1866—.

[45] According to an interview with her daughter, Mme M., 18 and 25 March 1975.

[46] APSCL, "Conseila. Enfants de Marie." The members of the central committee also discussed ejecting from the group members who did the waltz. They settled for taking the offenders (mostly the unmarried members of the society) aside and cautioning them against the evils of the waltz.

[47] I have determined this by counting the children of women in the fertility study; the number of men choosing a religious vocation was less

than half the number of women. On the national movement of women, in contrast with men, into religious orders, see Claude Langlois, "Les Effectifs des congrégations féminines au XIXe siècle. De l'enquête statistique à l'histoire quantitative," *Revue d'histoire de l'église en France* 60 (January-June, 1974), 39-64.

⁴⁸ A few biographies of nuns from the Nord include Auguste Hamon, *Les Auxiliatrices des âmes du purgatoire*, 2 vols. (Paris: Beauchesne, 1919), on Eugénie Smet, who had many biographers; Albert Delplanque, *Ames de religieuses. La Mère Eulalie, religieuse de la Sainte-Union des Sacrés-Coeurs* (Lille: Desclée, De Brouwer, et Cie., 1925). On Marie Wallaert-Brame, see Foucart, *Jules Brame* and his *La Famille Brame* (n.p., n.d.); for Marie Toulemonde, *Dame St.-Albéric Toulemonde.*

⁴⁹ Interviews with Mme M., 18 and 25 March 1975.

⁵⁰ Pierre Daudruy-Dubois, *La Famille Charvet*, I, 50.

⁵¹ See Thomas, *Herminie de la Bassemoûturie*, pp. 164 ff., and *Louise Charvet. Enfant de Marie*, p. 8.

⁵² From my own study of women in the Nord who became nuns. For these 110 women, the median age at taking vows remained constant until after World War I, when it rose.

⁵³ Ibid.

⁵⁴ Various invitations to religious investitures may be found in BML Fonds Humbert, cartons 7 and 8, congrégations religieuses. Sermons preached at these ceremonies, as well as other notices that they took place, appear in *La Semaine religieuse de Cambrai.*

⁵⁵ BML Fonds Humbert contains clippings, small booklets, and memorabilia testifying to the vigor of the many women's orders in the Nord.

⁵⁶ For example, Mme Bonduel-Bayart, as recounted in [Mme E. Bonduel-Bayart], *Ernest Bonduel (1863-1928)* (Paris: Taffin-Lefort, 1931), p. 24. Marie Toulemonde's first verse was directed to Henri V: "Illustre descendant d'une vaillante race / Venez sauver la France . . ." found in *Dame St.-Albéric Toulemonde*, p. 54.

⁵⁷ See APSCL, "Conseila. Enfants de Marie," meetings of 17 October 1870, 13 March 1871, 22 May 1871 and 11 November 1881; and Louis Quarré-Reybourbon, *L'Eglise et la paroisse du Sacré-Coeur de Lille* (Lille: Lefebvre-Ducrocq, 1898). The church today gives no clue that it owes its existence to the gift of public peace during the Franco-Prussian War. However, alumnae of the boarding school maintain the church's history through an oral tradition. They were the first to point out to me the importance of their grandmothers and great-grandmothers in its founding, although the public record ignores their contribution.

⁵⁸ On the Perpetual Rosary, see BML Fonds Humbert, cartons 34 and 35.

⁵⁹ Masquelier, *Mme Paul Feron-Vrau*, pp. 101-107.

⁶⁰ Ibid., p. 160. See also the League's publication, *Echo de la ligue pa-*

triotique des françaises; and for the history of the League itself, see Emmanuel Barbier, *Histoire du catholicisme libéral et du catholicisme social en France. Du concile du Vatican à l'avènement de S. S. Benoit XV (1870-1914)*, 5 vols. (Bordeaux: Cadoret, 1924), II, 515-516; IV, 141-143; V, 416-425. On the development of the League nationally, but especially in Paris, see also clippings at the Bibliothèque Marguerite Durand and in AN F⁷ 13215, 13216, 13218.

[61] As is demonstrated, for example in David Pivar, *The Purity Crusade* (Westport, Conn.: Greenwood, 1973).

[62] Typical of the many sermons preached to Northern women are: *Souvenir de la retraite donnée par Monseigneur Mermillod aux Enfants de Marie. Mars 1868* (Lille: L. Danel, 1868); *Souvenir du 23 juillet 1874 aux Enfants de Marie du Sacré-Coeur de Lille* (Lille: L. Danel, 1874); Abbé Fichaux (almoner at the Bernardine pensionnat), *Manuel d'instruction chrétienne* (Lille: A. Taffin-Lefort, 1906); E. Francqueville, *La Famille et l'église catholique ou l'influence de Jésus-Christ, de l'église et de la grâce sur la société domestique* (Lille: Imprimerie de St. Augustin, 1882).

[63] ADN M 154/35, police reports on Catholic politics, 1881, 1882, 1891, 1892.

[64] *Souvenir de la retraite donnée par Monseigneur Mermillod*, p. 29, in which he says that the ignorance of women in matters of religion, particularly theology, is striking. They are generous and devoted, but have little rigor in their understanding of the principles of religion.

Six. Society: Charity versus Capitalism

[1] Letter from Mme Alexandre Coget-Desurmont to Mme Boud, 3 September 1867, quoted in Foucart, *La Famille Brame*, n.p.

[2] Interview with Mme D., June 1976.

[3] Masquelier, *Mme Paul Feron-Vrau*, p. 26.

[4] Dubly, *Le Caducée et le carquois*, passim.

[5] Lambert, *Quelques familles*, p. 649 ff.

[6] René Reubrez, *Annuaire des échos mondains et Lille-Sélect, Lille, Roubaix, Tourcoing, Armentières* (Lille, 1906), in which one can find women who refused to list visiting hours.

[7] ADN M 141/31, prefect's report on women scheduled to meet the Empress Eugénie, 1867. This is a precious record on some of the most prominent women in the Nord; it includes general indications about their fortunes, family prominence, their habits, and sometimes quarrels, such as that in the Brame family.

[8] Legrand, *La Femme du bourgeois de Lille*, pp. 6, 15-19.

[9] *Lettres d'Alfred Motte-Grimonprez*, letter to Joseph Gillet, 21 June 1873, II, 323.

[10] Interview with Mme M., 18 and 25 March 1975.

[11] Ibid.

[12] Hannezo, *Les Barrois*, n.p.

[13] A program for one of these evenings, more gala than the usual ones, may be found ibid.

[14] The bills for these lessons can be found in BML, Fonds Humbert, carton 39.

[15] See "Comptabilité ménagère," June 1854, for example. Other women were well known for their musical skill, especially Mme Scrive-Lisnard on the harp and Mme Delcourt on the guitar.

[16] As one can see from Motte-Grimonprez's account of his wife's preparations or by examining "Comptabilité ménagère," in which one can always tell when Mme S. was planning something extraordinary by the entries for extra cooks and serving people, as well as for food, cards, and new dishes.

[17] Many of these rules can be found in Bourdon, *Politesse et savoir-vivre*, pp. 42-60 and passim.

[18] One may find evidence of the importance of reputation in novels written by the women of the Nord (see Chapter Eight), and ibid., p. 119: "Be attentive with older women, for it is they who determine the reputation of young people."

[19] See Dubly, *Le Caducée et le carquois*, passim. Mme Barrois regularly combined pleasure and business visits.

[20] "Comptabilité ménagère," which enumerates the cost of renting a *vinaigrette* or other means of transportation for the visit, and its purpose.

[21] Bourdon's *Politesse et savoir-vivre*, pp. 42-44, lists the occasions on which one owed visits. Mme R. in interviews, June and July 1976, gave almost the same list of occasions.

[22] Mme M. provided this account of what happened during a typical visit, and estimated the number of visits a woman would make on a typical afternoon, 18 and 25 March 1975.

[23] Official reports on charity in the Nord can be found in ADN X, Bienfaisance; in AMD Q, Bienfaisance; in AMR M, Bienfaisance. Among the many books on both public and private charitable institutions in the Nord one may consult Alfred Renouard, *Exposition universelle de 1889. Les Institutions ouvrières et sociales du département du Nord* (Lille: L. Danel, 1889); *Lille et la région du Nord en 1909*; A. Bologne, *L'Orphélinat de Don Bosco* (Lille, 1903); François Chon, *Notice historique sur la Société de Saint Vincent de Paul à Lille* (Lille: Lefort, 1883); A. Dassonville, *Quatre allocutions aux dames de la Croix-Rouge (1910-1911)* (Lille: La Croix du Nord, 1911); Chrétien Dehaisnes, *L'Oeuvre des layettes de la maternité Ste. Anne* (Lille: Lefort, 1890); Paul Delemer, *L'Assistance charitable à Lille* (Lille: René Giard, 1910); Descamps, *Lille, un coup d'oeil sur son agrandissement, ses institutions, ses industries*; Feron-Vrau, *Quarante ans d'action catholique*; J.-B. Godey, *Étude sur les crèches pour les petits*

enfants des ouvriers de Roubaix dédiée à Madame Constantin Descat
(Roubaix: A. Lesguillon, 1868); Aimé Houzé de l'Aulnoit, *Des comités
libres de charité* (Lille: Lefebvre-Ducrocq, 1881) and *Des avantages de la
création des caisses de secours en faveur des femmes nouvellement accouchées* (Lille: L. Danel, 1874); A. Huard, *Edouard Lefort* (Lille: A. Taffin-
Lefort, 1893); Edmond Leleu, *La Caisse des écoles de Lille, 1883-1921*
(Lille: Dhoossche, 1921); Charles Liagre, *Loos au XIXᵉ siècle* (Lille: Le-
febvre-Ducrocq, 1899); *Manuel des oeuvres catholiques de Lille* (Lille:
Bérgès, n.d.); *Notice sur Mlle Julie Flamen* (Lille: Ducolombier, 1876);
Charles Roussel-Defontaine, *Histoire de Tourcoing* (Lille: E. Vanaeckere,
1855); *Salles d'asile de Lille, 1864* (Lille: L. Danel, 1864); Louis Théry,
Des fondations charitables à Lille (Lyon: X. Jevain, 1901); Jules Brenne,
Lomme au temps des bourgeois (Paris: André Bomie, 1960); *Annales de
la charité; La Semaine religieuse du Diocèse de Cambrai*; Gabriel Piérard,
*La Croix-rouge française dans l'arrondisement de Valenciennes de 1870
à nos jours* (Valenciennes: Comité de Valenciennes, 1963); Pierrard, *La
Vie ouvrière*; Mme Jacques Prouvost, "La Femme à travers l'histoire de
Roubaix" (unpublished manuscript). There are also numerous notices of
individual philanthropists and many indications of private charity in the
genealogies listed in the bibliography.

[24] The last indication of official *dames de charité* for parishes that I have
found appears in *Souvenirs à l'usage des habitans de Douai* (Douai: Ceret-
Carpentier, 1843), p. 49, which lists those of 1829.

[25] Raymond de Bertrand, "Faits et usages des Flamands de France,"
Bulletin de l'Union Faulconnier IX (1906), 306, mentions that three or
four women from high society still held those "days" for the poor on the
first Wednesday or Friday of the month at the beginning of the twentieth
century in Dunkerque.

[26] Masquelier, *Mme Paul Feron-Vrau*, pp. 21 and 25.

[27] Such references to the feminine nature of charity may be found in
such disparate sources as *Semaine religieuse de Cambrai*, supplement,
1897, or Mme Paul Grendel [Julia Bécour], "Les Filles-mères," *Reveil du
Nord*, 30-31 May 1897.

[28] ADN M 222/370, Société de charité maternelle (police records).

[29] The following discussion focuses on the major organizations in the
Nord, and omits smaller or ephemeral ones such as the Société du prêt
du linge, the Oeuvre des orphélins de la guerre, the Croix-rouge (which
became a major organization only in the twentieth century), and the Société de Saint Vincent de Paul. The latter began as a male organization
to regularize poor visiting, and quickly developed parallel women's groups.
Although still in existence in the early twentieth century, the society's
women's branches seemed more active than the men's, and also did a good
deal of work for the men, especially in matters of fund raising. Records
of all these organizations may be found in ADN, Série X.

[30] Lists of members for certain societies may be found in ADN X 58/1-9, Crèches; ADN X 59/1-10, Société de charité maternelle; ADN M 222/527, Société de Saint Vincent de Paul, Dames, 1861; AMD Q 2/12 Loteries de bienfaisance 1861-1875. For Lille, where the largest number of women participated, see *Salles d'asile de Lille. 1864*, and *Société de charité maternelle de Lille* (Lille: L. Danel, 1884), a pamphlet found in vol. 73 of the collection *Miscellanea insulensia* of the Université catholique de Lille.

[31] One can confirm this by examining the departmental archives records of charity and social welfare programs or, in the case of Lille, by looking at Delemer, *L'Assistance charitable à Lille* for early twentieth-century differences.

[32] The best source on the Société de charité maternelle is ADN X 59/1-10 and ADN M 222/370, which contain annual reports of the organizations, their bylaws, and all communication with government officials. See also *Société de charité maternelle de Lille*; Jules Duthil, "Le Bazar de la maternité," in *Au jour le jour* (Lille: Imprimerie du *Nouveliste*, 1897), pp. 301-309, 401-406; and AMD Q 2/14-22, Société de charité maternelle, 1861-1890.

[33] ADN X 59/2, Société de charité maternelle, Lille.

[34] Brenne, *Lomme au temps des bourgeois*, p. 108.

[35] See ADN X 59/2, Société de charité maternelle, Comptes, subsides 1868-1883, especially the letter of Mme Mabille, President of Valenciennes' organization, in which she writes of distributing beds and bedding "aux familles que nous visitons et dont le couchage laissait tant à desirer; soit à cause du mélange des sexes; soit à cause du nombre d'enfants couchant tous, dans un seul et même lit." According to the statutes of the Maubeuge society, the *dames patronnesses* were officially charged "à la séparation des sexes dans le couchage des enfants, surtout arrivés à un certain âge et à leur séparation d'avec leurs parents." ADN X 59/8, Maubeuge, Statuts.

[36] See ADN X 59/1-10, which contains these stipulations in the bylaws of the various societies.

[37] Mathilde Bourdon, *La Charité en action* (Lille: L. Lefort, 1864), p. 73.

[38] See ADN X 59/1-10 for these stipulations in the bylaws of the various societies.

[39] Bourdon, *La Charité en action*, p. 73.

[40] For the general history of the *salles d'asile*, later called *écoles maternelles*, see Pauline Kergomard, *Ecoles maternelles de 1837 jusqu'en 1910, aperçu rapide* (Paris: Librairie classique Fernand Nathan, 1910); Emile Gossot, *Les Salles d'asile en France et leur fondateur Denys Cochin* (Paris: Didier, 1884). On their progress in various cities, see Henry Cochin, *Lamartine et la Flandre* (Paris: Plon, 1912), p. 294; de Bertrand, "Faits et usages des Flamands de France," *Bulletin de l'Union Faulconnier* IX, 303; *Salles d'asile de Lille, 1864*; Pierrard, *La Vie ouvrière*, pp. 333-336; and ADN Series M and T (Archives du Rectorat).

257

[41] ADN M 141/29, Salles d'asile, 1867.

[42] *Salles d'asile de Lille, 1864,* pp. 3-9, contains these rules as well as others governing the work of the *dames patronnesses.*

[43] Mathilde Bourdon recounts some of these tales in her *La Charité en action,* pp. 78-82.

[44] On the *crèches* in these cities the best source is ADN X 58/1-9. For the *crèches* in Roubaix, see Godey, *Etude sur les crèches de Roubaix* and AMR M IIe (1-2); in Douai, AMD Q 5/11; in Lille see the collection of pamphlets and clippings in BML Fonds Humbert, carton 3.

[45] Among other works on the history of *crèches* in France, I have consulted Jean-Baptiste Desplace, "De l'institution des crèches," *Annales de la charité,* Nouvelle série IV (January-June 1863), 165-175; and *Provision Made for Children under Compulsory School Age in Belgium, France, Germany, and Switzerland* (London: Wyman and Sons, 1909).

[46] This story has been pieced together from the assortment of material found in BML Fonds Humbert, carton 3. One can also consult AN F^15 3813 for official reports on the nurseries.

[47] For the story of Mme Wallaert-Descamps' negotiations with the city fathers of Lille, see *LCMPV,* meetings of 18 December 1869, pp. 234-235; 5 July 1870, pp. 286-287; 19 July 1870, pp. 336-342; 2 August 1870, pp. 358-363. Any of these sessions of the municipal council will show the resistance Mme Wallaert encountered when she attempted to found the *crèches.* Her efforts involved changing the use of money willed to the city by a member of the Wallaert family from the city council's project of a fund for workmen's compensation to the *crèches.* The history of the founding and of the original controversy is briefly reiterated in *LCMPV* meeting of 2 October 1896, when the new socialist municipal government again proposed creating a public day-care center.

[48] ADN X 57/4, Règlement de la journée dans les crèches de Lille.

[49] The male *patronage* has recently received attention in Pierrard, *La Vie ouvrière,* pp. 386-392, 404-412; and earlier in C. de Nicolay, *Madame la Comtesse de Grandville* (Lille: Lefort, 1867). On the various *ouvroirs* and *patronages* in the Nord, see ADN X 3/2, Etablissements d'assistance privés. Statistique 1891; AMD Q 2/13, Patronages des jeunes filles apprenties; H. Desmarchelier, *Histoire du décanat de la Madeleine de Lille (1229-1892)* (Lille: L. Quarré, 1892), pp. 299-310; *A la mémoire de Madame Delannoy-Desnoulez, Présidente de la conférence de la Société de Saint Vincent de Paul, du patronage des jeunes filles et de la salle d'asile de Sainte Catherine* (Lille: Imprimerie St. Augustin, n.d.). Pierrard suggests that the male *patronages* were not successful in attracting factory workers, but rather appealed to social-climbing shop clerks and the like. The female *patronages,* according to membership figures, attracted hundreds of young women, but the one with the largest membership was located in the parish of the Feron-Vrau factory. The Vraus and Feron-

Vraus often made participation in activities such as the *patronage* a condition of employment. We can also assume that the prizes instituted after the *patronages* had been in effect for several years were designed to keep young women active until they married. In Douai, such rewards were substantial, amounting to 100 francs deposited in a savings account.

⁵⁰ Charles Bernard, *Quelques mots en faveur du patronage des jeunes ouvrières prononcés en église Ste. Catherine de Lille* (Lille: Lefort, 1865).

⁵¹ Samples of this letter, whose phrasing remained the same from the 1870s to the 1890s, may be found in BML Fonds Humbert, carton 2, l'oeuvre des crèches. Mme Humbert was on the central committee for the day-care centers and served as treasurer, at least in the years 1879 and 1884.

⁵² Julia Bécour was foremost among them. See her caricature of the *dame patronnesse* in the character Clothilde in *Une heure d'oubli*.

⁵³ For the correspondence involved in awarding medals to leaders of the various societies, see ADN M 141/29, 34. Such ceremonies did detract from charitable efforts for the poor, as the letter from Mme Elise Delelis of Dunkerque demonstrates. She asked the prefect's wife for advice on what to wear to the reception, "la robe montante" or "la robe décolletée." But this was the other side of *caritas*: similar and correct clothing showed the unity of all upper-class women.

⁵⁴ ADN, Série X, besides providing statistics on the amount of aid distributed by the societies and the number of women and children assisted, gives indications of these social aspects of charity. For a description of one charity bazaar, see Duthil, "Le Bazar de la maternité," *Au jour le jour*, pp. 401-405.

⁵⁵ *La Révérende Mère Marie de la Providence, fondatrice de la société des auxiliatrices des âmes du purgatoire (1825-1871)* (Paris: J. Gabalda, 1919); Masquelier, *Mme Paul Feron-Vrau; Louise Charvet, Enfant de Marie, 1848-1877; Madame Théodore Aronio de Romblay. Pieux Souvenir*; "Mme Emile Delesalle," *Annales de l'archiconfrérie des mères chrétiennes* 4 (July 1896), 450-452; "Mme Thiriez-Dupont," *Dépêche du Nord*, 18 January 1884; Thomas, *Herminie de la Bassemoûturie*. These are just a few examples of books, pamphlets, and obituaries written after the deaths of Northern women.

⁵⁶ *Dépêche du Nord*, 18 January 1884.

⁵⁷ "Mme Emile Delesalle," *Annales de l'archiconfrérie des mères chrétiennes*, 451-452.

⁵⁸ See Aimé Houzé de l'Aulnoit, *Les Ecoles d'arts et métiers et l'orphélinat de Saint-Gabriel à Lille. Rapport au Congrès des Catholiques du Nord et du Pas de Calais, novembre 1884* (Lille: Lefebvre-Ducrocq, 1885). According to Renouard and Moy, *Les Institutions ouvrières et sociales du département du Nord*, p. 133, more than four hundred women were *dames patronnesses* of the orphanage.

[59] Masquelier, *Mme Paul Feron-Vrau*, p. 131, quoting a letter from Germaine Feron-Vrau in which she paid a convent to provide work for an unemployed carpenter.

[60] See, for example, Julia Bécour, *Fée Mab* (Paris: Société d'éditions littéraires, 1898).

[61] Mathilde Bourdon, *Marthe Blondel ou l'ouvrière de fabrique* (Paris: Putois-Cretté, 1863), p. iii.

[62] See, for example, her *Le Foyer* (Lille: Lefort, 1861), a story about the Comte de Charrière and his manor, where "master and servants lived together in a close union" and where "feudalism was nothing else than the legitimate and gentle authority of a father over the children" (pp. 6-7).

[63] *Dame St. Albéric Toulemonde*, p. 54.

[64] Police reports of these occasions took care to note if women attended, and those from the bourgeoisie usually did. See, for example, ADN M 154/14 on the mass for the soul of the Comte de Chambord, where "about five hundred people attended, mostly women and priests."

[65] The pronouncement on parliamentary government comes from Mathilde Bourdon, *Le Divorce* (Paris: C. Dillet, 1865), p. 16.

[66] One of the most disturbing charges against the *dames patronnesses* is found in a series of newspaper clippings found in ADN 1T 123/4. The article says that Mme S. gave a first communion dress to the daughter of a worker. When she discovered that the worker was not going to support the candidacy of her brother-in-law on the Catholic ticket, she demanded the dress be returned.

[67] A good part of this story can be found in Bernard Ménager, *La Laïcisation des écoles communales dans le département du Nord, 1879-1899* (Lille: Université des sciences humaines, des lettres et des arts, 1971). Ménager cites the relative lack of success in secularizing women's education.

[68] In fact, in Lille their withdrawal seemed to cause not the slightest dissatisfaction among city officials, who immediately appropriated 20,000 francs to cover the costs of providing school children with clothing—only one of the tasks of the *dames patronnesses*. See *LCMPV*, Meeting of 21 July 1882, pp. 686-687.

[69] On the new legislation and organization of the *salles d'asile*, see Albert Durand, *La Législation des écoles maternelles et des écoles primaires* (Paris: Ract et Falquet, 1882), pp. xxxii and 155, Decree of 21 August 1881, Article 10.

[70] Desmarchelier, *La Madeleine*, pp. 325-326.

[71] Quoted ibid.

[72] J. Dewez, *Histoire de la paroisse de St. André à Lille* (Lille: Nuez, 1899), p. 241.

[73] For a list of Catholic institutions in the Nord, see *Manuel des oeuvres catholiques de Lille* (Lille: Bergès, n.d.).

74 For the full debate in Lille, see *LCMPV*, Meeting of 20 March 1883, pp. 279-286.

75 On the problems of all Northern day-care centers with the departmental and national government because of their "lack of democratic principles," but especially because of their clericalism, see ADN X 57/5-8. The most fascinating parts of these files are the letters from Minister of the Interior Ernst Constans to the ladies, in which he discusses baby bottles and makes this the grounds for cutting their subsidies. In this, as in many other cases, Constans lived up to his reputation as the hatchet man of the Third Republic. The real grounds may be found in the reports of the inspector of the day-care centers to the Prefect.

76 See *Crèches de Lille* (Lille: Danel, 1871, 1873, and 1884) (pamphlets found in BML Fonds Humbert, carton 2, l'oeuvre des crèches); *Salles d'asile de Lille*; and *Société de charité maternelle de Lille* for membership lists.

77 These charges appear, for Lille, in *LCMPV*, Meeting of 21 December 1883, pp. 437-455, and for other cities in the Nord, ADN X 59/3, 8, and 10, Société de charité maternelle.

78 See letters ibid. Mme Berteau of Maubeuge said that the society would not accept the conseil général's subsidy if it meant that civil marriages would have to be recognized, letter of 11 October 1890. Mme Mabille of Valenciennes in a letter of 4 June 1888 said that the society would not eliminate the clause demanding religious marriages because it would add too large a number of women to its rolls.

79 See the lists of these organizations found in ADN Série M.

80 See ADN M 222/385, police report and *Statuts de la Société du denier des écoles laïques*. See also, for Lille, Edmond Leleu, *La Caisse des écoles de Lille, 1883-1921* (Lille: M. Dhoossche 1921), pp. 16-17, which describes an attempt to create new women's committees for supervising lunch programs. The proposal died for lack of support.

81 See *Conseil général du département du Nord session d'août 1884. Protection des enfants du premier âge. Rapport général de l'Inspecteur des enfants assistés* (Lille: L. Danel, 1884); ADN X 48/14, Société pour la protection des enfants en bas âge; AMD 5/15, 19, 20-21, Enfants assistés.

82 *LCMPV*, meetings of 27 July 1883, pp. 15-16, and 28 December 1883, p. 448.

83 Bécour's bitter account of the organization and of her dealings with male politicians appears in a long article under her pseudonym, Mme Paul Grendel, "Les Filles-mères," *Reveil du Nord*, 30-31 May 1897.

84 *LCMPV*, meeting of 23 November 1894. In that budget Article 96, which was the allocation for the committee, disappeared in favor of Article 95 to provide funds for the deaf, dumb, and blind. No record of any debate on the reallocation has been preserved.

85 On this organization, see ADN X 61/13, Commission extra-municipale

de la protection de la première enfance; and Delemer, *L'Assistance charitable*, p. 14.

⁸⁶ The Red Cross grew in importance among upper-class women in the twentieth century. See Maxime du Camp, *La Croix-rouge de France* (Paris: Crété, 1892); Piérard, *La Croix-rouge française dans l'arrondisement de Valenciennes*; Dassonville, *Quatre Allocutions aux dames de la croix-rouge*, which stresses the religious aspect of the organization.

Seven. Education: Innocence versus Enlightenment

¹ Masquelier, *Mme Paul Feron-Vrau*, pp. 8-32.

² *Dame St. Albéric Toulemonde*, p. 30.

³ *Maison d'éducation dirigée par les Dames Bernardines d'Esquermes à Lille* (Lille: Lefort, 1868), a booklet of the school's regulations, found in BML Fonds Humbert, carton 39.

⁴ Interview with Mme D., 27 May 1976.

⁵ Interviews with alumnae of Sacré-Coeur, 12 March 1974. Many of these alumnae were born around the turn of the century, a few even before that. These particular reports are corroborated in *Dame St. Albéric Toulemonde*, p. 30, in an interview with Mme D., 27 May 1976, and elsewhere.

⁶ See, for example, Toulemonde, *Naissance d'une métropole*, p. 182; Cuvelier-Verley, *Généalogie de la famille Cuvelier*, pp. 21-22; or Motte, *Les Motte*, p. 66.

⁷ See, for example, an account of the education of Octavie Smet, daughter of the mayor of Lille in 1830, in Lethierry d'Ennequin, *Une famille bourgeoise de Lille, ses alliances, ses seigneuries (1610-1930)* (Lille: Mercure de Flandre, 1930), p. 195-196.

⁸ Baunard, *Madame Camille Feron-Vrau*, p. 6.

⁹ Isoré, "Bourgeoises de Bergues en 1830," pp. 238-241.

¹⁰ On the Pensionnat Dames Delecourt see ADN 1T 122/4, which includes a floor plan of the establishment in 1856. On its later troubles, see *LCMPV*, meeting of 12 November 1877, p. 317.

¹¹ On the Bernardines, see ADN 6V/83; *Maison d'éducation dirigée par les Dames Bernardines; Fête du huitième centenaire de la naissance de Saint Bernard 1091-1891. Monastère de Notre-Dame de la Plaine, 20 août 1891*, found in *Miscellanea insulensea*, vol. 43. The biography of *Dame St. Albéric Toulemonde* is helpful for life at the boarding school.

¹² Motte, *Les Motte*, pp. 65-66.

¹³ On Sacré-Coeur, see ADN 6V/159; Louis Baunard, *Histoire de Madame Barat, fondatrice de la Société du Sacré-Coeur de Jésus*, 2 vols. (Paris: Poussielgue, 1876); Nicolay, *Madame la Comtesse de Grandville; Pensionnat des religieuses du Sacré-Coeur de Jésus, rue Royale, 66, à Lille, Prospectus* (Lille: Lefort, 1868). This last pamphlet is found in BML Fonds

Humbert, carton 39, which contains all Gabrielle Humbert's report cards and bills from the institution, as well as other clippings and memorabilia.

[14] See ADN 6V/182-185; Delplanque, *La Mère Eulalie. Religieuse de la Sainte-Union des Sacrés-Coeurs.*

[15] See *Souvenir de la bénédiction de la première pierre du nouvel établissement des dames de St. Maur* (Lille: Lefebvre-Ducrocq, 1869); *Souvenir du jubilé de vingt-cinq ans des dames de St. Maur, célébré à la Madeleine-les-Lille, le 17 juin 1880* (Lille: Lefebvre-Ducrocq, 1880).

[16] The picture can be found in *Dame St. Albéric Toulemonde*, p. 56.

[17] Abbé Deroubaix, quoted in *Souvenir du jubilé des dames de Saint-Maur*, pp. 6-8.

[18] The curriculum as well as the books used in courses may be found in ADN 2 T 937/2 and 1T 124/7. One can also look at Gabrielle Humbert's report card for a more complete list of categories in which students were graded, such as "maintien," "langage," "égards et politesse," "ordre et économie," BML Fonds Humbert, carton 39.

[19] Descriptions of these days are found in many sources, but my main source was interviews with alumnae of Sacré-Coeur de Lille, 12 March 1974.

[20] *Dame St. Albéric Toulemonde*, p. 60.

[21] Interview with alumnae of Sacré-Coeur de Lille, 12 March 1974.

[22] François de Salignac Fénelon, *L'Education des filles* (Paris: Librairie des bibliophiles, 1885), pp. 125-127. Fénelon was read, adhered to, and referred to by the women of the Nord and by educational authorities.

[23] This is a point made in Gaston Coirault, *Les Cinquante premières années de l'enseignement secondaire féminin 1880-1930* (Tours: Arrault, 1940), not only for convent schools, which occasionally taught a bit of Latin for religious purposes, but especially under the reformed system that was supposed to upgrade women's education while scrupulously avoiding the addition of Latin.

[24] The books mentioned below are those listed time and again not only in archival sources and on the list of approved books by the Maisons d'éducation chrétienne; they are those most remembered by women who spoke about their school days in interviews.

[25] *Maison d'éducation dirigée par les Dames Bernardines*, unpaginated.

[26] Interview with alumnae of Sacré-Coeur de Lille, 12 March 1974.

[27] *Dame St. Albéric Toulemonde*, p. 136, quoting her journal.

[28] For the ceremonies of prize days see *Fête du huitième centenaire de la naissance de Saint Bernard, 1891*; a program for a prize day at the Bernardine *pensionnat*, 1895, found in BML Fonds Humbert, carton 8; *Distribution des prix au pensionnat de Mademoiselle Brissez, à Lille, le 18 août 1853* (Lille: Blocquel-Castiaux, 1853), found in *Miscellanea insulensea*, vol. 68. Other information on the less public ceremonies comes from interviews with alumnae of Sacré-Coeur de Lille, 12 March 1974.

[29] Baunard, *Histoire de Madame Barat*, p. 409.

[30] Mathilde Bourdon wrote a book with this title (Paris: P. Lethielleux, 1868) and dedicated it to the mother superior of the Bernardines. But most women of the Nord I interviewed shared this sentiment about their school years.

[31] AN F[19] 3972, "Instructions complémentaires pour la loi du 10 avril 1867, en ce qui concerne l'enseignement secondaire des filles," 30 October 1867.

[32] Ibid., Rapport de l'association de l'enseignement secondaire des jeunes filles.

[33] Jules Michelet, *Du prêtre, de la femme, et de la famille* (Paris: Hachette, 1845).

[34] Jules Simon, "L'Enseignement primaire des filles en 1864," *Revue des deux mondes* 52 (15 August 1864), 948-968.

[35] AN F[1] 8755, report from Fleury, rector of the Academy of Douai to the Minister of Education, 15 January 1869; and *LCMPV*, Meeting of 10 July 1868, Cours d'instruction secondaire et création d'une école primaire supérieure pour les filles, Rapport au nom de la commission. The latter document shows the municipal council of Lille refusing at first to institute the courses. Later they acquiesced because of a greater demand.

[36] See articles in *Progrès du Nord*, 12 August 1867, 19 November 1867, 23 November 1867, 19 December 1867, 30 January 1868, 16 April 1868, 19 May 1868, 19 June 1868, and 20 January 1869, all of them favorable to Duruy's position. The last article announces the institution of courses.

[37] Recounting the troubles instituting the courses, the report from M. de Montigny in AN F[19] 8755 describes the cause (and subsequent ones) as follows: "There was, among the bourgeoisie, movement toward the école supérieure [for girls], but at all times many mothers resisted."

[38] Destombes, *Vie de son Eminence Le Cardinal Régnier, Archevêque de Cambrai*, II, 186. The Archbishop's messages were widely distributed in *La Semaine religieuse de Cambrai*, which added its own attacks on the courses.

[39] *Souvenir de la retraite donnée par Monseigneur Mermillod aux enfants de Marie. Mars 1868.*

[40] *La Femme chrétienne et française. Dernière réponse à M. Duruy et à ses défenseurs* (Paris: Duniol, 1868); *La Femme studieuse* (Paris: Duniol, 1869). Both were translated into English.

[41] See Coirault, *Les Cinquante premières années de l'enseignement secondaire féminin 1880-1930*; Paul Rousselot, *Histoire de l'éducation des femmes en France*, 2 vols. (Paris: Didier, 1883); Mona Ozouf, *L'Ecole, l'église et la République, 1871-1914* (Paris: Colin, 1963); and Fénelon Gibon, *L'Enseignement secondaire féminin* (Paris: Société générale d'éducation et d'enseignement, 1920).

[42] On the history of the Institut (then collège, then lycée) Fénelon see

LCMPV, meetings of 16 August 1876, 12 May 1877, 5 September 1877, 18 August 1882, 19 October 1883; and ADN 2T (Archives du rectorat), 935-937. These contain public debates, curriculum matters, accounts of internal problems, personnel matters, and lists of students.

[43] *LCMPV*, meeting of 12 May 1977.

[44] Ludovic Carrau, *De l'éducation. Précis de moral pratique* (Paris: Alcide Picard et Kaan, 1888), pp. 1-78.

[45] ADN 2T 936, liste nominative, Collège Fénelon, 1885-1886 (the series contains other such lists); and AN F^{19} 14185, which breaks down the professional background of girls' lycées for each city in the country.

[46] ADN 2T 935. This was the interpretation given by the inspector to the rector of the academy in a letter of 7 June 1884 on the problems of declining enrollment due to disciplinary troubles. The inspector added that if the teachers were from the same class as the students, they would not be working.

[47] ADN 2T 937 (2), letter from the director, Collège Fénelon, to the inspector, 13 August 1892. A municipal council meeting of 16 March 1897 centered on the continuing problem of students at Fénelon praying to the Virgin, pp. 226-227.

[48] See, for example, Louis Salembier, *Lettres sur les examens de jeunes filles* (Lille: B. Bergès, 1884).

[49] These arguments and criticisms, which follow Dupanloup's closely, can be found, among other places, in the diocesan newspaper, *La Semaine religieuse de Cambrai*. Criticisms notwithstanding, in the midst of the controversy the convents took it upon themselves to strengthen their programs. They did this by introducing expurgated versions of hitherto distasteful authors such as Voltaire, and by adding new courses, such as psychology. The latter, as far as I can tell from reading texts by such authors as Salembier (who instructed Northern girls), was the old "morale" reworked.

[50] *APSCL*, "Conseila. Enfants de Marie du Sacré-Coeur," meeting of 15 July 1880.

[51] *Souvenir des dames de Saint Maur*, pp. 9-10

[52] See, for example, *ASJPC*, "Diaire de l'archiconfrérie des mères chrétiennes," meeting of 30 April 1880, containing this notice: "Christian mothers, so rightly alarmed for the spiritual health of their children . . . are invited most urgently to multiply their visits to the Holy Sacrament and their hours of adoration."

[53] See ADN 6V/83, 159, 182-185.

[54] The story appears in Harvey Goldberg's *The Life of Jean Jaurès* (Madison: University of Wisconsin Press, 1962).

[55] See Lucien Detrez, *Le Palais épiscopal de Lille* (Lille: Raoust, 1938), p. 91, for other people involved in the consortium.

[56] Interview with Mme L., 24 May 1976.

Eight. The Domestic Myth

[1] The most complete list of Bourdon's approximately two hundred works is found in the catalogue of the Bibliothèque nationale, and Hippolyte Verly, *Essai de biographie lilloise contemporaine. 1800-1869* (Lille: Leleu, 1869), pp. 23-25, gives a sketch of her life. Obituaries in the *Echo du Nord*, 27 December 1888; Jules Duthil *Au jour le jour*, pp. 444-445; and *Le Progrès du Nord*, 28 December 1888, reveal the general esteem with which she was viewed by the community. From archival sources one can find various organizations to which Bourdon belonged, where she lived in Lille, and information about her second husband: BML Fonds Humbert, carton 1 Biographie; ADN M 222/527 Société de St. Vincent de Paul, Section des dames; *Salles d'asile de Lille. 1864*, p. 21. According to the material found in Fonds Humbert, Hercule Bourdon began his career as a St. Simonian and later converted to Catholicism. This suggests that Bourdon not only saw the problems of male indifference to religion in other families in the Nord, but that she experienced it in her own, and was able to effect a conversion. See also an important local review of her work by Géry Legrand, future mayor of Lille, in "Le Roman catholique, lettre à Mme Bourdon (Mathilde Froment)" *La Revue du Mois*, 1(July 1861): 371-380. Bourdon's work was always reviewed in national periodicals.

Biographical information on Julia Bécour can be found in *Les Diction-naires départementaux, Nord* (Paris: 1893); *Souvenir 1840-1917 sur la tombe de Madame Bécour le 19 juillet 1917* (Lille: Delemar et Dubar, 1917); on her charitable activities see Paul Delemer, *L'Assistance chari-table*, p. 14; and ADN X 61/13 Oeuvre des mères abandonées. Several notices about Bécour and her books are located in BML Fonds Humbert.

The most comprehensive studies of De Gaulle are the brief notices in works on her famous grandson. See Georges Cattui, *De Gaulle* (Porrentruy: Aux Portes de la France, 1944); Paul-Marie de la Gorce, *De Gaulle entre deux mondes* (Paris: Fayard, 1964); and Brian Crozier, *De Gaulle* (New York: Scribner's, 1973).

[2] For the theoretical underpinnings of this chapter I have relied heavily on Ian Watt, *The Rise of the Novel: Studies in Defoe, Richardson and Fielding* (Berkeley and Los Angeles: University of California Press, 1964); Leslie Fiedler, *Love and Death in the American Novel* (New York: Stein and Day, 1966); Kenneth Burke, *A Grammar of Motives* (New York: Pren-tice-Hall, 1954) and Kenneth Burke, *A Rhetoric of Motives* (New York: Braziller, 1955); the works of Northrop Frye and Ernest Cassirer; and Elaine Showalter, *A Literature of Their Own* (Princeton: Princeton Uni-versity Press, 1977).

[3] Paris: Ambroise Bray, 1862, p. 71.

[4] Paris: Blériot, 1866, p. 82.

[5] Lille: Ch. Tallandier et Gaujac, 1891, p. 5.

[6] Baltimore: Kelly, Piet and Co., 1876, p. 1.
[7] Paris: Gaume frères, 1838, p. 54.
[8] New York: Catholic Publication Society, 1875, p. 4.
[9] Bourdon, *Femme et mari*, p. 123.
[10] Ibid., p. 122.
[11] Paris: Société d'éditions littéraires, 1898, p. 180.

Bibliography

Archival Sources

Archives départementales du Nord

Série M—Police
M 132/17-18 Notables
M 141/28-33 Voyage de l'empereur et de l'impératrice à
  Lille, 1867
M 153/18bis Assemblée générale des Catholiques du
  Nord et du Pas de Calais
M 154/13-16 Fêtes royalistes variées
M 154/35 Politique catholique
M 217/1-6 Patronages et cercles
M 222/370 Société de charité maternelle
M 222/376 Société de St. Vincent de Paul, Section des
  dames
M 222/385 Société du denier des écoles laïques
M 222/527 Société de St. Vincent de Paul, Section des
  dames
M 222/539 Salon des négociants
M 222/773 Société d'éducation et d'enseignement
M 222/777 Ligue de l'enseignement
M 222/779 Société laïque des amis de l'enfance de
  Lille-Vauban
M 551/7 Prêts à l'industrie (1861-1869)
M 551/8 Faillites
M 557/5 Expositions
M 613/1 Contraventions de la loi de 1841

Série 1T—Instruction publique

1T 30/14 Cours d'instruction secondaire pour les jeunes filles. 1869.

1T 30/16 Revue d'enseignement des femmes

1T 30/17 Pensionnat secondaire. Demandes d'ouverture et renseignements

1T 116/11 Comité de patronage. Salles d'asile

1T 122/4 Ouvertures de pensionnat. 1830-1870

1T 123/2-9 Enseignement libre

1T 124/7 Ouverture de l'école primaire libre

1T 124/15 Pensionnats libres

1T 124/16 Salles d'asile

Série 2T—Archives du rectorat
2T 935 Collège Fénelon. 1879-1884
2T 937 (1-2) Collège Fénelon

Serie V—Congrégations
6V 83 Dames Bernardines
6V 159 Dames du Sacré-Coeur de Jésus

Serie X—Bienfaisance
X 3/2 Etablissements d'assistance privés. 1890

X 3/3 Etablissements du Département du Nord ayant un charactère charitable, reconnus d'utilité publique au cours de XIXe siècle. Renseignement statistique 1899

X 3/4 Etablissements privés. 1905

X 48/14 Enfants en bas âge

X 57/3-8 Société des crèches

X 58/1-9 Crèches

X 59/1-9 Société de charité maternelle

X 61/9 Oeuvre des orphélins de la guerre

X 61/10 Office central lillois des institutions sociales et charitables

X 61/11 Assistance maternelle et infantile

X 61/15 Commission extra-municipale de la protection de la première enfance

X 61/16 Fédération nationale des oeuvres de protection
de la maternité et de l'enfance
X 79/1 Maternité Boucicaut

Archives nationales de France

F¹⁵ (Hospices et secours) 3813 Crèches. Société de
charité maternelle
F¹⁷ (Instruction publique) 8755 Cours secondaire; 8775
Institut Fénelon; 10882; 12434²; 13940 Reforme de
l'enseignement, 1884-1904; 14185 Population
scolaire.
F¹⁹ (Cultes) 3971; 3972
F²¹ (Monuments publiques) 1202 Théâtre de Lille

Archives municipales de Douai
Q 2/11-22 Bienfaisance
Q 5/11 Rapport á la Parfaite Union sur la crèche
Q 5/15-21 Enfants assistés

Archives municipales de Roubaix
M II F Maternité Boucicaut
M IIᵉ (1-2) Crèches
F II ga Prud'hommes. Fabrique de Roubaix
F II gb 1 Prud'hommes—Registre de déliberations
F II ge 4 Conseil des Prud'hommes—Contestations
1837-1841

Bibliothèque municipale de Lille
Fonds Humbert
Fonds Lefebvre
Mss. 1158 "Comptabilité ménagère d'une famille lilloise
très connue, dont le chef fût commandant des
canonniers. Curieux document commmencé en 1843
et qui s'arrête en 1858, donnant des détails
intéressants sur les dépenses d'une maison
bourgeoise aux XIXᵉ siècle"
Fonds Quarré-Reybourbon
Fonds Gentil

Archives de la Société de Jésus, Province de Champagne
   "Diaire du Ministre,"—extracts provided by Le Père
      Hugues Beylard
   "Diaire de l'archiconfrérie des mères chrétiennes, 1868-
      1962"

Archives du Pensionnat du Sacré-Coeur de Jésus à Lille
   "Conseila, 1868-1882. Compte-rendu des séances.
      Enfants de Marie du Sacré-Coeur"

Genealogies

Archives du Batut. N.p., n.d.

Barry, Charles. *Généalogie des Serret.* N.p., n.d.
Bernard, Jean and Henri. *Généalogie de la famille Bernard,
   1575-1924.* Lille: Desclée, de Brouwer et Cie., 1928.
Bernard-Maître, Henri. *Généalogie de la famille Bernard.*
   Paris: L. Durand et fils, 1952.
———, and Pierre Daudruy. *La Famille Dubois.* 2 vols.
   Fécamp: Durand, 1954.
Bigo d'Halluin, Auguste. *Généalogie de la famille Bigo.* Lille:
   L. Danel, 1887.
———. *Généalogie de la famille Masurel.* Lille: L. Danel,
   1899.
Bommart, Th. *Généalogie de la famille Bommart de Douai.*
   4 vols. Lille: L. Danel, 1878-1893.
———. *Généalogie de la famille Crépy.* 4 vols. Lille: L. Da-
   nel, 1883-1908.
Bruchet, Andrée and M. Decroix. *Généalogie de la famille
   Mathon.* St. Omer: L. Lorez, 1934.
Cattaert, Auguste. *Essai généalogique et biographique sur
   la famille Cattaert.* Paris: Emile Lechevalier, 1899.
Cuny, Jean. *Généalogie Delobel.* N.p., 1971.
Cuvelier-Verley, Albert G. J. *Généalogie de la famille Cu-
   velier d'Oresmieux, 1535-1927.* Lille: Société d'études
   de la province de Cambrai, 1927.

Daudruy-Dubois, Pierre. *La Famille Charvet.* 2 vols. *Fécamp:* Durand, 1964.

——. *Généalogie de Baecque.* Fécamp: Durand, 1947.

——, and Fernand Decroix. *Baillescourt et la famille Proyart.* Fécamp: Durand, 1957.

Denis du Péage, Paul. *Mélanges généalogiques.* Lille: Société d'études de la province de Cambrai, 1911.

——. *Notes généalogiques.* Lille: Société d'études de la province de Cambrai, 1922.

——. *Recueil de généalogies lilloises.* 4 vols. Lille: Société d'études de la province de Cambrai, 1906-1909.

Foucart, Jacques. *La Famille Brame.* N.p., n.d. [1964].

——. *Jules Brame.* N.p., 1964.

Généalogie de la famille Lesage. Lille, 1899.

Généalogie de la famille Waymel. Lille, 1885.

Gennevoise, E. *Notes généalogiques. La famille Lorthois de Tourcoing, 1600-1910.* Lille: Lefebvre-Ducrocq, n.d.

Hache, Victor. *Généalogie des familles de Lille, Armentières et environs.* Roubaix: 1921—.

Hannezo, Gérard. *Histoire d'une famille du Nord. Les Barrois.* N.p., n.d.

Houzé de l'Aulnoit, A. *Famille Houzé de l'Aulnoit et ses alliances.* Lille: Lefebvre-Ducrocq, 1892.

Lefebvre, Léon. *Notices généalogiques: famille Ducrocq.* Lille: L. Danel, 1882.

Lestienne, Paul. *Généalogie Dassonville.* Lille: Société d'études de la province de Cambrai, 1924.

——. *Famille Cordonnier-Reys.* Lille: Danel, 1913.

Lethierry d'Ennequin. *Une famille bourgeoise de Lille, ses alliances, ses seigneuries (1610-1930).* Lille: Mercure de Flandre, 1930.

Mennynck, Auguste de, and Marie Boutemy-Cabillaux. *Notes historiques et généalogiques.* Lille, 1887.

Motte, Gaston. *Les Motte. Etude de la descendance Motte-Clarisse, 1750-1950.* Roubaix: Verschave, 1952.

Scrive, Marcel. *Antoine Scrive-Labbe et sa descendance.* Angers: Editions de l'ouest, 1945.

Souvenir de famille: jubilé de cinquante ans de M. et Mme Auguste Bernard-Beaussier, M. et Mme Louis Decroix-Beaussier. Lille: E. Reboux, n.d.

Souvenir de famille. Marriage de Mlle Jeanne Boutemy avec M. Joseph Tisseyre célébré à Lys-les-Lannoy, le 25 mai, 1896. Lille: Lefebvre-Ducrocq, 1896.

Spriet, Charles. *Tableau généalogique.* Lille: Lefebvre-Ducrocq, 1886.

Théry, Adolphe. *Les Bernard: une famille d'industriels qui passe en 20 ans de 489 à 983 membres.* Paris: Spes, 1929.

Théry, G. *Généalogie de la famille Théry-Leclercq.* Lille, 1888.

Trelcat, A. *La Famille Despret.* Lille: Société d'études de la province de Cambrai, 1929.

Contemporary Printed Sources

A la mémoire de Madame Delannoy-Desnoulez, Présidente de la conférence de la Société de Saint Vincent de Paul, du patronage des jeunes filles et de la salle d'asile de Sainte Catherine. Lille: Imprimerie St. Augustin, n.d.

Adhémar, La Comtesse d'. *La Femme catholique et la démocratie française.* Paris: Perrin et Cie., 1900.

———. *Nouvelle éducation de la femme dans les classes cultivées.* Paris: Perrin et Cie., 1896.

Album-souvenir des fêtes jubilaires de La Croix du Nord, 1889-1914. Lille: Imprimerie de La Croix du Nord, 1914.

Alfred-Julien Thiriez, filateur de coton, chévalier de la légion d'honneur, 1833-1903. Lille: Danel, 1914.

Allard, Georges. *Rapport sur l'enseignement primaire libre dans le Nord.* Lille: Lefebvre-Ducrocq, 1884.

Anthoine, Emile. *A travers les écoles. Souvenirs posthumes.* Paris: Hachette, 1887.

———. *L'Instruction primaire dans le département du Nord de 1868 à 1877.* Lille: C. Robbé, 1878.

Ardouin-Dumazet, V.-E. *Voyages en France.* Volume 18: *Région du Nord: Flandre et le littoral du Nord.* Paris: Berger-Levrault, 1899.

Arnous, Paul. *Pierre Legrand 1834-1905.* Paris: Plon, 1907.

Assemblée générale des catholiques du Nord et du Pas de Calais tenue à Lille du 22 au 26 novembre 1882. Lille: Lefebvre-Ducrocq, 1883.

Aux parents. Lille: P. Lagrange, 1899.

Backer, Félix de. *Vie de Mme Van Der Meersch (Julie Behaghel).* Paris: Le Coffre fils, 1876.

Bajart, Léonce. *L'Industrie des tulles et dentelles en France.* N.p., n.d.

Barat, Madeleine Louise Sophie. *Recueil de pensées et de maximes.* Paris: V. Goupy, 1866.

Baunard, Louis. *La Bénédiction paternelle et maternelle.* Lille: Lefebvre-Ducrocq, 1882.

————. *Les Deux frères. Cinquante années de l'action catholique à Lille. Philibert Vrau, Camille Feron-Vrau 1829-1908.* Paris: La Bonne Presse, 1910.

————. *Ernest Lelièvre et les fondations des petites-soeurs des pauvres d'après sa correspondance 1826-1889.* Paris: Vve. Ch. Poussielgue, 1905.

————. *Histoire de Madame Barat, fondatrice de la Société du Sacré-Coeur de Jésus.* 2 vols. Paris: Poussielgue, 1876.

————. *Kolb-Bernard, sénateur du Nord, 1798-1888.* Paris: Librairie Ch. Poussielgue, 1899.

————. *Madame Camille Feron-Vrau.* Paris: Maison de la Bonne Presse, 1914.

Bécour, Theophile. *De l'empirisme, ses causes, ses dangers et moyens de le combattre.* Lille: L. Danel, 1878.

Bernard, Charles. *Quelques mots en faveur du patronage des jeunes ouvrières pronouncés en église Ste. Catherine de Lille.* Lille: Lefort, 1865.

Berne, A. de. *Mémoires d'un octogénaire parisien tour à tour citoyen de Lyon et de Lille.* Paris: H. Chapelliez, 1889.

275

Blocquel, Simon. *La Bonne cuisine*. Paris: Charles Douniol, 1862.

——. *Guide des femmes de ménage, des cuisinières, et des bonnes d'enfants*. Paris: Delarue; Lille: Blocquel-Castiaux, 1841.

——. *Le Nécessaire des dames. Véritable trésor de la toilette, de la santé, et d'économie domestique*. Paris: Delarue; Lille: Castiaux, n.d.

——. *Nouvelle sémiographie. Langage allégorique, emblématique ou symbolique des fleurs et des fruits, des animaux, des couleurs, etc. Ouvrage dedié aux dames*. Paris: Delarue; Lille: Blocquel-Castiaux, 1857.

Blocquel, Mme Simon. *L'Art de confectionner des fleurs artificielles*. Lille: Blocquel, n.d.

Bologne, A. *L'Orphélinat de Don Bosco*. Lille, 1903.

Bouly, Eugène. *Les Sciences, les lettres, et les arts à Cambrai*. Cambrai: P. Levêque, 1844.

Bourdon, Mathilde. *Aux jeunes personnes. Politesse et savoir-vivre*. Paris: Lethielleux, 1864.

——. *La Charité en action*. Lille: Lefort, 1864.

——. *De la confiance en Dieu dans les calamités publiques*. Lille: Lefort, 1849.

——. *Etudes historiques. Marie Tudor et Elizabeth, reines d'Angleterre*. Paris: Putois-Cretté, 1868.

——. *Histoire d'Elisabeth, reine d'Angleterre*. Plancy: Société de Saint-Victor, 1852.

——. *Histoire de Marie Stuart*. Paris: S. Victor, 1853.

——. *L'Homme propose et Dieu dispose*. Lille: Lefort, 1849.

——. *Journée chrétienne de la jeune fille*. 2 vols. Paris: Putois-Cretté, 1867.

——. *Le Mois des serviteurs de Marie*. Paris: Putois-Cretté, 1863.

——. *Nouveaux conseils aux jeune filles et jeunes femmes*. Paris: Blériot, 1897.

——. *Le Pouvoir de la prière*. Lille: Lefort, 1857.

————. *Sainte Jeanne de Valois, fondateur des Annonciades.* Lille: Lefort, 1851.

————. *Saint Thomas de Cantorbéry.* Lille: Lefort, 1852.

Brun-Lavainne, E. *Mes souvenirs.* Lille: Lefebvre-Ducrocq, 1855.

————. [H. Prévault]. *Traité de la tenue des livres.* Lille: Lefort, 1835.

Cambon, Paul. *Correspondance, 1870-1924.* Paris: Grasset, 1940.

Camp, Maxime du. *La Croix rouge de France.* Paris: Crété, 1892.

Capon, Alphonse. *Petit François, moeurs lillois.* Paris: J. Tallandier, 1908.

Carnoy, H. *Dictionnaire biographique des hommes du Nord.* Paris: Imp. de l' "Armorial francais," 1899.

Carrau, Ludovic. *De l'éducation. Précis de morale pratique.* Paris: Aleide Picard et Kaan, 1888.

Catéchisme à l'usage du diocèse de Cambrai. Cambrai: Deligne et Lenglet, 1887.

Catéchisme de Cambrai. Lille: A. Taffin-Lefort, 1909.

Cent ans d'industrie chimique: les établissements Kuhlmann, 1825-1925. Paris, n.d.

Centenaire des enfants de Marie du Sacré-Coeur. Lille: SILIC, 1932.

Chevallier, Chanoine Gustave. *Mgr. Sonnois Archevêque de Cambrai.* Cambrai: O. Masson, 1920.

Chon, François. *Notice historique sur la Société de Saint Vincent de Paul à Lille.* Lille: Lefort, 1883.

————. *Promenades lilloises.* Lille: L. Danel, 1888.

Cochin, Henry. *Lamartine et la Flandre.* Paris: Plon, 1912.

Coisne, Madame André (née P. Bécour). *Coups de griffe.* Lille: Librairie Nouvelle, 1911.

Coulon, Alphonse-Marie. *Histoire de Halluin.* Courtrai: Eugène Beyaert, 1904.

Couplets de M. Paul Bernard à l'occasion du mariage de sa soeur. Chantés par M. Riguier-Delaunay. Lille: L. Danel, 1879.

Craux, Madame Gustave. *Antoine Brasseur. Histoire de sa vie.* Lille: L. Danel, 1897.

Croix, Charles. *Avesnes, ses rues, ses maisons.* Avesnes: Editions de l'Observateur, 1950.

Dame St. *Albéric Toulemonde, sur les deux ailes de la simplicité et de la pureté.* Found in: Archives de la Société de Jésus, Province de Champagne.

Danel, L. *Compte-rendu du banquet offert par M. et Mme Danel à leurs ouvriers.* Lille: Danel, 1878.

Dassonville, A. *Quatre allocutions aux dames de la Croix-Rouge (1910-1911).* Lille: La Croix du Nord, 1911.

Decottignies, Louis. *Poésies.* Lille: Imp. de Leloux, 1841.

de Gaulle, Josephine. *Histoire de saint Joseph, Patron de l'Eglise catholique, sa vie et son culte,* Lille: Lefort, 1874.

———. *Le Libérateur de l'Irlande, ou Vie de Daniel O'Connell.* Lille: Lefort, 1851.

———. *Vie de général Drouot.* Lille: Lefort, 1848.

Dehaisnes, Mgr. Chrétien. *L'Oeuvre des layettes de la maternité Ste. Anne.* Lille: Lefort, 1890.

Dehocq, Abbé Paul. *Aperçu historique sur la confrérie du Très St. Sacrament de Saint Etienne à Lille, 1603-1905.* V. Ducoulombier, 1906.

Delahaye-Théry, Madame Eugène. *Les Cahier noirs.* Rennes: Editions de "la province," 1934.

Delemer, Paul. *L'Assistance charitable à Lille.* Lille: René Giard, 1910.

———. *Noces d'or de la conférence de St. Vincent de Paul de Saint-André à Lille.* Lille: H. Morel, 1908.

———. *Notice sur la famille Delemer.* Lille, 1913.

Delplanque, Albert. *Ames de religieuses: la mère Eléonore.* Lille: Desclée, De Brouwer et Cie., 1925.

———. *Ames de religieuses. La Mère Eulalie, religieuse de la Sainte-Union des Sacrés Coeurs.* Lille: Desclée, De Brouwer et Cie., 1925.

———. *Ames de religieuses: la mère Josephine.* Lille: Desclée, De Brouwer, et Cie., 1924.

Dépret, Louis. *Lille. Notes historiques et contemporaines.* Paris: Hachette, 1867.

——. *Scénarios.* Lille: Petit, 1874.

——. *Silhouettes de villes.* Paris: Hachette, 1874.

Derode, V. *Histoire de Lille et de la Flandre wallonne.* Lille: Vanaeckere, 1848.

Descamps, Ange. *Lille, un coup d'oeil sur son agrandissement, ses institutions, ses industries.* Lille: L. Danel, 1878.

Descamps, Emile. *Allocution prononcé au mariage de M. Jules Scrive-Loyer et Mlle Germaine Bigo.* Lille: L. Danel, 1900.

Desmarchelier, H. *Histoire du décanat de la Madeleine de Lille (1229-1892).* Lille: L. Quarré, 1892.

——. *Les Trois des Rotours.* Lille: L. Danel, 1901.

Destombes, C. J. *Vie de son Eminence le Cardinal Régnier Archevêque de Cambrai.* 2 vols. Lille: Lefort, 1885.

Deule, O. de la. *Lille en 1895.* Lille: Imprimerie du Nouvelliste et de la Dépêche, 1896.

Dewez, Abbé J. *Histoire de la paroisse de St. André à Lille.* Lille: Nuez et Cie., 1899.

Dieudonné, Christophe. *Statistique du département du Nord.* 3 vols. Douai: Marlier, 1804.

Drioux, Abbe Claude. *La Morale pratique.* Paris: Poussielgue frères, 1888.

Dubly, Henry-Louis. *Le Caducée et le carquois.* Lille: Mercure de Flandre, 1926.

Dumotit, Arsène. *Dépopulation et civilisation: étude demographique.* Paris: Lecrosnier et Babé, 1890.

Dupanloup, F. *La Femme chrétienne et française. Dernière réponse à M. Duruy et à ses defenseurs.* Paris: Charles Duniol, 1868.

——. *La Femme studieuse.* Paris: Charles Duniol, 1869.

Dupont, J.-B. *Mémoire sur les moyens d'améliorer la santé des ouvriers à Lille.* Paris: Delarue, 1826.

——. *Topographie historique, statistique et médicale de l'arrondisement de Lille.* Paris: Delarue, 1833.

Durand, Albert. *La Législation des écoles maternelles et des écoles primaires*. Paris: Ract et Falquet, 1882.

Durant, Clément. *La Femme dans l'histoire de Lille du VIIe siècle au XXe siècle (620-1918)*. Lille: Mercure de Flandre, 1928.

Duthil, Jules. *Au jour le jour*. Lille: Imprimerie du Nouvelliste, 1897.

Eustache, G. *Manuel pratique des maladies des femmes*. Paris: J.-B. Ballière, 1881.

———. *La Puériculture*. Paris: J.-B. Ballière, 1903.

Exhortations en faveur des salles d'asile. Lille: L. Lefort, 1840, 1844, 1862.

Extrait des Annales du pensionnat des Dames Bernardines d'Esquermes, Fêtes du huitième centenaire de la naissance de St. Bernard. Lille: 1891.

Faucheur-Deledicque, Narcisse. *Mon histoire: à mes chers enfants et petits-enfants*. Lille: L. Danel, 1886.

Félix, R. P. *Paternité et maternité dans l'éducation*. Lille: Desclée, De Brouwer et Cie., 1886.

Femmes fortes dans les temps modernes. Portraits et récits offerts aux jeunes filles chrétiennes. Lille: Maison St. Joseph, 1896.

Fénelon, François de Salignac. *Les Aventures de Télémaque, fils d'Ulysse*. With an introduction by Abbé J. Martin. Paris: Poussielgue frères for the Alliance des maisons d'éducation chrétienne, 1880.

———. *Education des filles*. With an introduction by Octave Gréard. Paris: Librairie des bibliophiles, 1885.

Ferguson, S. *Histoire du tulle et des dentelles mécaniques en Angleterre et en France*. Paris: E. Lacroix, 1862.

Feron-Vrau, Paul. *Centenaire de la maison Ph. Vrau et Cie*. Lille: La Croix du Nord, 1919.

———. *Quarante ans d'action catholique*. Paris: Imprimerie Paul Feron-Vrau, 1921.

Fichaux, Louis. *Manuel d'instruction chrétienne*. Lille: A. Taffin-Lefort, 1906.

Franciosi, Charles de. *Hommage à Monsieur Louis Danel.* Lille: L. Danel, 1877.

Francqueville, E. *La Famille et l'église catholique ou l'influence de Jésus-Christ, de l'église et de la grâce sur la société domestique.* Lille: Imprimerie de St. Augustin, 1882.

Gagneur, M.-L. *Le Calvaire des femmes.* Paris: Le Siècle, 1877.

Ghesquière, H. *La Femme et le socialisme.* Lille: Imprimerie ouvrière for Comité des femmes de Lille, 1893.

Godey, J.-B. *Etude sur les crèches pour les petits enfants des ouvriers de Roubaix dédiée à Madame Constantin Descat.* Roubaix: A. Lesguillon, 1868.

Gossot, Emile. *Les Salles d'asile en France et leur fondateur Denys Cochin.* Paris: Didier, 1884.

Grandidier, F. *Vie du R. P. Guidée.* Amiens: Lambert-Caron, 1877.

Grar, Edouard. *Histoire de la recherche, de la découverte et de l'exploitation de la houille dans le Hainaut français, dans la Flandre française et dans l'Artois.* Valenciennes: Prignet, 1847-1851.

Gréard, Octave. *L'Enseignement secondaire des filles.* Paris: Delalain, 1882.

Gréville, Madame Henri. *Instruction morale et civique des jeunes filles.* Paris: E. Weill et G. Maurice, 1882.

Helin, Abbé M. *Célébration du mariage de Benjamin Charvet et Mlle Henriette Gennevoise en l'église Saint-Michel à Lille, 11 janvier 1892.* Neuville-sous-Montreuil: Imprimerie de E. Duquat, 1892.

L'Histoire locale au jour le jour. Lille: L. Quarré, 1890.

Histoire régionale. Vols. 1-44. Collection of booklets found in the library of the Université catholique de Lille.

Houbron, Georges. *Le Type féminin en Flandre; essai ethnographique. Extrait du Bulletin de la Société de Géographie de Lille.* Lille: L. Danel, 1903.

Houdoy, Jules. *La Filature du coton dans le Nord de la France.* Paris: A. Rousseau, 1903.

Houzé de l'Aulnoit, Aimé. *Des avantages de la création des caisses de secours en faveur des femmes nouvellement accouchées.* Lille: L. Danel, 1874.

———. *Des comités libres de charité.* Lille: Lefebvre-Ducrocq, 1881.

———. *Les Devoirs de l'assistance publique vis-à-vis des indigents.* Paris: F. Levé, 1890.

———. *Les Ecoles d'arts et métiers et l'orphélinat de Saint-Gabriel à Lille. Rapport au Congrès des Catholiques du Nord et du Pas de Calais, novembre 1884.* Lille: Lefebvre-Ducrocq, 1885.

Huard, A. *Edouard Lefort.* Lille: A. Taffin-Lefort, 1893.

d'Ideville, Henry. *Lettres flamandes.* Paris: A. Pougin, 1876.

Josson, Louise. *Rapport fait à l'archiconfrérie des mères chrétiennes. Assemblée générale de Notre-Dame de Sion. Le 5 février 1864.* Paris: Au secrétariat de l'archiconfrérie, 1864.

———. *Rapport fait à l'archiconfrérie des mères chétiennes dans la chapelle de Notre Dame de Sion.* Paris: Olmer, 1859.

Jouy, V.-J. Etienne. *L'Hermite en province.* Paris: Pillet, 1826.

Kergomard, Pauline. *Ecoles maternelles de 1837 jusqu'en 1910, aperçu rapide.* Paris: Librairie classique Fernand Nathan, 1910.

Kuhlmann, F. *Exposition des produits de l'industrie. Rapport du jury départemental du Nord.* Lille: L. Danel, 1844.

———. *Exposition nationale des produits de l'industrie agricole et manufacturière de 1849. Rapport du jury départemental du Nord.* Lille: L. Danel, 1849.

Lallemand, Léon. *Un péril social. L'Introduction de la charité légale en France.* Paris: Société d'économie sociale, 1891.

Lami, E.-O. *Voyages pittoresques et techniques en France et à l'étranger.* Paris: Jouvet et Cie., 1892.

Lataud, L. *Histoire de Ferrière-la-Grande.* Lille: Camille Robbe, 1908.

Leclercq-Bernard, H. *Véritable guide des maîtres et patrons, ainsi que des employes, ouvriers et domestiques des deux sexes.* Lille: L'auteur, 1871.

Leclercq-Huet, Madame J., et al. *Les Richesses éducatrices du foyer chrétien.* Lille: René Giard, 1921.

Legougeux, Louis. *Souvenirs lillois.* Lille: Danel, 1904.

Legrand, Pierre. *Le Bourgeois de Lille.* Lille: Lefebvre-Ducrocq, 1851.

————. *La Femme du bourgeois de Lille.* Lille: Lefebvre-Ducrocq, 1852.

Leleu, Edmond. *La Caisse des écoles de Lille, 1883-1921.* Lille: M. Dhoossche, 1921.

LeLiepvre, Abbé Ernest. *Charles Kolb-Bernard: souvenirs intimes de son neveu.* Le Havre: Imprimerie du Commerce, 1893.

Lepreux, G. *Nos journaux. Histoire et bibliographie de la presse périodique dans le département du Nord.* Douai: L. and G. Crépin frères, 1896.

Lettres d'Alfred Motte-Grimonprez 1827-1887. 3 vols. Paris, 1952.

Leuridan, Th. *Histoire de la fabrique de Roubaix.* Roubaix: Vve. Béghin, 1864.

Liagre, Charles. *Loos au XIXe siècle.* Lille: Lefebvre-Ducrocq, 1899.

Lille et la région du Nord en 1909. 2 vols. Lille: L. Danel, 1909.

Louise Charvet, enfant de Marie 1848-1877. Simples souvenirs dédiés à sa famille. Lille: J. Lefort, 1877.

Madame Théodore Aronio de Romblay. Pieux souvenir. Lille: L. Danel, n.d.

Manuel des oeuvres catholiques de Lille. Lille: Bergès, n.d.

Manuel du Négociant. Paris: Baudouin, 1808.

Marie du Sacré-Coeur. *La Formation catholique de la femme contemporaine.* 2nd edition. Paris: X. Rondelet, 1899.

Maternal Schools in France. Washington, D.C.: U.S. Government Printing Office, 1882.

Max-Hilaire. *La Vie douaisienne.* Douai: Crépin, 1903.

Mémorial du mariage de Monsieur le Vicomte Guy Dauger et de Mademoiselle Gabrielle Bernard. Lille: L. Danel, 1899.

Mermillod, Gaspard. *Mission de la femme chrétienne dans le monde. Retraite donnée par Monseigneur Mermillod aux enfants de Marie du Sacré-Coeur d'Amiens.* Lille: Desclée, De Brouwer et Cie., 1893.

Michelet, Jules. *Du prêtre, de la femme, et de la famille.* Paris: Hachette, 1845.

———. *La Femme.* Paris: Calmann-Lévy, 1854.

Molière, J.-B. *Les Femmes savantes.* With an introduction by Abbé Figuière. Paris: Poussielgue frères, 1888.

Monseigneur Duquesnay et le denier des écoles catholiques de Lille. Souvenir du 26 mars 1882. Lille: Desclée, De Brouwer et Cie., 1882.

Nicolay, C. de. *Madame la Comtesse de Grandville.* Lille: Lefort, 1867.

Notice sur Mlle Julie Flamen. Lille: Ducoulombier, 1876.

Oeuvre de nouvelles églises de Lille. Rapport lu le mercredi 28 février 1877 dans une réunion du comité catholique. Lille: Ducoulombier, 1877.

Origine et commencements de l'oeuvre des églises pauvres à Lille. Lille: J. Lefort, 1868.

Ortille, E. *Lettre sur les dangers de la prostitution clandestine adressée à M. le Maire de Lille.* Lille: C. Lagache, 1881.

Pariset, M. *Nouveau manuel complet de la maîtresse de maison.* With a supplement by Mme Celnart and Gacon-Dufour. Paris: Roret, 1852.

Pauline Fauchille-Prévost. Funeral card. Lille: 1902.

Pharaon, Florian. *Voyage impériale dans le nord de la France.* Lille: Danel, 1867.

Pilard, Charles. *Deux mois à Lille.* Lille: Imprimerie de Madame Bayart, 1868.

Pimodan, Comte de. *Simples souvenirs, 1859-1907.* Paris: Plon, 1908.

Poilloue de St. Mars, Gabrielle [Comtesse Dash]. *Les Femmes à Paris et en province.* Paris: M. Levy frères, 1868.

Poradowska, Marguerite. *Le Mariage du fils Grandsire.* Paris: Hachette, 1894.

Provision Made for Children under Compulsory School Age in Belgium, France, Germany, and Switzerland. London: Wyman and Sons, 1909.

Quarré-Reybourbon, Louis. *Edouard Van Hende, 1819-1900.* Lille: L. Danel, 1901.

———. *L'Eglise et la paroisse du Sacré-Coeur de Lille.* Lille: Lefebvre-Ducrocq, 1898.

———. *Esquermes, La Madeleine-les-Lille.* Lille: Six-Horemans, 1875.

Ratisbonne, Théodore. *Nouveau manuel des mères chrétiennes.* Paris: Vve. Poussielgue et fils, 1866.

Ravet-Anceau. *Annuaire du commerce, de l'industrie, et d'administration.* Lille: Danel, 1852—.

Renouard, Alfred. *Exposition universelle de 1889. Les Institutions ouvrières et sociales du département du Nord.* Lille: L. Danel, 1889.

Reubrez, René. *Annuaire des échos mondains et Lille-Sélect, Lille, Roubaix, Tourcoing, Armentières.* Lille, 1906.

La Révérende Mère Marie de la Providence, fondatrice de la société des auxiliatrices des âmes du purgatoire (1825-1871). Paris: J. Gabalda, 1928.

Roussel-Defontaine, Charles. *Histoire de Tourcoing.* Lille: E. Vanaeckere, 1855.

Rousselot, Paul. *Histoire de l'éducation des femmes en France.* 2 vols. Paris: Didier et Cie., 1883.

Salembier, Abbé Alfred. *A la mémoire du chanoine L. Salembier, 1849-1913. Souvenirs d'un frère.* Lille: La Croix du Nord, n.d.

Salembier, L. *Henri-Dominigue Lacordaire. Conférence*

285

faite aux jeunes filles qui suivent les cours de l'Université catholique de Lille, 1900-1901. Besançon: Imprimerie catholique de l'est, 1909.

———. *Instruction des jeunes filles.* Lille: Ducoulombier, 1889.

———. *Lettres sur les examens de jeunes filles.* Lille: B. Bergès, 1884.

———. *Notions de psychologie à l'usage des jeunes filles.* Paris: Poussielgue frères, 1890.

———. *Vie de Jeanne d'Arc dediée aux enfants des écoles catholiques.* Lille, Paris: J. Lefort, 1892.

Salles d'asile de Lille. 1864. Lille: L. Danel, 1864.

[Scrive-Loyer, Jules]. *Portraits bourgeois contemporains.* Lille, 1886.

Sède, Baron de. *Voyage de LL. MM. L'Empereur et l'Impératrice dans le Nord de la France.* Arras: Auguste Tierny, 1867.

Ségur, Anatole de. *Paul Marie Charles Bernard, 1840-1874.* Paris: Tolra, 1875.

———. *Vie de l'Abbé Bernard.* Paris: Bray et Retaux, 1883.

Ségur, Comtesse de (née Sophie Rostopchine). *Après la pluie le beau temps.* Paris: Hachette, n.d.

———. *Evangile d'une grand'mère.* Paris: Société liturgique, 1866.

———. *François le bossu.* Paris: Hachette, 1908.

———. *Les Malheurs de Sophie.* Paris: Hachette, 1922.

———. *Pauvre Blaise.* Paris: Hachette, 1861.

———. *Les Vacances.* Paris: Hachette, 1858.

Seilhac, Léon de. *La Grève du tissage de Lille.* Paris: Arthur Rousseau, 1910.

Sévigné, Marie de. *Letters of Madame de Sévigné to her daughter and her friends.* 2 vols. Edited by Richard Aldington. London: George Routledge and Sons, 1937.

———. *Lettres choisies de Madame de Sévigné.* Paris: Poussielgue frères, 1884.

Silhouettes lilloises: extraites du journal Le Diable Rose. Lille: A. Degans, 1873.

Simon, Jules. "L'Enseignement primaire des filles en 1864." *Revue des deux mondes* 52 (1864): 948-968.

——. *L'Ouvrière*. 4th edition. Paris: Hachette, 1862.

Les Soeurs de la Charité maternelle de la residence de Lille. Lille: A. Béhague, 1874.

Les Soeurs franciscaines de la propagation de la foi. Lille: H. Morel, 1898.

Souvenir de la bénédiction de la première pierre du nouvel établissement des dames de St. Maur. Lille: Lefebvre-Ducrocq, 1869.

Souvenir de la retraite donnée par Monseigneur Mermillod aux enfants de Marie. Mars 1868. Lille: L. Danel, 1868.

Souvenir du 23 juillet 1874 aux Enfants de Marie du Sacré-Coeur de Lille. Lille: L. Danel, 1874.

Souvenir du jubilé de vingt-cinq ans des dames de Saint Maur, célébré à la Madeleine-les-Lille, le 17 juin 1880. Lille: Lefebvre-Ducrocq, 1880.

Souvenir 1840-1917 sur la tombe de Madame Bécour le 19 juillet 1917. Lille: Delemar et Dubar, 1917.

Souvenirs à l'usage des habitants de Douai. Douai: Ceret-Carpentier, 1843.

Technical Instruction in France. Washington, D.C.: U.S. Government Printing Office, 1882.

Thellier de Poncheville, Charles. *Le Rôle social de la femme, conférence faite à la VIᵉ session de la semaine sociale de France.* Lyon: Chronique social de France, 1910.

Théry, G. *De l'avocat d'office en matière de divorce.* Paris: Pillet et Demoulin, 1886.

——. *Le Mariage et la loi civile.* Lille: Desclée, De Brouwer et Cie., 1880.

Théry, Léon. *De la combinaison du régime de la communauté avec le régime dotal.* Cambrai: F. et P. Déligne, 1897.

Théry, Louis. *Des fondations charitables à Lille.* Lyon: X. Jevain, 1901.

Thomas, Henri. *Herminie de la Bassemoûturie.* Tournai: Casterman, 1867.

Le Très Révérend Père Marie-Théodore Ratisbonne. Fondateur de la société des prêtres et de la congrégation des religieuses de Notre Dame de Sion. Paris: Vve. Ch. Poussielgue, 1903.

Une âme réparatrice. Madame Marie-Lucie Vrau, veuve de Monsieur Camille Feron-Vrau, 1839-1913. Lille: Desclée, De Brouwer et Cie., 1914.

Valdelièvre, Pierre. *Les Heures émues.* Paris: Beffroi, 1912.

Vandame, H. *Oeuvre de Notre Dame de la Treille et Saint-Pierre. Compte-rendu de la période trentenaire, 1876-1908.* Lille: Lefebvre-Ducrocq, 1908.

Vandeputte, A. J. *Almanach du commerce de département du Nord.* Lille: Vandeputte, 1846.

Verly, Hippolyte. *Essai de biographie lilloise contemporaine. 1800-1869.* Lille: Leleu, 1869.

———. *Les Tablettes d'un bourgeois de Lille.* Lille: A. Leleux, 1874.

———. *Souvenirs d'une vieille barbe.* Lille: Librairie centrale, 1892.

Villars, Paul. *Silhouettes municipales.* Lille: LaVie flamande illustrée, 1908.

Ville de Lille. Conseil municipal. *Procès-verbaux des séances.* Lille: Jules Petit, 1870-1900.

Villemot, Antoine. *Documents, publications et ouvrages récents, relatifs à l'éducation des femmes et à l'enseignement secondaire des jeunes filles.* Paris: P. Dupont, 1889.

Villermé, Louis. *Tableau de l'état physique et moral des ouvriers employés dans les manufactures de coton, de laine et de soie.* Paris: Renouard, 1840.

La Violette du Louvencourt (Marie Robyn 1842-1858). Dunkerque: Lorenzo, 1860.

Wailly, N. de, ed. *Imitation de Jésus-Christ.* Angers: A. Burdin, 1885.

Watteeuw, L. *Tourcoing au XIXe siècle.* Tourcoing: Imprimerie Watteeuw, 1904.

Zola, Emile. *Germinal.* Translated by Leonard Tancock. Harmondsworth: Penguin, 1974.

Novels

Bécour, Julia. *Blidie ou les marionnettes humaines.* Paris: E. Dentu, 1881.
————. *De dix-huit à vingt ans. Journal d'une jeune fille.* Paris: A.-L. Guyot, n.d.
————. *La Famille Desquiens. Scènes des moeurs lilloises.* Lille: C. Lagache, 1882.
————. *Fée Mab.* Paris: Société d'éditions littéraires, 1898.
————. *Histoire de la princesse Violette.* Paris: Librairie d'éducation A. Hatier, 1893.
————. *L'Ile des mécontents.* Paris: Charles Delagrave, 1895.
————. *Leur supériorité.* Cahors: A. Coueslant, 1905.
————. *Livre de lecture courante. Geneviève et Michel.* Lille: Camille Robbe, 1890.
————. *Ma mie Georgette.* Lille: E. Dujardin, 1894.
————. *Roman d'une libre penseuse. Elfa.* Paris: A.-L. Guyot, 1897.
————. *Sur la pente.* Cahors: Coueslant, 1904.
————. *Tante Sébastienne.* Lille: Imprimerie A. Massart, 1889.
————. *Le Trousseau de la poupée.* Paris: Librairie d'éducation A. Hatier, 1893.
————. *Une heure d'oubli.* Lille: Ch. Tallandier et Gaujac, 1891.
————. *Un mariage fabuleux.* Lille: Imprimerie A. Massart, 1890.
————. *Les Voix lointaines. Le Stage (Paroles de là-bas).* Paris: P.-G. Leymaire for the Librairie des Sciences Psychiques, 1905.
Bourdon, Mathilde. *Agathe ou la première communion.* Paris: Putois-Cretté, 1869.
————. *L'Ainée et la cadette.* Lille: Lefort, 1876.

Bourdon, Mathilde. *Andrée d'Effauges*. Paris: Putois-Cretté, 1869.

———. *Anne-Marie*. Paris: P. Lethielleux, 1868.

———. *Antoinette Lemire*. Paris: Putois-Cretté, 1861.

———. *Les Béatitudes ou la science du bonheur*. Paris: Librairie Ambroise Bray, 1869.

———. *Les Belles années*. Paris: P. Lethielleux, 1868.

———. *Le Chercheur d'or*. Lille: Lefort, 1851.

———. *Denise*. Paris: Putois-Cretté, 1864.

———. *Le Divorce*. Paris: C. Dillet, 1865.

———. *L'Empire de la vertu*. Paris: Leclerc et Cie., 1850.

———. *Etudes et notices historiques*. Paris: Bray et Retaux, 1879.

———. *La Famille Clairval*. Lille: L. Lefort, 1859.

———. *La Famille Reydel*. Paris: Henri Allard, 1870.

———. *Femme et mari*. Paris: Librairie Blériot, 1886.

———. *Le Foyer*. Lille: L. Lefort, 1861.

———. *Le Legs d'une mère*. Lille: L. Lefort, 1851.

———. *Léontine*. Paris: Ambroise Bray, 1862.

———. *La Machine à coudre*. Lille: J. Lefort, 1869.

———. *Marthe Blondel ou l'ouvrière de fabrique*. Paris: Putois-Cretté, 1863.

———. *Le Ménage d'Henriette*. Paris: Bray et Retaux, 1871.

———. *Quelques nouvelles*. Lille: L. Lefort, 1864.

———. *Real Life*. Baltimore: Kelly, Piet and Co., 1876.

———. *Les Roses sans épines*. Lille: L. Lefort, 1869.

———. *Types féminins: fille, soeur, épouse, mère, religieuse*. Paris: Putois-Cretté, 1869.

———. *Une faute d'orthographe*. Paris: Putois-Cretté, 1864.

———. *Les Veillées du patronage*. Paris: Putois-Cretté, 1864.

de Gaulle, Josephine. *Adhémar de Belcastel*. New York: Catholic Publication Society, 1875.

———. *Deux belles-mères*. Paris: Casterman, 1864.

———. *Marie et Laure*. Paris: Gaume frères, 1838.

———. *Nouvelles soirées d'une mère*. Paris: LeClere, 1860.

Periodicals

Annales de la charité
Annales de l'archiconfrérie des mères chrétiennes
Annuaire statistique du département du Nord
Bulletin de l'Union Faulconnier
La Cordée du Patriarche
Echo de la ligue patriotique des françaises
L'Echo du Nord
*Echo des modes de Lille. Journal de la société élégante du
   département du Nord*
Fleur bleue
Mémoires de la Société archéologique d'Avesnes
*Mémoires de la Société d'agriculture, des sciences et des
   arts de l'arrondissement de Valenciennes*
Mémoires de la Société dunkerquoise
Polybion
Le Progrès du Nord
Le Propagateur du Nord
Le Réveil du Nord
La Revue du mois
La Revue du Nord
La Semaine religieuse du Diocèse de Cambrai
La Vie lilloise

Modern Secondary Sources

André-Delastre, Louise. *Marie de la Providence*. Paris: Imprimerie de l'Apostolat, 1958.
Ameye, Jacques. *Tourcoing ma ville*. Tourcoing: La Brouette, 1968.
Barthes, Roland. *Système de la mode*. Paris: Seuil, 1967.
[Bonduel-Bayart, Mme E.] *Ernest Bonduel 1863-1928*. Paris: Taffin-Lefort, 1931.
Brenne, Jules. *Lomme au temps des bourgeois*. Paris: André Bomie, 1960.
Camier, M. "Cambrai sous la Monarchie de Juillet." D.E.S. thesis, Université de Lille, 1956.

Camescasse, Valentine. *Souvenirs de Madame Camescasse.* Paris: Plon, 1924.

Carter, Edward II et al. *Enterprise and Entrepreneurs in Nineteenth- and Twentieth-Century France.* Baltimore: Johns Hopkins University Press, 1976.

Charbon et sciences humaines. Paris: Mouton, 1966.

Codaccioni, Félix-Paul. *Lille, 1850-1914, contribution à une étude des structures sociales.* Lille: Service de reproduction des thèses de l'université, 1971.

Coirault, Gaston. *Les Cinquante premières années de l'enseignement secondaire féminin 1880-1930.* Tours: Arrault, 1940.

Cunnington, C. W., and Phillis Cunnington. *English Women's Clothing in the Nineteenth Century.* Boston: Plays, 1970.

Cunnington, Phillis. *Costume in Pictures, 1750-1850.* London: Faber and Faber, 1970.

Dassonneville, Danielle. "Le Patronat lillois de 1815 à 1870." Maîtrise d'histoire, Université de Lille, 1971.

Daumard, Adéline. *La Bourgeoisie parisienne de 1815 à 1848.* Paris: S.E.V.P.E.N., 1963.

Delooz, Pierre. *Conditions sociologiques de la sainteté canonisée.* 2 vols. Liège: Université de Liège, Faculté de droit, 1960.

Demont, Adrien. *Souvenances. Promenades à travers ma vie.* Arras: Nouvelle société anonyme du Pas de Calais, 1927.

Demont-Breton, Virginie. *Les Maisons que j'ai connues.* Paris: Plon, 1926-1930.

Denain-Anzain, livre d'ordre de la société. Paris, 1949.

Dubly, Henry-Louis. *Vers un ordre économique et sociale. Eugène Mathon, 1860-1935.* Paris: Blondin, 1946.

Duroselle, Jean-Baptiste. *Les Débuts du catholicisme social en France: 1822-1870.* Paris: Presses universitaires de France, 1951.

Duveau, Georges. *La Vie ouvrière en France sous le Second Empire.* Paris: Gallimard, 1946.

292

Falcucci, Clément. *L'Humanisme dans l'enseignement secondaire*. Toulouse: Privat, 1939.

Fohlen, Claude. *L'Industrie textile au temps du Second Empire*. Paris: Plon, 1956.

Gendarme, René. *La Region du Nord: essai d'analyse économique*. Paris: A. Colin, 1954.

Gibon, Fénelon. *L'Enseignement secondaire féminin*. Paris: Société générale d'éducation et d'enseignement, 1920.

Gille, Bertrand. *Recherches sur la formation de la grande entreprise capitaliste (1815-1848)*. Paris: S.E.V.P.E.N., 1959.

———. *La Banque en France au XIXe siècle*. Paris: Droz, 1970.

Gillet, Marcel. *Les Charbonnages du nord de la France au XIXe siècle*. Paris: Mouton, 1973.

Guerande, Paul. *Le Petit monde de la Comtesse de Ségur*. Paris: Les Seize, 1964.

Guillaume, P. *La Population de Bordeaux au XIXe siècle*. Paris: A. Colin, 1972.

Hamon, Auguste. *Les Auxiliatrices des âmes du purgatoire*. 2 vols. Paris: Beauchesne, 1919.

Hamon, Augustin, *Les Maîtres de la France*. 3 vols. Paris: Editions sociales internationales, 1936-1937.

Henry, Louis. *Manuel de la démographie historique*. Geneva: Droz, 1967.

———. *Les Familles genevoises*. Paris: Presses Universitaires de France, 1956.

Horvath, Sandra Ann. "Victor Duruy and French Education, 1863-1869." Ph.D. dissertation, Catholic University of America, Washington, D.C., 1971.

Hufton, Olwen. "Women and the Family Economy." *French Historical Studies* 9 (Spring 1975): 1-22.

Laffey, John F. "Municipal Imperialism in Nineteenth Century France." *Historical Reflections / Réflexions historiques* 1 (June 1974): 81-114.

Laloux, Jacques. *Le Rôle des banques locales et régionales du Nord de la France dans le développement industriel et commercial.* Paris: Giard, 1924.

Lambert-Dansette, Jean. *Quelques familles du patronat textile de Lille-Armentières, 1789-1914.* Lille: Raoust, 1954.

Langlois, Claude. "Les Effectifs des congrégations féminines aux XIXe siècle. De l'enquête statistique a l'histoire quantitative." *Revue d'histoire de l'église en France* 60 (January-June 1974): 39-64.

Larnac, Jean. *Histoire de la littérature féminine en France.* Imprimerie Nicholas Renault et Cie., 1929.

Lasserre, André. *La Situation des ouvriers de l'industrie textile dans la région lilloise sous la Monarchie de Juillet.* Lausanne: Nouvelle Bibliothèque de droit et de jurisprudence, 1952.

Legein, Michel. "La Bourgeoisie à Dunkerque 1800-1886." Thesis, Université de Lille, 1975.

Maisons et meubles flamands. Paris: Hachette, 1929.

Marnata, F. *Les Loyers des bourgeois de Paris, 1860-1958.* A. Colin, 1961.

Masquelier, H. *Une apôtre de la ligue patriotique des françaises: Madame Paul Feron-Vrau, née Germaine Bernard, 1869-1927.* Paris: Maison de la Bonne Presse, 1931.

Mémoires de Monseigneur J. B. Carlier. Lille: Desclée, De Brouwer et Cie., 1925.

Ménager, Bernard. *La Laïcisation des écoles communales dans le département du Nord, 1879-1899.* Lille: Université des sciences humaines, des lettres et des arts, 1971.

Miscellanea insulensea. Multivolumed collection of local pamphlets found at the Université catholique de Lille.

Moraze, Charles. *La Situation industrielle et financière du Nord de 1857 à 1870.* Paris: Bulletin de la Société d'histoire moderne, 1938.

Motte, Fernand. *Souvenirs personnels d'un demi-siècle de vie et de pensée, 1886-1942.* Lille: S.J.L.I.C., n.d.

Motte, Gaston. *Motte-Bossut. Une époque. Lettres de famille 1817-1883.* N.p., n.d.

———. *Motte-Bossut, un homme, une famille, une firme.* Tourcoing: Frère, 1944.

Nord industriel. Spécial pionniers. 1966.

Ozouf, Mona. *L'Ecole, l'église et la République, 1871-1914.* Paris: A. Colin, 1963.

Parent, Paul. *L'Architecture civile à Lille au XVIIᵉ siècle.* Lille: Raoust, 1925.

Peignage Amédée Prouvost et cie. 1851-1951. Roubaix, 1951.

Perrot, Marguerite. *Le Mode de vie des familles bourgeoises.* Paris: A. Colin, 1961.

Piérard, Gabriel. *La Croix-Rouge française dans l'arrondisement de Valenciennes de 1870 à nos jours.* Valenciennes: Comité de Valenciennes, 1963.

Pierrard, Pierre. *Lille et les lillois: essai d'histoire collective contemporaine (de 1815 à nos jours).* Paris: Bloud et Gay, 1967.

———. *La Vie ouvrière à Lille sous le Second Empire.* Paris: Bloud et Gay, 1965.

Prouvost, Mme Jacques. "La Femme à travers l'histoire de Roubaix." Unpublished paper.

Rollet, Henri. *L'Action sociale des catholiques en France (1871-1914).* 2 vols. Paris: Boivin, 1947.

Le Sacerdoce d'une mère. Lille: R. Giard, 1944.

Salembier, Joseph. *Anthologie de 50 poètes contemporains de la Flandre française.* Lille: Raoust, 1954.

Saint-Léger, Alexandre de. *La Foire et la braderie.* Lille: L. Danel, 1929.

———. *Les Mines d'Anzin et d'Aniche pendant la Révolution.* 4 vols. Paris: Leroux, 1935-1938.

———. *Notre pays à travers les âges.* Lille: Robbe, 1913.

Schnerb, Robert. *Rouher et le Second Empire.* Paris: A. Colin, 1949.

Talmy, Robert. *Une forme du catholicisme social en France:*

L'Association catholique des patrons du Nord, 1884-1895. Lille: Morel et Corduant, 1962.

Tolédano, André D. *La Vie de famille sous la restauration et la monarchie de juillet.* Paris: A. Michel, 1943.

Toulemonde, Jacques. *Naissance d'une métropole: Roubaix et Tourcoing au XIXe siècle.* Roubaix: Frère, 1964.

Tudesque, A.-J. "La Bourgeoisie du Nord au milieu de la Monarchie de Juillet." *Revue du Nord* 46 (October-December, 1959): 277-285.

Un Centenaire: Enfants de Marie du Sacré-Coeur. Paris: J. De Gigord, 1932.

Vahe, Anne-Marie. "La Bourgeoisie douaisienne au temps du Second Empire." D.E.S. thesis, Université de Lille, 1959.

Van Gennep, A. *Le Folklore de la Flandre.* 2 vols. Paris: Maisonneuve, 1935-1936.

Vanier, Henriette. *La Mode et ses métiers: frivolités et luttes des classes 1830-1870.* Paris: Armand Colin, 1960.

Warenghien, Le Baron de. *Souvenirs et fragments.* Paris: Plon, 1925.

Zeldin, Theodore. "The Conflict of Moralities: Confession, Sin and Pleasure in the Nineteenth Century." In Theodore Zeldin, ed., *Conflicts in French Society,* London: George Allen and Unwin, 1970.

Index